77TH ANNUAL REPORT

OF THE

INTERSTATE COMMERCE COMMISSION

FISCAL YEAR ENDED JUNE 30, 1963

Civil Engng.

Doc,
IC 1.1
. V. 77
1963
Set 2

U.S. GOVERNMENT PRINTING OFFICE

WASHINGTON : 1964

For sale by the Superintendent of Documents, U.S. Government Printing Office
Washington, D.C., 20402 - Price $1.75 (cloth)

INTERSTATE COMMERCE COMMISSION

LAURENCE K. WALRATH, *Chairman*
ABE McGREGOR GOFF, *Vice Chairman*
HOWARD G. FREAS
KENNETH H. TUGGLE
EVERETT HUTCHINSON
RUPERT L. MURPHY
CHARLES A. WEBB
CLYDE E. HERRING
JOHN W. BUSH
WILLIAM H. TUCKER
PAUL J. TIERNEY

HAROLD D. McCOY, *Secretary*

II

CONTENTS

Interstate Commerce Commissioners (left to right) Tucker, Herring, Murphy, Tuggle, Goff (Vice Chairman), Walrath (Chairman), Freas, Hutchinson, Webb, Bush, Tierney.

REPORT OF THE
INTERSTATE COMMERCE COMMISSION

WASHINGTON, D.C., *December 31, 1963.*

To the Senate and House of Representatives:

The Interstate Commerce Commission submits herewith its 77th Annual Report to the Congress. A statement of appropriations and aggregate expenditures for the 1963 fiscal year ended June 30, 1963, is contained in appendix D to this report.

With important exceptions, the other material in the report also deals with the period between July 1, 1962, and June 30, 1963. The exceptions mainly are the references to legislative actions by the First Session of the 88th Congress and legislative recommendations for consideration by the Second Session of this Congress. Various formal proceedings also are discussed beyond the end of fiscal 1963 in situations where subsequent actions may have significantly altered narration of earlier occurrences.

The customary arrangement of this report has been modified somewhat in order to present more clearly the authority and responsibility of the Commission, the significant issues considered, and our recommendations for improvement and refinement of this complex regulatory area. Because of extensive use of this report for research and operational planning by economic and transportation interests, the basic format has been retained where possible.

The chapter on Commission organization is followed by a summary and analysis of the fiscal year's activities and recommendations for the future. Thereafter follow detailed discussions of the formal proceedings, traffic and earnings of carriers, regulatory and administrative activities, and court litigation.

1

THE COMMISSION

Commissioner Laurence K. Walrath was elected by the members of the Interstate Commerce Commission to serve as Chairman for calendar year 1963. He succeeded former Chairman Rupert L. Murphy. Commissioner Abe McGregor Goff, the Vice Chairman, was elected by Commission members in March 1963 to serve for the remainder of the calendar year, succeeding former Vice Chairman Donald P. McPherson whose term of office as a Commissioner had expired. The 11 members of the Commission, who serve 7-year staggered terms, their date of initial oaths of office, and States of legal residence, are as follows:

Howard G. Freas of California	Aug. 18, 1953
Kenneth H. Tuggle of Kentucky	Sept. 1, 1953
Everett Hutchinson of Texas	Feb. 1, 1955
Rupert L. Murphy of Georgia	Dec. 30, 1955
Laurence K. Walrath of Florida	Mar. 29, 1956
Abe McGregor Goff of Idaho	Feb. 12, 1958
Charles A. Webb of Virginia	Sept. 30, 1958
Clyde E. Herring of Iowa	Sept. 21, 1959
John W. Bush of Ohio	Apr. 3, 1961
William H. Tucker of Massachusetts	Apr. 3, 1961
Paul J. Tierney of Maryland	Mar. 29, 1963

A detailed outline of the Commission's staff organization appears in appendix A.

As part of a broad reorganization plan which became effective in early March 1961, the Commission realigned and consolidated the decisional functions into the present three Divisions known, respectively, as Divisions 1, 2 and 3. Division 1 deals with operating rights; Division 2, with rates, tariffs and valuation; and Division 3, with finance, safety and service.

Each Division is composed of three members, with the senior Commissioner in the Division serving as its Chairman. Division meetings are arranged to suit the convenience of members, or the Chairman of the Division may call special conferences as required. In addition, a Division may take action in constructive sessions through voting by notation.

Employee Boards

Nineteen employee boards have been delegated matters for initial decision. Decisions of the boards may be appealed to the appropriate Division and a decision at the latter stage is then administratively final and there is no right of review by the entire Commission. The 19 boards are: Fourth Section Board, Board of Suspension, Temporary Authorities Board, Transfer Board, three Finance Boards, three Motor Carrier Boards, two Safety and Service Boards, Special Permission Board, Released Rates Board, two Operating Rights Boards, and a Review Board in each of the three proceedings bureaus.

The review boards of the proceedings bureaus are the Operating Rights Review Board, Rates and Practices Review Board, and Finance Review Board. These review boards were established following the September 1961 legislative amendment to section 17 of the Interstate Commerce Act. We have delegated to these boards authority to handle proceedings or classes of proceedings that do not involve issues of general transportation importance. Unlike other employee boards, the review boards act in cases which have required the taking of testimony at public hearings or the submission of evidence by opposing parties in the form of affidavits. The board's action is administratively final if no appeal is made to the appropriate appellate division. In the event of appeal, the Appellate Division's action is administratively final. These review boards are already making a noteworthy contribution toward reducing the heavy burden of proceedings work which heretofore rested entirely on the Division.

ANALYSIS OF DEVELOPMENTS—RECOMMENDATIONS FOR THE FUTURE

REVIEW OF PROGRESS

The technological evolution of the sixties continues to shape the national economy's quadrants—agriculture, industry, labor, and transportation. Technology's effect upon public transportation, however, is unique. Unlike other basic economic components, for-hire transport is identified as a public utility and, thus, is regulated in the public interest. Transportation is now beginning to obtain many benefits from improved equipment, advanced operational methods, and more refined research, but beneficial results have not been realized across the board. One side effect has been a distending overcapacity, leading to intensified competition among regulated for-hire carriers of the same and other modes. Experimentation and innovations in ratemaking and the move towards mergers, particularly by railroads, are close concomitants of the margin existing between potential and actual service. The resulting conflicts have involved issues extremely complex and growing in aggregate number.

This Commission entered the 1960's confronted with an expanding backlog of proceedings requiring decision and a workload so unwieldy that the regulatory process was in danger of becoming a barrier to progress of for-hire carriage, instead of serving the public interest by encouraging its advancement. A restructuring of the Commission's organization and streamlining of its procedures were clearly necessary to meet these challenges. A reorganization in depth was effected in 1961 and has been continuously updated. Procedures were modified to permit staff level boards to decide issues of routine and minor significance.

The employee boards now fully integrated into the stream of the decisional process, contribute markedly to our ability to keep pace with the heavy caseload, for they decide adversary-type proceedings at a rate of about 700 a year. As a result of the realignment Commissioners, previously confronted by an overwhelming number of cases requiring their personal review, have been able to devote more time to issues of broad public policy.

Modernization of our organization and procedures came none too soon to meet the recently encountered variety of new and intricate issues, many involving wide economic areas and large geographical regions. In one proceeding alone, public hearings ran almost con-

4

tinuously for 140 days. The 16-foot record, completed this year, consisted of some 16,000 pages of transcript by 152 witnesses. The case was decided by a three-Commissioner Division only 76 days after the record was closed, but a court order in effect at that time prevented use of the rates approved by the Division.

Last year our hearing examiners, Commissioners, and the joint boards whose memberships include State regulatory officials, presided 4,624 times at public hearings and oral arguments across the Nation. Many of these cases represented consolidations of dozens of proceedings embracing similar issues. Public attendance at these hearings and arguments often was in the hundreds. Half a million pages of transcript were entered into the records of these formal proceedings.

The greater share of the massive number of resulting decisions and rulings was an outgrowth of some 260,000 applications, pleadings, complaints, and protests of individuals, carriers, and shippers and not from actions initiated by the Commission. The broad rulemaking and investigation proceedings instituted by this agency generally were inaugurated to provide for development of definitive policy criteria in important areas such as piggyback operations and carriers' reporting requirements.

In fiscal year 1963 we reduced the average elapsed time for disposition of formal proceedings cases to 6.9 months, a 21-percent improvement over the time required 2 years ago (see appendix B). This reduction, with practically no increase in the formal proceedings-work staff, was accompanied by final action on 7,605 cases and was accomplished despite receipt of 10,655 new cases, the highest in our history. Although the transportation and shipping environments and the general public brought more cases and more complicated issues to the Commission for settlement, there was no regulatory lag, beyond that generally considered to be the minimum established within the law as a guaranty for the "due process" to which every party is entitled. Regulated carriers' introduction of the new rates, services, and equipment required to match shipper needs and meet competition was and is tempered only by safeguards sufficient to protect the public interest, and not by decisional delay caused by cumbersome procedures. We have no control over the number of cases presented to us, nor of the 5- to 10-percent increase confronting the Commission each year. As there appears to be no slackening of this trend, maintaining this average minimum decisional period of less than 7 months, with our staff limitations, is expected to become one of our severest challenges. We are investigating the possibility of further refinement of procedural shortcuts which may be possible under present law and others which would require legislative enactment. In addition, we are studying other avenues of possible improvement, including increased automation of our operations.

Concern over the status of public transportation and its capability
to keep pace with and support the national economy was clearly enunciated in the 1962 and 1963 transportation messages of the President.
The controversial nature of the issues prevailing in this vital sector
was illustrated by the extensive congressional hearings necessary to
explore the depth of the problem. The most serious conflicts in this
legislative program concerned regulated railroad competition against
economically unregulated motor carrier movement of agricultural
products and barge transportation of bulk commodities. The President recommended that equality of competitive opportunity would be
advanced by freeing railroads in these two areas from the present
minimum rate authority of the Interstate Commerce Commission or,
alternatively, extending motor carrier and inland waterway regulation
into the agricultural and bulk commodity fields, respectively. The
Commission supported the latter proposal, in accord with our previous
recommendations that agricultural commodity exemptions should be
extended only to highway vehicles of no more than three axles and the
entire bulk exemptions for water carriers should be repealed.

The difficulties experienced in attempting to adapt and modernize
the Interstate Commerce Act to be responsive, equitably, to the transportation conflicts of this era in many ways mirror similar problems
examined by the Senate's Cullom Committee nearly 80 years ago.
The record of the years of congressional testimony necessary before the
Act to Regulate Commerce was enacted in 1887 strikingly parallels the
record which documents issues of this past year: What commodities
should be regulated; What tariffs should be made public; What minimum restraints of carriers are necessary to prevent discrimination and
abuse of the public; What degree of regulation can be imposed and still
leave carriers sufficiently unfettered to exercise the managerial discretion and zeal so imperative for advancement of interstate commerce?
These questions were not completely answered this year, but we consider a record was developed which clearly illuminated the issues and
upon which the necessary amendments to the Interstate Commerce
Act can now be realized.

In diverse areas of the Federal Government there is growing awareness that laws affecting transportation are urgently in need of modification. As a consumer of transportation, the Federal Government
has become the country's biggest shipper, spending an estimated $5
billion annually.

While only a part of our total surface transportation is regulated
by the Interstate Commerce Commission, this portion is the foundation
upon which most for-hire domestic surface carriage is keyed. It
involves the sinews of public commerce: Railroads; Trucks and
buses; Oil pipelines; Inland and coastal waterway barges; Great

Lakes and deep sea shipping between States; Freight forwarders; and Express companies. In calendar year 1962, carriers economically regulated by the Commission accounted for an estimated 1,393,871 million ton-miles and 801,367 million passenger-miles with revenues of $20.0 billion. Revenues increased to $20.4 billion in fiscal 1963. While these totals confirm the substantial accomplishments of regulated carriers, we continue to be alarmed over the diversion of intercity freight to unregulated and unlawful carriage and thus renew our legislative recommendations in this area (see page 12). In the enforcement area, over 1,200 motor carrier investigations were made, the largest number conducted in any year of the Commission's history. These violations included bogus leasing, buy-and-sell schemes, illegal cooperatives, rebates and concessions, and infractions of the safety rules.

The phenomenal development of transportation technology often seems analogous to a transport renaissance, but beyond the economic and technical advancements the social and humanitarian effects upon various areas of labor employment and public safety are of concern to this Commission. Even though there are more than 82 million vehicles on the highways, and some 92 million motor vehicle operators' licenses in force, the tragic price of mobility is exorbitantly prohibitive when tolled against the annual loss of some 41,000 citizens killed in traffic and 4½ million injured. Although these accidents represent a monetary loss of some $7 billion and an incalculable cost in human suffering, there has been progress in this area. In perspective, the loss is being held to about the level of 1941 despite, two decades later, a 40-percent increase in population, 75 percent more drivers, 126 percent more vehicles, and 130 percent more miles of vehicle travel annually.

In addition to active participation on the President's Interdepartmental Highway Safety Board, we continued to promote and monitor the safety practices prescribed for the 2 million vehicles of some 140,000 motor carriers (private, exempt and regulated), in addition to our traditional efforts in railroad safety matters. In rail and highway safety programs, we devoted special attention to ensuring that carriers adhered strictly to our rules regarding movement of hazardous cargoes, particularly those of an extremely dangerous nature such as radioactive materials, unstable and explosive elements, toxic and poisonous gases, and highly flammable liquids.

For reasons of both safety and improvement of highway operations, we were encouraged by the construction progress of the 41,000-mile interstate system, more than one-third of which was open to traffic by the close of the fiscal year. Scheduled for completion in 1972 and designed to accommodate traffic needs of 1975, this impressive undertaking will more than double the modern highway mileage of the United States. It will be the Nation's key highway network, serving both defense and interstate commerce needs. Although it is impossible to prophesy the extent or dimension of the impact upon surface carriers, the regulatory problems engendered could be severe, if the system accounts for 20 percent of all highway traffic as estimated. For this reason, detailed study and preliminary planning for our anticipated work in this area are underway.

Highway advancements are being competitively paced by developments among the other modes of transport, such as introduction of reduced railroad rates on commodities suitable for integral or unit train operations and the institution of new cars designed and programmed for special service, often involving large aggregate volumes. Oil pipelines, particularly, are benefiting from progressive uses of automation. Inland waterway operators are increasingly adapting their procedures and equipment to changing requirements of shippers.

To anticipate and keep pace with such developments affecting regulated carriers, we have updated various traditional approaches to regulation. We are actively seeking, through research and planning, new methods to handle complex and unprecedented problems that are being shaped by technological advancement, automation, over-capacity, and introduction of novel competitive practices. For this reason, we created a Committee on Policy and Planning of three Commissioners who report to the Commission through its Chairman and are responsible for processing basic policy and planning problems to a level where they will be ready for analysis and action. In addition, we continued the active liaison program with the other transportation regulatory agencies—the Civil Aeronautics Board and Federal Maritime Commission. Meeting regularly, as requested by the President in his Transportation Message of 1962, the three agency Chairmen sought coordinated solutions for improvement of the regulatory process. Top level staff groups were designated to study and develop consistency of regulatory treatment, particularly in the fields of terminal area operations, through routes and joint rates, freight forwarders, brokers and consolidators, audits and cost finding, economic analysis and statistical data, and containerization.

Our probings for insight into the emerging role that regulation should carry out in this climate of shifting economic patterns and progressive technology included participation in studies of the Common Market's handling of inter-member surface transport rules and Japan's ultra-high speed, New Tokaido rail line being constructed between Tokyo and Osaka. In addition, we were host to scores of foreign officials who observed the operation of our regulatory process and kept us informed of comparative means of resolving surface transport problems, many of which are gravitating to similar identities.

PRACTICE AND PROCEDURE

A total of 30,254 persons have been admitted to practice before the Commission's bar since its establishment in 1929. Some 68 percent of the practitioners have been admitted as attorneys, members of the bar of the highest court of their States. The remainder were admitted as nonlawyers. During the past year 611 applicants were admitted to practice, 80 percent of whom were attorneys. The 122 persons who qualified as practitioners by passing our written examination represented some 58 percent of the 211 nonlawyers taking the test in the 1963 fiscal year.

In the procedural area we prescribed special rules (49 C.F.R. 1.244) governing applications for grandfather certificates of registration and special rules (49 C.F.R. 1.245) providing for new certificates authorizing a single-State motor common carrier to engage in interstate commerce within that State (see page 43). Another addition to the rules (49 C.F.R. 1.246) added minor refinements involving the posting of notices and procedures for discontinuance or change of train or ferry service.

Perhaps the most significant impact on all regulatory agency procedural development was occasioned by the 30 recommendations in the final report of the Administrative Conference of the United States, December 15, 1962.[1] Various recommendations applicable to the Interstate Commerce Commission already were incorporated in our procedures, such as No. 8 which called for establishment of a continuing means of observation and improvement of agency procedures. At the close of the fiscal year, others, such as the matter of ex parte communications, were being prepared for inclusion in our rules or were under active consideration.

The Administrative Conference also urged, and we supported, enactment of legislation creating a permanent Conference so that Federal agencies may cooperatively, continuously and critically examine their administrative processes and related organizational problems.

LEGISLATIVE ACTIVITIES

Our legislative activities during the past year, as in previous years, dealt with a wide variety of measures affecting the jurisdiction and functions of the Commission.

We closely followed and actively participated in extensive hearings in both the House and Senate on companion bills (H.R. 4700 - S. 1061 and H.R. 4701 - S. 1062) which would implement many of the proposals contained in the President's 1962 transportation message to Congress as supplemented on March 5, 1963.

---

[1] S. Doc. 24, 88th Cong., 1st sess.

With respect to the so-called "omnibus bill" (H.R. 4701 - S. 1062), we favored and urged enactment of those sections concerned with experimental rate, classification, and documentation systems; co-operative highway enforcement agreements between the Commission and the States; and extension of civil forfeiture provisions of the act to include safety violations and unlawful operations by motor carriers. While supporting in principle those provisions of the omnibus bill which would establish an interagency joint board, the Commission, acting in concert with the Civil Aeronautics Board and the Federal Maritime Commission, drafted and submitted to the House and Senate commerce committees substitute provisions to accomplish the same end.

With respect to the so-called "minimum rate deregulation" bill (H.R. 4700 - S. 1061), we expressed the view that the desired goal of achieving equality of competitive opportunity among the carriers of the various modes will best be realized by extending rather than restricting or limiting the applicability of the reasonable regulatory provisions of the Interstate Commerce Act. This approach was recommended by the President as an alternative to his "deregulation" proposal.

The railroad work rules dispute which threatened to tie up the Nation's railroads and seriously disrupt the national economy, was another matter which required a considerable amount of attention. The Commission followed with great interest the hearings in both the House and Senate on joint resolutions (H.J. Res. 565 and S.J. Res. 102) introduced at the request of the President which would have assigned to the Commission the difficult task of arbitrating this dispute. In testifying on these resolutions, we stated that we would accept and exert our best efforts to meet this added responsibility should the Congress decide that this would be a proper solution. Ultimately, the Congress assigned this task to a special seven-man arbitration board composed of two members representing labor and management, respectively, and three public members.

A number of measures recommended by us in last year's annual report were the subject of hearings in which we appeared and testified. These measures included S. 1063 which would authorize the Commission to prescribe incentive per diem charges as a means of encouraging the acquisition of an adequate national freight car fleet (Legislative Recommendation No. 2); S. 1033, which would broaden the scope of the Standard Time Act by providing that the standard time of the zones shall be the exclusive measure of time and by adding more definite standards, requirements for observance, penalties for violation, and provisions for administration and enforcement (Legislative Recommendation No. 1); and H.R. 2090 and its companion S. 684, which would clarify certain provisions of part IV of the Interstate

Commerce Act, and place transactions involving unifications or acquisitions of control of freight forwarders under the provisions of section 5 of the act (Legislative Recommendation No. 15).

We also supported S. 1664, a bill designed to establish a permanent Administrative Conference charged with the continuous improvement of the administrative procedures of the Federal agencies, expressing our belief that the proposed Conference would constitute a proper forum for the attainment of this goal.

Additional hearings in which members of the Commission or its staff actively participated involved such diverse subjects as appropriations, urban mass transit, civil rights, admission to practice before Federal administrative agencies, a proposed partial exemption from regulation of the transportation of accidentally wrecked or disabled motor vehicles by towing, and a measure which would permit physically handicapped individuals to operate commercial motor vehicles subject to certain conditions. In summary, we appeared and testified at 17 hearings involving a total of 24 bills during the first session of the 88th Congress. Laws enacted during the first session of the current Congress relating to our jurisdiction and functions or affecting carriers subject to our regulation include Public Law 88–51 (H.R. 5795) which relieved the Postmaster General for a 3-year period from the statutory prohibition against withdrawal of funds from the Treasury when revenues from fourth-class mail do not come within 4 percent of the cost of service unless steps are taken, including a request for the Commission's consent, to establish rates necessary to bring fourth-class revenues in line with the costs of service therefor; Public Law 88–67 (S. 1031) which repealed the Inland Waterways Corporation Act; Public Law 88–108 (S.J. Res. 102) which provided for arbitration of the railroad work rules dispute; and Public Law 88–208 (H.R. 2906) which would exempt from economic regulation the emergency towing of accidentally wrecked or disabled motor vehicles.

Responding to 95 requests from various congressional committees and subcommittees for reports and comments on bills, resolutions and other matters before them, constituted an important part of our legislative activities during the past year. We also presented our views, at the request of the Bureau of the Budget, on three bills, nine draft bills, one proposed Executive Order, and two enrolled bills. In addition, we submitted 16 draft bills to the Congress together with statements of justification, to implement the legislative recommendations contained in our last annual report.

Keyed to our legislative activities was the work of members of our congressional liaison staff in attending, as observers for the Commission, the many congressional committee hearings in which we testified or in which we had a broad general interest. As a result of these efforts we found ourselves in a better position to be helpful to the committees in presenting our direct testimony and in responding to questions raised by committee members and their counsel.

Also found to be mutually beneficial were the courtesy calls paid early in the session by our Chairman, Vice Chairman, and members of our legislative and liaison staffs on the chairmen of the committees and subcommittees with which our work brings us into closest contact. The general discussion of a large variety of topics at these meetings gave all concerned a clearer understanding of, and a greater insight into, the problems expected to be encountered during the year. Following these meetings, members of the liaison staff met from time to time with committee and subcommittee counsel and other staff members to lend such assistance as they could in the consideration of particular matters, including pending legislation.

In order to be as helpful as possible, our liaison staff also conferred on a number of occasions with the staffs of individual members of both Houses, with industry representatives and with representatives from other departments and agencies on matters coming within the Commission's jurisdiction and functions. In addition, members of our liaison staff handled an increasing number of telephone inquiries from congressional and other sources covering all aspects of our regulatory activities. Approximately 1,425 such inquiries were received during the year, representing an increase of some 400 over last year. During the same period, our liaison staff responded to almost 500 letters from individual members of the Congress for information and materials pertaining to our work.

LEGISLATIVE RECOMMENDATIONS

Our new recommendations, explained below, for the most part are procedural in nature and, if enacted, would enable the Commission to utilize its time and staff more effectively. We therefore urge early and favorable consideration of these proposals which will, as in the past, be implemented by draft legislation. In addition we urge enactment of S. 2152, a measure which would strengthen the Commission's hand in dealing with the problems presented by the rapid growth of illegal for-hire and gray area transportation and in which is embodied several of our own recommendations.

We are also renewing all of last year's recommendations. For convenience of reference, the substance of these proposals is summarized below under a separate heading, together with a cross-reference to last year's report. Also shown is the status, as of the end of the session, of each bill introduced to give effect thereto.

NEW RECOMMENDATIONS

1. We recommend that part II be amended so as to authorize the Commission to exempt from the requirements of that part, or any provision thereof, such service and transportation as may be determined by the Commission in appropriate rulemaking proceedings to be of such nature, character, or quantity as not substantially to affect or impair uniform regulation of motor carriers engaged in interstate or foreign commerce in effectuating the national transportation policy.

With a number of exceptions specifically enumerated in the statute, the regulatory provisions of part II now embrace all for-hire motor transportation of passengers or property in interstate or foreign commerce. As a consequence, the Commission regularly is called upon to apply and enforce the requirements of part II with respect to certain motor carrier operations and activities which contribute but slightly to the national transportation system and which cannot be said to be of significance in the overall design of regulation contemplated by the Interstate Commerce Act. For example, the interstate motor movement of such commodities as homing pigeons or trash and garbage would appear to be of such nature, character, or quantity as not substantially to affect or impair uniform regulation, and exemption of such transportation from regulation would in no wise hinder the effectuation of the national transportation policy or affect materially the welfare of regulated transportation. Likewise, the exclusion from interstate regulation of local mass transit motorbus operations conducted within precisely defined territorial limits would in certain circumstances appear to have little or no effect upon uniform regulation of that segment of the for-hire industry.

This recommendation does not contemplate a marked departure from previous legislative techniques. In this connection, comparable exempting authority is set forth in section 204(a) (4a) of the Interstate Commerce Act as to motor carriers lawfully engaged in operation solely within a single State, while the Civil Aeronautics Board is empowered by 49 U.S.C. section 1386 to create somewhat similar exemptions from air carrier economic regulation.

2. We recommend that section 17(2) be amended so as to authorize the Commission to delegate to qualified individual employees, including transportation economists and specialists, those matters which have not involved the taking of testimony at a public hearing or the submission of evidence by opposing parties in the form of affidavits.

In addition to a voluminous number of formal cases, the Commission's responsibilities under the act extend to numerous matters of a highly routine and specialized nature. For example, matters relating to extensions of time for filing annual, periodical, or special reports; rejection of tariff publications for failure to give lawful notice or failure to comply with the Commission's regulations; and orders assigning cases for hearing, extending dates for the filing of pleadings, and postponing compliance dates. Under the present provisions of section 17(2), however, the Commission may delegate such functions only to three-man boards composed of "examiners, directors or assistant directors of bureaus, chiefs of sections, and attorneys."

In our judgment, enactment of the proposed legislation would enable us to utilize key employees more effectively and would contribute significantly to improved overall administrative efficiency in the processing of matters of the type described.

3. We recommend that section 1(22) be amended so as to include within the exemption from the Commission's jurisdiction contained in that section, the acquisition and operation of spur, industrial, team, switching or side tracks, located or to be located solely within one State.

Spur, industrial, etc. . . ., tracks are usually located in terminal or station areas. They are mostly short in length and of relatively little monetary value. Applications seeking approval of their acquisition are usually for the purpose of rendering necessary service to an industry or industries. They are nearly always granted. Under these circumstances, the processing and consideration of the applications only add to the workload of the Commission and require expenditure of money and time of both the carrier involved and the Commission which could be better devoted to other purposes.

4. We recommend that section 5(1) be amended so as to exempt contracts, agreements, or combinations affecting the transportation of household goods to which any common carrier by motor vehicle may be a party with other such carrier or carriers for the pooling or division of traffic, service, or earnings.

The pooling provisions of the act require a hearing and approval by the Commission before the described "contracts, agreements, or combinations" may lawfully be entered into. Regulation of household goods carriers under such provisions has not been practical. Combinations whereby they divert, surrender, or exchange shipments, allocate or control solicitation, use service facilities and instrumentalities or employees cooperatively, and divide proceeds of diverted traffic, are so flexible that before agreements can be filed and approved, many are terminated or changed and new arrangements entered into. In our opinion, the proposed exemption is required by these special circumstances.

5. We recommend that section 220(f) of the Interstate Commerce Act, section 8 of the Locomotive Inspection Act, and section 4 of the Accident Reports Act be amended so as to (a) incorporate in the Locomotive Inspection Act a prohibition against use in a damage suit of any report sent by a carrier under that act; (b) prohibit the introduction in evidence in any damage suit of the report submitted to the Commission by its accident investigators; (c) prohibit expert opinion testimony by the Commission's accident investigators in damage suits; and (d) restrict factual testimony by the Commission's accident investigators to cases where factual evidence is not reasonably available from other sources.

This Commission faces the same problem as the Civil Aeronautics Board in regard to efforts of litigants to compel Commission employees who have investigated an accident to testify in damage suits. Accordingly, our recommendation follows the same lines as that proposed in companion bills (S. 1136 and H.R. 5200) introduced during the first session of the 87th Congress at the request of the CAB.

A related problem faced by the Commission involves efforts of litigants to compel the production of the reports submitted by Commission investigators and, in the case of rail accidents, of the reports submitted by the carriers. The Commission has consistently refused to produce such reports on the ground that they are confidential and at least within the policy of the statutes which prohibit the use in a damage suit of the Commission's report of investigation. For the most part we have been able to successfully resist efforts to compel such disclosures. However, the literal terms of the three statutes do not cover the report of Commission investigators, as distinguished from the Commission's report of investigation, and the Locomotive Inspection Act does not literally cover the report submitted by the carriers. In our opinion, enactment of a clear statutory provision would obviate this problem, with a resultant saving in the time which the Commission's legal staff must devote to such matters.

6. We recommend that section 20a(12) be amended so as (a) to eliminate the necessity for prior approval of the Commission for a person to hold the position of officer or director of more than one carrier when such carriers are in a single integrated system of carriers lawfully operated under common control, and (b) to make it clear that the prohibition against the holding by "any person" of the position of officer or director of more than one carrier applies to the holding of such positions by different

members, officers, employees, or directors of the same firm, co-partnership, corporation, association, or joint stock association, or to the representation of a person on the board of directors of more than one carrier through an agent or nominee.

At the present time approval is granted as a matter of course for a person to serve as an officer or director of two or more carriers in a single system, it being considered that the findings contemplated by the statute properly may be made under such circumstances. The requirement that application be made and processed in these situations casts an unnecessary burden upon the carriers and the Commission. During the years 1960 to 1962, inclusive, 642 interlocking directorship applications were filed. Of these, only about 2 percent involved positions with unaffiliated carriers.

Concerning (*b*) above, the prohibition against the same person serving as an officer or director of more than one railroad, without prior approval of the Commission, is partly defeated by the fact that, for example, several partners in a firm may lawfully serve as directors on several railroads without approval by the Commission. Evasion through the use of affiliated persons should be precluded by the proposed amendment.

7. We recommend that procedures for judicial review of orders of the Commission be changed so as to provide: (*a*) that review be upon appeals to the United States Court of Appeals in all cases where at present a special three-judge court is used; (*b*) that review be permitted in any judicial circuit wherein the party or any of the parties filing the request for review have their residence or principal office; (*c*) that final review by the Supreme Court of the United States be only by petition for a writ of certiorari; (*d*) that a limit of 60 days be imposed as the time within which a petition for review must be filed in any case for which the present statutory provisions do not fix a period for filing petitions for review, such 60-day period to run from the date of entry of the order appealed from or entry of an order denying reconsideration thereof where petitions for reconsideration are allowed by the Commission's rules, whichever is later; (*e*) that appeals be commenced by the filing of a petition for review in the form of a notice of appeal; (*f*) that anyone seeking review be required to serve notice of appeal upon all parties to the proceeding before the Commission, the Department of Justice, and the Commission; (*g*) that when several appeals are taken from the same order of the Commission, venue be determined by the first notice of appeal to be filed, and all subsequent appeals be considered as taken to the same court, consolidated therewith, and

handled as one appeal; and (*h*) that review proceedings be brought against the Commission as defendant, rather than against the United States, with the Department of Justice to have the right to intervene in any proceeding.

This recommendation embraces certain proposals of the Administrative Conference of the United States and our Special Advisory Committee of Interstate Commerce Commission Practitioners; and, with respect to (*h*) above, a recommendation contained in our 75th and several prior Annual Reports. In our judgment, enactment of the proposed legislation would improve present procedures for judicial review of Commission orders and would result in significant savings in time, effort, and expense.

RECOMMENDATIONS RENEWED FROM PRIOR REPORT

8. **Would authorize the Commission to prescribe per diem charges on a basis that would provide an incentive to the carriers to procure and maintain an adequate national supply of freight cars. (Recommendation No. 2 in the 76th Annual Report.)**

S. 1063 and H.R. 2092 were introduced in the Senate and House, respectively, at our request, and hearings were held on S. 1063 before the Freight Car Shortage Subcommittee of the Senate Commerce Committee. No further action was taken on these measures.

The urgency for enactment of this legislation is presently greater than at any time since it was first recommended. The Nation is faced with one of the most serious boxcar shortages in its history. Shortages are also being recorded daily in the supply of hopper cars, covered hoppers, and flatcars. These shortages are having a dire effect on our economy.

There is no uncertainty as to the reason for these shortages—the national car supply has dwindled to a new low for this century, despite the fact that carriers are making a determined effort to repair and rebuild cars. Purchases are confined primarily to equipment of a specialized nature, which obviously will not tend to reduce the existing shortages, as only a few big shippers are afforded relief by the new cars acquired. In 1962 a total of 30,232 new cars came on line but 87,436 were scrapped. In the first 4 months of 1963 the loss continued at the rate of over 3,000 units per month.

Little assistance can be expected from the institution of the new multilevel per diem system scheduled by AAR to become effective for the Nation's railroads on January 1, 1964. This system is based generally on the concept of adequate compensation to owners of cars purchased, on the basis of cost, but compliance with the plan is voluntary and some carriers have not accepted it.

On the other hand, the proposed legislation will enable the Commission to prescribe and promulgate reasonable per diem charges. It will also serve as an additional incentive for those carriers willing to contribute their share to the Nation's supply to acquire new cars. Per diem charges are too low to reflect the value of such cars to their owners, especially during car shortages. The present per diem charges of $2.88 per car today do not cover the full current costs and risks of ownership, not to mention profit, and are considerably below the amount which a car owner could earn daily by use of the car on its own railroad. This policy in practice discourages construction of new freight cars and, in effect, places a premium upon inadequate car ownership and will continue to do so as long as it is cheaper to rent a car than it is to own one.

In our opinion, Congress should authorize the Commission in fixing car rentals to give consideration to "the adequacy of the national freight car supply" and prescribe such reasonable charges as will encourage the "acquisition and maintenance" of a car supply adequate to serve the needs of the Nation's commerce and the national defense.

9. Proposes that a uniform system of time standards and measurement be established for the United States; that the observance of such time standards be required for all purposes; that careful consideration be given to the question of whether the Commission is the most appropriate agency to administer the provisions of any future law relating to standard time; and, in the event the present Standard Time Act (15 U.S.C. 261–264) is not changed or amended so as to provide a more efficient and effective system of time regulation, that the Commission be relieved of the responsibility for its administration. (Recommendation No. 1 in the 76th Annual Report.)

At our request, S. 1033 and H.R. 4702 were introduced in the Senate and House, respectively. Hearings were held on S. 1033 which was reported out favorably with amendments by the Senate Commerce Committee. No further action was taken on these measures.

10. Would substitute gross operating revenue for the number of vehicles owned or operated as a more reliable test for determining whether a proposed unification or acquisition of control of motor carriers is exempt from section 5. (Recommendation No. 3 in the 76th Annual Report.)

No action has been taken on bills S. 674 and H.R. 2087, introduced in the Senate and House, respectively, at our request.

11. Would eliminate from section 19a requirements that the Commission determine (1) the present value of land, (2) the valuation of property held by carriers for purposes other than for use in common carrier service, and (3) the amount, value, and

disposition of aids, gifts, grants, and donations and the amount and value of concessions and allowances made by carriers in consideration thereof, and would make optional the requirement that the Commission keep itself informed of changes in the quantity of the property of carriers following the completion of the original valuation of such property. (Recommendation No. 4 in the 76th Annual Report.)

S. 675 and H.R. 2596 (also H.R. 2598) were introduced in the Senate and House, respectively, at our request. No further action was taken on these measures.

12. Would authorize the Commission, after investigation and hearing, when necessary and desirable in the public interest, to require the establishment of through routes and joint rates between motor common carriers of property and between those carriers and common carriers by rail, express, and water. (Recommendation No. 5 in the 76th Annual Report.)

S. 676 and H.R. 2088 were introduced in the Senate and House, respectively, at our request. Although no further action was taken on these measures, our recommendation is involved in hearings which were held on S. 1062 and H.R. 4701 in the Senate and House, respectively.

13. Would provide (a) that agricultural cooperatives and shipper associations shall be entitled to exempt status under sections 203(b)(5) and 402(c), respectively, only upon application and proof of eligibility, and (b) that sections 220 and 412 be amended to permit the Commission or its duly authorized agents to inspect the books, records, and other documents kept or maintained by such cooperatives and associations. (Recommendation No. 6 in the 76th Annual Report.)

Bills S. 677 and H.R. 3770 were introduced in the Senate and House, respectively, at our request, to give effect to this recommendation, but no further action was taken.

14. Would limit the application of the agricultural and other commodity exemptions to providing direct assistance to farmers, ranchers, and fishermen in the transportation of their products to local markets. Appropriate grandfather rights would be afforded carriers now operating under the exemptions. (Recommendation No. 7 in the 76th Annual Report.)

Bills S. 925 and H.R. 5201 were introduced in the Senate and House, respectively, at our request. While no further action was taken on these measures, our recommendation is involved in hearings which were held on S. 1062 and H.R. 4701 in the Senate and House, respectively.

15. Would authorize the Commission to award reparations against motor carriers and freight forwarders for damages aris-

ing from violations of parts II and IV of the act, respectively. (Recommendation No. 8 in the 76th Annual Report.)

No action, as yet, has been taken on bills S. 678 and H.R. 2594 introduced in the Senate and House, respectively, at our request. This recommendation, however, is involved in hearings which were held on S. 1062 and H.R. 4701 in the Senate and House, respectively.

16. Would make more definite the Commission's authority to prescribe regulations governing the safety of operations and equipment of private carriers of property by motor vehicle. (Recommendation No. 9 in the 76th Annual Report.)

Bills to implement this recommendation were introduced in the Senate and House, respectively, at our request, as S. 679 and H.R. 2597. No hearings on these measures have, as yet, been scheduled.

17. Proposes that section 212(a) be amended (1) to make willful noncompliance with *any* lawful rule or regulation of the Commission ground for suspension, change, or revocation of motor carrier operating authorities, (2) to conform the revocation procedure therein prescribed to that provided in section 410(f), and (3) to provide for suspension on short notice of motor carrier operating authorities for noncompliance with the Commission's insurance regulations. (Recommendation No. 10 in the 76th Annual Report.)

Bills S. 680 and H.R. 2093 were introduced in the Senate and House, respectively, at our request to implement this recommendation, but no further action has been taken.

18. Would permit in motor carrier enforcement proceedings under section 222(b) the service of process upon carriers and the joining of any other necessary party without regard to where the carrier or other party may be served. (Recommendation No. 11 in the 76th Annual Report.)

Bills S. 681 and H.R. 2091 were introduced in the Senate and House, respectively, at our request, but no further action has been taken on these measures. However, our recommendation is involved in hearings which were held on S. 1062 and H.R. 4701 in the Senate and House, respectively.

19. Would amend section 222(h) so as to (*a*) extend the civil forfeiture provisions therein to unlawful operations and safety violations by motor carriers, (*b*) permit the Commission to institute forfeiture actions directly in the courts, and (*c*) increase substantially the amount of the forfeitures prescribed. (Recommendation No. 12 in the 76th Annual Report.)

No action, as yet, has been taken on bills S. 682 and H.R. 2094 introduced in the Senate and House, respectively, at our request. This recommendation, however, is also involved in the hearings which were held on S. 1062 and H.R. 4701 in the Senate and House, respectively.

20. Would authorize the Commission to deny, revoke, or suspend motor carrier operating authorities and brokers' licenses, or to require divestiture of interest, where such authority or license has been used in the commission of a crime affecting the fitness of the carrier or broker to engage in public transportation. (Recommendation No. 13 in the 76th Annual Report.)

Bills to implement this recommendation were introduced, at our request, in the Senate and House as S. 683 and H.R. 2595, respectively. No further action has been taken on these measures.

21. Would repeal the water carrier bulk commodity exemption in section 303(b), but with provisions preserving the rights of those carriers presently engaged in operations under such exemption. (Recommendation No. 14 in the 76th Annual Report.)

S. 926 and H.R. 5549 were introduced in the Senate and House, respectively, at our request, to implement this proposal but no further action was taken on these measures. Our recommendation, however, is involved in the hearings which were held on S. 1062 and H.R. 4701 in the Senate and House, respectively.

22. Would revise and clarify provisions of part IV of the act relating to ownerships, control, and operation of freight forwarders in common with carriers of other modes to the end that future transactions involving such relationships be made subject to the provisions of section 5 of part I. (Recommendation No. 15 in the 76th Annual Report.)

Bills S. 684 and H.R. 2090 were introduced at our request, in the Senate and House, respectively, to implement this recommendation. Following hearings before the Subcommittee on Transportation and Aeronautics, a substitute bill, H.R. 5445, was reported out favorably by the House Committee on Interstate and Foreign Commerce. S. 684 was the subject of hearings before the Surface Transportation Subcommittee of the Senate Commerce Committee. After being reported out favorably by that Committee, the bill was recommitted to the Committee for further consideration. No further action was taken on these measures.

23. Would eliminate the mandatory oath requirement for certain reports, applications, and complaints filed with the Commission. (Recommendation No. 16 in the 76th Annual Report.)

Bills S. 685 and H.R. 2089 were introduced, at our request, in the Senate and House, respectively, to implement this recommendation, but no further action has been taken.

MANAGEMENT

In our last annual report we made reference to the creation of three new employee boards: Finance Review Board, Rates and Practices Review Board, and Operating Rights Review Board. As these boards did not become fully operative until January of 1962, we withheld comment on their effectiveness. Since their creation, the performance of these boards in handling the less important cases has fully justified their formation. During the fiscal year ended June 30, 1963, these boards disposed of 590 cases. Each of these previously would have required the personal attention of at least three Commissioners.

In carrying out our total responsibilities, recognition has been given to the rapidly developing techniques and advantages of data processing and related management sciences. This interest was supported by establishing a Section of Systems Development to replace the Automatic Data Processing Staff referred to in our last report. Among priority work is the continuing development of automated procedures to replace burdensome manual computations traditionally used to develop transportation cost information.

Late in December of 1962, the Commission upgraded its data processing equipment by installing an RCA 301 electronic digital computer system. The RCA 301 configuration consists of a basic processor with a 10,000 character high-speed memory, six magnetic tape stations, a card reader and card punch, and a high-speed printer. Some conventional electrical accounting machines were retained for auxiliary operations. The new system replaces a random access data processor and two EAM installations. To take full advantage of this increased data processing capability, we combined all the data processing equipment and staff engaged in its operation in a new Data Processing Branch to centralize operations.

We use the ADP installation for processing most of our statistical information, including the continuous rail carload waybill sample, financial and operating reports filed by carriers, the inventory of Motor Carrier Authorities, as well as the payroll, personnel records, budget and fiscal accounting, and the Central Status System.

The upgraded installation is expected to improve the Commission's information services, provide faster responses to data requirements, provide increased capacity for growing workloads, and open the way for more comprehensive analysis of available data. There was no significant increase in annual machine rental cost, and the sizable workload incident to the conversion to the new equipment was being absorbed by the existing staff. Conversion of the data processing operations from the old to the new equipment was well advanced by the end of the fiscal year.

Our management information system was expanded and improved during the year to monitor properly the Commission's ever increasing workload of formal cases. A significant improvement made in this system (Central Status System) was the incorporation of a fully automated method of identifying any case in which a processing lag develops. The system differentiates between each type of formal case handled by the Commission and identifies, by date, each step of processing. To insure timely action for correcting any out-of-line conditions which are identified, representatives in the office of the Commission's Chairman and the office of each Division Chairman were designated as work expediters. These representatives and the director of each proceedings bureau are furnished periodic computer listings of all cases failing to meet processing target dates and necessary corrective action is initiated on the cases within their respective areas of control. As a corollary to the Central Status System, our Examiner Work Reporting System is being revised to permit full integration of the two information systems. This will provide a clear indication of the specific areas of administrative handling that must be improved in order to eliminate any unnecessary delays between the various steps of active processing.

The Commission's Staff Committee on Organization, Operation and Procedure devoted special attention to the area of proceedings work. At the end of the fiscal year, we were considering permanent adoption of a now temporary system wherein each proceedings bureau digests the important cases decided within each month. These are made available to inform the staff of the policy enunciated in current important decisions and for use as a research tool in connection with specific case assignments.

The Commission's overall analysis of its data collection activities is continuing. Our Staff Committee on Reduction of Paperwork Burden which was created in 1959, has reviewed 56 reports. As a result, 13 reports were discontinued or consolidated with others; reporting incidence of 11 reports was changed from monthly to quarterly; and data content of 11 reports was reduced. The cumulative effect of the foregoing has resulted in carrier respondents being relieved from filing some 445,000 reports annually including elimination of more than 33.5 million reportable items. At yearend, we had commenced examination of our annual reporting requirements.

A study was completed of the utilization of motor vehicles in connection with performance of the Commission's field programs. It confirmed initial indications that savings could be obtained through use of General Services Administration motor pool vehicles, on a rental basis, rather than authorizing employees to use their privately owned automobiles at a reimbursable mileage rate. Commencing in July 1963, for a period of 18 months, General Services Administration vehicles will be assigned on a regular basis to the Bureau of Safety and Service field staff. Ultimately, the rental vehicles will be assigned to all locomotive inspectors, signal and train control inspectors, and safety and service agents. Rental vehicles will be assigned to field employees of other bureaus (except the Bureau of Motor Carriers) who consistently perform high monthly mileage travel. Field employees of the Bureau of Motor Carriers will continue to use Commission motor vehicles for that bureau's field programs.

In the field of personnel management, special emphasis was given to the equal employment opportunity program, more effective utilization of employees, employment of women, strengthening of management-labor relationships, hiring of the handicapped, and recruitment of specialty skills. More visits were made to high schools to recruit stenographers and typists, and to law schools and colleges to recruit attorneys and accountants. The Commission was given special recognition by the Civil Service Commission for making 1.91 percent of our appointments during the year from the physically handicapped group. Considerable effort was devoted to the issuing of regulations and publications for guidance of supervisory and operating personnel in specific areas of personnel management.

The "ICC Newsletter," a monthly employee publication was inaugurated in August 1962, and replaced similar publications formerly issued by bureaus and offices. The newsletter is proving its anticipated value in encouraging all Commission personnel to better understand and carry out the Commission's functions.

Our last annual report mentioned that the General Services Administration had completed a study of the Commission's mail handling and messenger procedures and that we were in the process of implementing recommendations included in the study report. To date, centralized messenger service has been established for all bureaus and offices. Central briefing of incoming material has been reduced to less than 9 percent of the total mail handling time. These improvements in mail handling and messenger service have enabled us to reassign nine positions to other Commission activities. Some additional savings in manpower also have resulted from improved recordkeeping in the area of mail handling.

By late spring of 1963, we had established and published in manual form, requirements with respect to the composition, organization and use of advisory committees. Such committees were reorganized or reconstructed in accordance with the provisions of Executive Order 11007. In line with that order, a list of the committees with the names and affiliations of members, description of its function and statement of the dates of its meetings is contained in appendix C.

In our last report we noted that a survey of space utilization of the ICC Building had been conducted. To alleviate the acute space assignment problem, uniform standards for space allocation were adopted and, as a means of releasing storage space for conversion to offices, an intensive program of records disposition was commenced. More than 12,500 cubic feet of records were transferred to Federal Record Centers and an additional 8,000 cubic feet of records destroyed. These actions resulted in releasing for reuse storage equipment valued in excess of $60,000. A further reduction of approximately 10,500 cubic feet of records housed in Federal Records Centers resulted from the enactment of records disposal schedules. During the year more than 11,400 square feet of storage area in the building was remodeled into office and general purpose space by the General Services Administration. That agency expects to complete the remainder of this project during the current year. We have realloted space in accordance with our occupancy standards and by the end of the year had relocated six of our bureaus and parts of others in permanent quarters.

In the interests of increasing production; reducing processing time; and improving the quality of work, a comprehensive study was made of our printing plant operations, with emphasis on such factors as equipment and plant layout, workload and workflow, job control, and staffing. The installation of more modern bindery, platemaking, printing, folding, and collating equipment is expected to provide the Commission with improved printing plant services.

During April of 1963, we revised our method of reproducing Commission decisions. Heretofore, decisions selected for printing in bound volumes were first typeset and reproduced in pamphlet form by the Government Printing Office. These decisions now are transcribed on automatic typewriters and reproduced by offset process in our printing plant. While it is too soon to determine anticipated monetary savings from the new system, printed decisions in pamphlet form produced thus far under the revised system are available for distribution to subscribers 1 week following the release of the decision by the Commission. Formerly subscribers encountered a delay of from 90 to 180 days awaiting publication of printed decisions.

More than 300 items of office furniture and equipment with a total acquisition value in excess of $24,000 were acquired at no cost to the Commission through General Services Administration's excess property utilization program.

APPROPRIATIONS AND EMPLOYMENT

The following statement shows average employment and total appropriations for the fiscal years 1940 to 1964 for activities included under the current appropriation title "Salaries and Expenses."

Year	Appropriation	Average employment	Year	Appropriation	Average employment
1940	$8,948,000	2,649.3	1952	$11,264,035	1,889.5
1941	9,077,960	2,734.9	1953	11,003,500	1,849.4
1942	9,212,750	2,658.6	1954	11,284,000	1,837.9
1943	9,336,377	2,359.4	1955	11,679,655	1,859.1
1944	8,873,900	2,076.0	1956	12,896,000	1,902.2
1945	8,833,700	1,957.5	1957	14,879,696	2,090.1
1946	8,733,738	2,058.3	1958	17,412,375	2,237.8
1947	10,496,200	2,240.4	1959	18,747,800	2,268.1
1948	10,713,000	2,247.7	1960	19,650,000	2,343.6
1949	11,300,317	2,217.8	1961	21,451,500	2,386.1
1950	11,416,700	2,161.0	1962	22,075,000	2,399.7
1951	11,408,200	2,072.3	1963	23,502,800	2,412.8
			1964	24,670,000	[1] 2,419.6

[1] Estimated.

The appropriation of $23,502,800 for the 1963 fiscal year beginning July 1, 1962, represented an increase of $1,427,800 over the appropriation for the previous fiscal year, of which $896,800 was for pay increases under Public Law 87–793. The balance of the increase, or $531,000 was primarily for continuance of the 1962 fiscal year operating level, for planned purchases and services which were deferred, and for full year cost of increased per diem rates. The 1963 fiscal year appropriation did not provide for additional positions to handle the increased workload of the Commission. (See appendix D for statement of appropriation and obligation for the fiscal year ended June 30, 1963.)

FINANCE PROCEEDINGS

Merger cases, both rail and motor, continued to require the largest portion of the time of employees of the Bureau of Finance.

RAILROADS

Unifications

During the year, 17 additional requests to unify railroad properties were filed under section 5 of the act. Seven of the applications were approved. Cases still pending are marked by an asterisk in the table below. Those approved were (1) the purchase by the Georgia and Florida Railway Company, a subsidiary of the Southern Railway Company, of the properties and franchises of the Georgia and Florida Railroad (Alfred W. Jones, Receiver); (2) merger of the Nesquehoning Valley Railroad and the Tresckow Railroad into the Lehigh Coal and Navigation Company, commonly known as the Lehigh and Susquehanna Railroad, with all of the properties then being acquired by the Reading Company; (3) purchase by the Central Railroad Company of New Jersey of the properties of the Wilkes-Barre and Scranton Railway Company; (4) the merger of the Shenango Valley Railroad Company and the Stewart Railroad into the Mahoning and Shenango Valley Railroad Company, all of which are subsidiaries of the Central Railroad Company of New Jersey; (5) purchase by the Norfolk, Franklin, and Danville Railway Company, a newly organized company controlled by the Norfolk and Western Railway Company, of the properties of the Atlantic and Danville Railway Company (Seaborn J. Flournoy, Trustee); (6) merger into the Atchison, Topeka and Santa Fe Railway Company of its subsidiary, the California, Arizona and Santa Fe Railway Company; and (7) merger into the Illinois Central Railroad Company of its wholly owned subsidiary, the Chicago, Memphis and Gulf Railroad Company.

In the Georgia and Florida purchase, a condition was imposed requiring only the minimum protection afforded by the statute for railway employees who might be adversely affected. In this connection, the report stated:

We have no power to require consummation of the transaction and, if such is to be accomplished, it must be upon terms acceptable to the applicants. At the

27

same time, as indicated, we must accord the employees the full protection required by the applicable statute. Under the circumstances, we will impose conditions substantially in the language of the statute * * *.

That transaction has been consummated, thereby insuring continued service to the public, and the acquiring carrier has also paid off government guaranteed loans of approximately $2 million.

Of the applications pending at the beginning of the year, authority has been granted for the Chesapeake and Ohio Railway Company to acquire control of the Baltimore and Ohio Railroad, subject to conditions for the protection of railway employees and for the maintenance of existing routes and channels of trade for the protection of other railroads. The order of the Commission approving the transaction has been sustained by a three-judge district court in Michigan; however, railway employee groups have appealed the decision to the United States Supreme Court.

The Southern Railway Company was authorized to acquire control of the Central of Georgia Railway Company, subject to conditions for the maintenance of existing routes and channels of trade for the protection of other railroads and subject to conditions for the protection of railway employees. The conditions imposed represented a revision of those imposed in similar prior cases, principally in connection with the arbitration of disputes. Neither the railroad nor the employee organization is satisfied with the conditions, the former contending that requirements would increase the financial and managerial burden of the carriers, whereas the employee organization alleged that the conditions imposed afford the employees less protection than those imposed in prior similar proceedings.

Acquisition by the Detroit, Toledo and Ironton Railroad Company of control of the Ann Arbor Railroad Company, subject to conditions for the protection of railway employees and for the maintenance of through routes and channels of trade for the protection of other carriers, also was approved. The proceeding has been reopened for reconsideration solely with respect to employee conditions.

Also authorized was the merger of the Southern Pacific Terminal Company into the Southern Pacific Company and the acquisition of control by the Boston and Maine Railroad of the Stoney Brook Railroad Corporation.

The following table shows the number of proposals involving railroad unifications pending at the end of the reporting year:

Finance Docket No.	Nature of transaction
21334	Acquisition by Atchison, Topeka & Santa Fe Ry. Co. of control of Western Pacific R. Co.
21314	Acquisition by Southern Pacific Co. of control of Western Pacific R. Co.
22382*	Acquisition by Atchison, Topeka & Santa Fe Ry. Co. of control of Oklahoma City-Ada-Atoka Ry. Co.
22465	Merger into Atchison, Topeka & Santa Fe Ry. Co. of Gulf, Colorado & Santa Fe Ry., Panhandle & Santa Fe Ry. Co., and Kansas City, Mexico & Orient Ry. Co.
21478	Merger into a new company, the Great Northern Ry. Co., of the Northern Pacific Ry. Co., Chicago, Burlington & Quincy R. Co., Pacific Coast R. Co., and lease by that company of Spokane, Portland & Seattle Ry. Co.
21313	Acquisition by Illinois Central R. Co. of control of Louisville & Nashville R. Co.
21892	Acquisition by Illinois Central R. Co. of control of Chicago & Eastern Illinois R. Co.
21755	Acquisition by Missouri Pacific R. Co. of control of Chicago & Eastern Illinois R. Co.
21510	Merger of New York, Chicago & St. Louis R. Co. into Norfolk & Western Ry. Co.
21511	Acquisition of control and lease of Wabash R. Co. by Norfolk & Western Ry. Co.
21512	Purchase by Norfolk & Western Ry. Co. of about 106 miles of line of the Connecting Ry. Co.
21920	Acquisition by Norfolk & Western Ry. Co. of control of Akron, Canton & Youngstown R. Co.
22235*	Lease by Norfolk & Western R. Co. of properties of Pittsburgh & W. Va. Ry. Co.
21989	Merger of New York Central R. Co. into Pennsylvania R. Co.[1]
21215	Merger of Atlantic Coast Line R. Co. into Seaboard Air Line R. Co.
22274*	Acquisition by Texas & Pacific Ry. Co. of control of Kansas, Oklahoma & Gulf Ry. Co., Midland Valley R. Co., and Oklahoma City-Ada-Atoka Ry. Co.[2]
22621*	Merger of Boston & Maine R. into Boston & Maine Corp., a noncarrier.
22432*	Acquisition by New York Central R. Co. of further control of Indiana Harbor Belt R. Co.
22167*	Acquisition by New York Central R. Co. of further control of Pittsburgh & Lake Erie R. Co.
22644*	Purchase by New York Central R. Co. of certain properties of Penndel Co.
22375*	Acquisition by Georgia-Pacific Corp., a noncarrier, of control of Ashley, Drew & Northern Ry. Co.
22365*	Lease by Illinois Terminal R. Co. of portion of properties of Philadelphia, Baltimore & Washington R. Co.

[1] The following railroads have sought to be included in this merger: Boston & Maine Railroad, Brooklyn Eastern District Terminal, Delaware & Hudson Railroad Corp., Erie-Lackawanna Railroad Co., New York, New Haven & Hartford Railroad Co. Trustees, and New York, Susquehanna & Western R. Co.
[2] Inclusion is sought by the Missouri-Kansas-Texas Railroad Company.
*These applications were filed during fiscal year 1963 and are still pending.

An examiner recommended approval, subject to conditions, of the application to merge the Atlantic Coast Line Railroad Company into the Seaboard Air Line Railroad Company. Exceptions to the examiner's report were filed and the entire Commission heard oral argument.

Hearings were concluded on the application of the Great Northern Railway Company, Northern Pacific Railway Company, Chicago, Burlington and Quincy Railroad Company and the Pacific Coast Railroad to merge into the Great Northern Pacific and Burlington Lines, Inc., and for the latter to lease the properties of the Spokane, Portland and Seattle Railroad Company. The public hearings required 82 days and involved a transcript of over 15,000 pages, presented by 623 witnesses, and 243 exhibits.

In the matter of the separate applications of the Southern Pacific Company and the Atchison, Topeka and Santa Fe Railway Company for authority to acquire control of the Western Pacific Railroad Company, an examiner's report and recommended order were served in September. He would approve the application of the Santa Fe over that of the Southern Pacific.

An examiner's report also was in process of preparation on the separate applications of the Missouri Pacific Railroad Company and the Illinois Central Railroad Company for authority to acquire control of the Chicago and Eastern Illinois Railroad. Over 25 days were required to complete the hearing in that proceeding.

An examiner's report recommended approval, subject to certain conditions, of the applications of the Norfolk and Western Railway Company to merge into it the New York, Chicago and St. Louis Railroad Company, the lease of the Wabash Railroad, the acquisition of control of the Akron, Canton and Youngstown Railroad and of the Pittsburgh and West Virginia Railway Company.

Hearings on the proposed merger of the Pennsylvania Railroad Company and the New York Central Railroad Company continued. By the end of the fiscal year 107 days of hearing had been required. Hearings were held in Washington, D.C., and 16 other cities located in Illinois, Missouri, Indiana, Ohio, Pennsylvania, New York, and New Jersey. (Hearings were finally concluded in Washington on October 2, 1963.)

We issued our report in a proceeding, which had been reopened upon petition of the Denver and Rio Grande Western Railroad Company seeking modification of the conditions imposed in an order entered by the Commission on February 6, 1923. These conditions required the preferential solicitation of traffic by the Southern Pacific Company via the Union Pacific Railroad Company through the Missouri River and Ogden, Utah. We found that in view of the long-continued reliance placed upon the conditions, it would be unreasonable and unjust to grant the modification sought in the absence of a compelling showing that, because of changed conditions, the public interest so required.

Railroads continued their efforts to increase their use of other carriers' trackage in an effort to reduce expenses by eliminating duplicate tracks between common points. Applications for trackage rights, operating agreements, and joint use of facilities approved during the fiscal year totaled 29, involving about 520 miles of railroad, compared with 22 applications approved in the prior year, involving about 480 miles of line.

Appendix E shows that 52 applications under section 5(2) involving mergers, purchases, joint use of facilities, acquisition of control, and acquisition of trackage rights were granted, an increase of 16 over those granted in the prior fiscal year.

Thirteen applications to hold the positions of officer or director of two or more railroads were pending at the beginning of the year and 178 such applications were received. Of these, 1 was dismissed, 1 denied and 179 were granted, while 10 are pending. A petition seeking modification of a prior order was denied. Another, seeking reconsideration of a denial order, is pending.

Abandonments and Construction

The continued increase in the number of applications to abandon lines of railroad indicated managerial awareness of the financial drains of nonproductive lines having little public interest or support. A total of 127 applications were filed for permission to abandon 1,937 miles of line compared with 122 applications filed last year involving 1,616 miles, and 98 applications filed during the fiscal year ending June 1961 involving 1,140 miles. We granted 110 applications, permitting abandonment of 1,688 miles. One of the applications granted involved the abandonment by the Rutland Railway Corporation of its entire line of railroad of approximately 391 miles. In 6 separate applications, the Southern Pacific Company was authorized to abandon a total of 216 miles of railroad located in the States of New Mexico (114 miles), Texas (64 miles), California (32 miles), and Oregon (6 miles).

Twenty applications were filed to construct about 164 miles of railroad compared to only 8 applications filed last year to construct about 14 miles. Two short-line railroads came into existence by acquisition of lines of railroad. The Chattahoochee Industrial Railroad instituted operations in Georgia over approximately 15 miles of line, and the Marquette and Huron Mountain Company, Inc., of Michigan instituted operation over approximately 24 miles of railroad in that State. Also the Port Authority Trans-Hudson Corporation, a newly formed wholly owned subsidiary of The Port of New York Authority, was authorized to acquire and operate the Hudson Rapid Tubes Corporation, whose lines extend from Jersey City and Hoboken, N.J., to New York, N.Y.

The number of certificates issued and other pertinent information concerning proceedings on applications for abandonment, construction, acquisition, and operation of lines of railroad are set forth in appendix C.

There is an increasing interest in the creation of multiple-State authorities to acquire and operate transportation facilities, both rail and motor, in an endeavor by local authorities to solve the problems of mass transportation of passengers in metropolitan areas. These actions follow one of our recommendations in a general investigation conducted by the Commission in *Railroad Passenger Train Deficit*, 306 I.C.C. 417.

Passenger Train Discontinuances

The number of proposals under section 13a (1) of the act, involving discontinuance or change in operation or service of trains between

States was less than the number filed last year. A total of 13 proposals to discontinue 31 trains were filed by 11 railroads. Investigations were instituted concerning all but two proposals involving three trains. During the year, 5 railroads were permitted to discontinue operation of 14 passenger trains. Partial continuance was required of one railroad involving two passenger trains. The proposals of two railroads to discontinue seven trains were denied, and the proposals of three railroads to discontinue eight trains were dismissed.

There was also a decline in the number of petitions filed under section 13a(2), involving discontinuance or change in the operation or service between points in a single State. Only 1 railroad filed a its petition to discontinue two other trains, and denied a petition proposing to discontinue 12 trains during the prior year. In these cases we permitted one railroad to discontinue one train and dismissed its petition to discontinue two other trains, and denied a petition of another railroad to discontinue two trains. The following table shows the number of proposals handled during the year, and the action taken in those cases:

Carrier	Trains involved	Investigated	Final action
Baltimore & Ohio R. Co	3	Yes	A
Do	2	Yes	A
Chesapeake & Ohio Ry. Co	2	Yes	A
Chicago & North Western Ry. Co	4	Yes	P
Chicago, Milwaukee, St. Paul & Pacific R. Co	2	Yes	D
Chicago, Rock Island & Pacific R. Co	2	Yes	A
Erie-Lackawanna R. Co	3	Yes	P
Do	2	Yes	P
Missouri Pacific R. Co	4	Yes	D
Do	2	Yes	C
New York Central R. Co	2	No	A
Do	1	No	A
New York, Chicago & St. Louis R. Co	2	Yes	A
Pennsylvania R. Co	2	Yes	D
Do	5	Yes	C
Soo Line R. Co	2	Yes	P
Southern Pacific Co	2	Yes	C
Do	2	Yes	P
Union Pacific R. Co	4	Yes	P

A—Discontinuance permitted.
C—Continuance required in whole or in part.
D—Dismissed.
P—Case pending as of July 1, 1963.

Issuance of Securities and Assumption of Obligations

The number of applications filed by railroads and the aggregate amount of securities authorized increased substantially. Corresponding figures for motor carriers, however, showed a slight decrease.

Authority was granted to issue securities in the principal and par amount of $545,485,164. Also 2,963,763 shares of no-par-value common stock were authorized. Motor carrier issues accounted for $75,148,043 of the principal and par amount and 2,842,958 of the no-par-value shares. Corresponding figures for the previous year were

$258,739,112 and 1,455,229 no-par-value shares of which $98,168,818 principal and par amount and 1,380,229 no-par-value shares were to be issued by motor carriers. One application was filed under section 20b, by Erie-Lackawanna Railroad Company.

Authority was granted for the assumption of obligation and liability with respect to $276,346,712, total principal amount, of securities, of which $204,391,650 was with respect to railroad equipment-trust certificates. The coupon rate of these certificates ranged from $3\frac{7}{8}$ to $4\frac{3}{4}$ percent, the selling price from 98.105 to 99.745 percent of the principal, plus accrued interest, and the average annual cost of the proceeds for the various assumptions ranged from 4.02 to 4.77 percent. None of the rates reached last year's high of 5.20 percent. This year's low was 0.08 percentage point lower than last year's, and in general the trend was downward.

Two special applications for exemption from competitive bidding under the provisions of Ex Parte No. 158, *In re Competitive Bidding in Sale of Securities*, 257 I.C.C. 129, were granted.

During the year 190 applications and 49 petitions involving securities were filed, and 185 applications and 50 petitions were decided. Included were 100 applications filed by railroads or companies controlling railroads, and 90 filed by motor carriers or their noncarrier parent companies. Of the former, 6 applications were filed for the purpose of financing, in whole or in part, railroad acquisition transactions under section 5, while 26 applications were filed for similar motor carrier transactions.

In *Illinois Terminal R. Co. Bonds*, 317 I.C.C. 595, decided November 21, 1962, authority was granted for an issue of bonds by the Illinois Terminal Railroad Company which contained restrictions preventing the call of the bonds for an initial 5-year period. In that, and several other cases containing similar call restrictions, which were approved, the carriers justified such restrictions by pointing out that they are frequently used in connection with the sale of industrial and utility issues and that the carriers must compete for their funds in the same money market. Also, that institutional investors, who form the largest market for such bonds, do not care to devote the time and study required in deciding whether to purchase bonds if the bonds are subject to call at an early date. These decisions represent some relaxation of the view expressed in *Southern Ry. Co. Bonds*, 295 I.C.C. 782, decided July 31, 1958, that, as a general rule, bonds should be redeemable at any time upon payment of a reasonable redemption premium.

In *Bi-State Development Agency of Mo.-Ill. Met. Dist., Bonds*, 317 I.C.C. 641, Division 3 granted for lack of jurisdiction, the applicant's motion to dismiss its application for authority to issue transit bonds. Applicant is a bi-State agency, created as a "body corporate and

34   INTERSTATE COMMERCE COMMISSION

politic," governed by a board of commissioners under a compact between the States of Missouri and Illinois, approved by Congress, with powers to plan and develop the St. Louis bi-State metropolitan district; own and operate various types of public works projects, including passenger transportation facilities; and borrow money and issue securities upon prescribed terms. In creating a public passenger transit system, the applicant proposed to issue transit revenue bonds, a portion of the proceeds of which were to be used in the purchase of properties of companies providing local transit service in the district, including several which are subject to the jurisdiction of the Commission. Division 3 found that the applicant was not a "carrier" by railroad or motor vehicle, and issuance of securities by it prior to its engaging in transportation as such a carrier did not require approval of the Commission, because it could not be considered as a "corporation organized for the purpose of engaging in transportation," subject to part II of the act within the meaning of section 214 relating to issuance of securities. The agency has pending an application under section 5 of the act for authority to purchase the properties of the several carriers involved. Legislative Recommendation No. 1, this report, is made to exempt such State-owned motor transport agencies engaged in passenger operations from regulation under the Interstate Commerce Act.

Reorganizations

On October 2, 1962, we ratified the appointment of a trustee of the property of The Boston Terminal Corporation, debtor, in proceedings pending in the U.S. District Court for the District of Connecticut for reorganization of The New York, New Haven & Hartford Railroad Co., principal debtor, and The Boston Terminal Corporation, secondary debtor, pursuant to section 77 of the Bankruptcy Act. The New Haven owns 70 percent and The New York Central Railroad Co., 30 percent of the capital stock of The Boston Terminal Corporation. The petition of The Boston Terminal Corporation was the only petition for reorganization of railroads under section 77 filed during the year.

In The New Jersey & New York Railroad Co. reorganization proceeding, the Commission approved a modified plan of reorganization. The court has not yet approved the plan.

On July 17, 1962, the Commission ratified the appointment of a substitute trustee of the property of the Boston & Providence Railroad Corporation, debtor, in proceedings pending in the U.S. District Court for the District of Massachusetts for reorganization of the debtor pursuant to section 77.

No plan of reorganization was filed in The Atlantic & Danville Railway Co. reorganization proceeding, referred to in our last three reports. However, on October 29, 1962, the Commission, as noted previously, authorized, under section 5 of the act, the acquisition of the properties of the Atlantic & Danville by the Norfolk, Franklin & Danville Railway Co., a subsidiary of the Norfolk & Western Railway Co.

Appendix F contains a list of railroads in reorganization or receivership, and summaries of railroad mileage involved in such proceedings at the end of 1960, 1961 and 1962, and at stated intervals since 1895.

Guaranty of Loans

The Commission's authority under part V terminated June 30, 1963, except with respect to applications then pending and guaranties previously made. No legislation has been introduced to renew the program. Five recently filed applications involving $38.5 million were pending at yearend.

From the time of enactment of part V in August 1958 to the end of this fiscal year, a total of 41 applications were received from 16 carriers for loan guaranties aggregating $286.6 million. Withdrawals and amendments filed by various applicants reduced this total to $267.1 million. Thirty-six of the 41 applications received have been processed, and, as indicated above, 5 applications for $38.5 million are now pending. Twenty-nine were approved, 3 were approved in part and denied in part, 2 were denied, and 2 were withdrawn. Of the $500 million aggregate principal amount of loan guaranties which the Commission was authorized to make, $220,472,360 (or 44.1 percent) had been approved as of June 30, 1963. The following table lists the railroads that have received guaranties and the total amounts authorized for the individual roads, as well as the amounts sought in applications pending at yearend.

Loan guaranties approved

Railroad	Number of applications	Total amount guaranteed
Boston & Maine	4	$8,000,000
Central of New Jersey	1	15,000,000
Chicago & Eastern Illinois	2	14,800,000
Erie-Lackawanna	1	15,000,000
Georgia & Florida	2	1,934,960
Lehigh Valley	5	21,823,000
Missouri-Kansas-Texas	2	22,000,000
Monon	1	5,000,000
New York Central	1	40,000,000
New Haven	4	23,159,400
New Haven trustees	2	12,500,000
New York, Susquehanna & Western	2	855,000
Norfolk Southern	2	7,400,000
Pittsburgh & West Virginia	2	3,000,000
Reading	1	30,000,000
Total	32	220,472,360

Loan guaranty applications pending

Railroad	Number of applications	Amount of guaranty requested
Missouri-Kansas-Texas	1	$12,000,000
Erie-Lackawanna	1	15,000,000
Boston & Maine	1	1,000,000
Central of New Jersey	1	5,000,000
Monon	1	5,500,000
Total	5	38,500,000

At the close of the 1963 fiscal year, $184.5 million of the loans had been disbursed. Repayments of $8.7 million had been made on outstanding loans. On June 29, 1963, all loans guaranteed for the receiver of the Georgia and Florida Railroad were repaid as a result of purchase of the properties and franchises of that railroad by certain subsidiaries of Southern Railway Company.

Of the total amount of loans guaranteed to yearend, $220.5 million, $1.0 million was for future maintenance expenditures; $170.3 million was for reimbursement of capital expenditures made after January 1, 1957; $36.2 million was for future capital expenditures; and $13.0 million was for refinancing of capital expenditures made after January 1, 1957.

Although the financial position of many of the Nation's railroads has improved since 1958, certain of the railroads in the eastern district are still operating at revenue and income levels below those experienced in 1957. It is apparent that some of these eastern district railroads have survived since 1958 only with the help of loans guaranteed under part V.

Generally, railroads have been able to obtain part V loans at rates of interest only slightly above the New York prime rate. While unsecured loans are authorized, practically all loans guaranteed to date have been secured by collateral.

One railroad defaulted on its part V loans. Early in 1961 the New Haven Railroad went into receivership. At that time it had outstanding loan guaranties under part V with an unpaid principal balance of $21,796,480, and $14,375,000 thereof, plus interest thereon of $300,740, was paid to the lenders with funds obtained through a supplemental appropriation. The remainder of $7,421,480, covering certain equipment obligations, was assumed by the trustees. Since their appointment, guaranties of loans totaling $12.5 million have been authorized for the trustees of the New Haven. Such loans are secured by trustees certificates and constitute an expense of administration by the court having jurisdiction and as such constitute (with one minor exception) a direct first lien on all of the properties of the debtor railroad. Only $8.0 million of such guaranties to the trustees had been disbursed at yearend; and the trustees obtained, with our consent, an extension to December 1, 1963, of the time within which they could take down the remaining $4.5 million.

Among the provisions of part V that will continue in effect are those with respect to modifications, with our consent, during the term of the guaranty as to rate of interest, time of payment of principal or interest, security or other terms and conditions of the guaranties. Several requests have been received and it is anticipated there will be many instances where railroads and lenders will find it necessary or desirable to seek further modifications during the period of the guaranties. Practically all of the guaranties authorized thus far are for the maximum 15 years provided in part V.

MOTOR CARRIER UNIFICATIONS

Although there was an increase in the number of motor carrier applications filed, compared with the prior year, the number of applications denied increased 42 percent over the previous year, reflecting, principally, a somewhat stricter view by the Commission of the fitness of applicants.

With the enactment of Public Law 87–805 (76 Stat. 911), it was necessary to revise our rules governing transfers of operating rights (not subject to section 5 of the act) to cover transfers of certificates of registration and claimed grandfather rights within a single State under section 206(a)(6) and (7), as amended, effective October 15, 1962.

We received or reopened 1,379 applications involving motor carriers under sections 5 and 210a(b), and transfer cases, an increase of 108 over the previous year; and 15 investigations were instituted under section 5(7) compared to 13 in fiscal year 1962. Orders were entered disposing of 1,349 applications, an increase of 56 over the previous year, and 18 investigations were terminated. Of the applications disposed of, 1,012 were granted in whole or in part, a decrease of 17 from the previous year, 225 were denied, an increase of 67 over the previous year, and 112 were dismissed. Applications granted included 207 under section 5, a decrease of 53 from the previous year, 119 under the 20-vehicle exemption of section 5(10), 579 transfers to new entities, and 107 grants of temporary authority. Approvals under section 5 represented only 69 percent of those acted upon under that section compared to 76 percent the previous year. Approvals under the transfer rules represented 78 percent compared to 82 percent the previous year. The percentage of applications for temporary authority granted was 71 percent for both years. Employee boards disposed of 1,161 proceedings, and 49 hearing officers' recommended orders became effective. Petitions disposed of totaled 326. Four hundred ninety-five proceedings were pending as of July 1, 1963, an increase of 28 over those pending at the beginning of the period.

Of the applications approved under section 5, 37 involved 25 of the 100 largest motor carriers of property (based on 1962 revenues reported to us). Data concerning these authorizations are given in appendix E. Six of the authorizations involved mergers of subsidiaries or other system reorganizations. Acquisitions by subsidiaries of some of the largest carriers, which are not themselves among the 100 largest, are not included.

The 100 largest carriers of property are an active but variable group. Only 72 carriers have been continuously in the group during the past 5 years. During this period 84 carriers in the group have been involved in 191 unifications, representing 16 percent of the applications granted under section 5.

The following table shows the percentage distribution of carriers on the basis of revenues reported for 1957 to 1961, inclusive.

By order of December 7, 1962, in Ex Parte No. MC–51, Pooling by Motor Common Carriers of Household Goods, the Commission discontinued the rulemaking proceeding. See Legislative Recommendation No. 4, this report.

In *Gilbertville Trucking Co.* v. *United States*, 371 U.S. 115, the Supreme Court remanded for further proceedings our order embraced in *L. Nelson & Sons Transp. Co.—Control and Merger*, 80 M.C.C. 257, insofar as it required one of the respondents to divest himself of his stock in Gilbertville Trucking Co., Inc. The Court was of the opinion that consideration should have been given to a less drastic method of terminating the violation of law. In our report on further consideration, in *L. Nelson & Sons Transp. Co.—Investigation of Control*, 93 M.C.C. 22, we modified the order to accept, in lieu of such divestiture, a request for revocation of the operating authority of L. Nelson & Sons Transportation Co., and a statement showing that Gilbertville would not be controlled, managed or operated in a common interest with any other carrier.

Concentration in motor carrier of property industry, 1957–61

Revenue group	1957	1958	1959	1960	1961	1957	1958	1959	1960	1961
	General commodity carriers									
	Number of carriers					Revenues (millions of dollars)				
	6,602	6,236	5,952	6,290	6,312	$3,666.8	$3,690.2	$4,257.2	$4,293.5	$4,483.1
	Percentage distribution									
Over $10,000,000	0.97	1.11	1.40	1.29	1.47	32.84	34.71	39.48	39.78	43.43
$5,000,001 to $10,000,000	1.35	1.31	1.76	1.62	1.57	17.09	15.72	16.77	16.67	15.42
$2,500,001 to $5,000,000	2.50	2.66	2.84	2.62	2.58	15.84	15.82	14.07	13.62	12.79
$1,000,001 to $2,500,000	4.82	5.24	5.44	5.26	5.34	13.75	13.98	12.18	12.33	11.79
$500,001 to $1,000,000	5.98	6.29	6.65	6.01	5.89	7.50	7.51	6.70	6.40	5.88
$300,001 to $500,000	5.47	5.31	5.88	5.72	5.31	3.79	3.49	3.22	3.28	2.92
$200,001 to $300,000	5.32	5.55	6.13	6.07	6.54	2.33	2.28	2.08	2.14	2.24
$100,001 to $200,000	13.43	13.44	14.67	14.41	14.42	3.45	3.27	2.95	3.03	2.90
$50,001 to $100,000	13.43	13.68	13.27	13.75	13.85	1.76	1.70	1.35	1.46	1.42
$25,001 to $50,000	15.51	15.47	15.26	15.22	14.50	1.03	0.96	0.78	0.83	0.76
Up to $25,000	31.22	29.94	26.70	28.03	28.53	0.62	0.56	0.42	0.46	0.45
Total	100.00	100.00	100.00	100.00	100.00	100.00	100.00	100.00	100.00	100.00
	Household goods carriers									
	Number of carriers					Revenues (millions of dollars)				
	1,581	1,644	1,515	1,635	2,187	$359.2	$382.2	$434.8	$462.1	$492.2
	Percentage distribution									
Over $10,000,000	0.32	0.36	0.40	0.43	0.32	39.12	41.78	41.48	43.52	40.61
$5,000,001 to $10,000,000	0.32	0.36	0.59	0.55	0.41	9.41	10.57	15.64	14.08	13.14
$2,500,001 to $5,000,000	0.57	0.49	0.46	0.55	0.27	9.02	7.95	6.12	6.81	4.52
$1,000,001 to $2,500,000	1.07	1.16	1.32	1.16	1.01	6.71	7.41	7.43	5.71	6.96
$500,001 to $1,000,000	1.58	1.28	1.72	1.77	1.55	5.04	3.82	4.18	4.16	4.64
$300,001 to $500,000	2.66	2.74	3.89	4.34	3.38	4.43	4.55	5.23	5.75	5.75
$200,001 to $300,000	5.63	4.50	4.62	3.49	3.57	6.13	4.76	3.93	3.03	3.83
$100,001 to $200,000	13.91	13.44	13.93	16.33	15.27	8.77	8.24	7.00	8.13	9.58
$50,001 to $100,000	18.53	17.70	18.88	17.31	16.05	5.82	5.47	4.71	4.46	5.17
$25,001 to $50,000	23.34	23.05	22.38	22.33	23.46	3.82	3.64	2.88	2.93	3.88
Up to $25,000	32.07	34.92	31.81	31.74	34.71	1.73	1.81	1.40	1.42	1.92
Total	100.00	100.00	100.00	100.00	100.00	100.00	100.00	100.00	100.00	100.00
	Other special commodity carriers									
	Number of carriers					Revenues (millions of dollars)				
	6,501	6,102	6,228	6,414	6,533	$1,783.8	$1,844.9	$2,206.4	$2,295.4	$2,371.8
	Percentage distribution									
Over $10,000,000	0.15	0.21	0.32	0.34	0.26	6.94	10.88	14.69	17.36	15.64
$5,000,001 to $10,000,000	0.55	0.46	0.61	0.56	0.60	12.93	10.14	11.22	10.73	11.69
$2,500,001 to $5,000,000	1.35	1.38	1.45	1.47	1.44	15.52	15.71	14.64	14.72	13.95
$1,000,001 to $2,500,000	3.98	4.00	4.85	4.71	4.88	20.44	20.13	20.47	19.73	20.76
$500,001 to $1,000,000	6.20	6.39	7.21	6.97	7.12	14.85	14.86	14.21	13.53	13.76
$300,001 to $500,000	8.03	7.60	7.77	7.61	8.02	10.62	9.85	8.52	8.31	8.61
$200,001 to $300,000	6.46	6.59	7.19	8.53	6.66	5.37	5.37	4.98	4.76	4.50
$100,001 to $200,000	14.08	14.18	14.63	13.92	14.60	6.85	6.68	5.98	5.56	5.80
$50,001 to $100,000	13.67	13.45	14.00	14.03	14.34	3.40	3.34	2.84	2.83	2.88
$25,001 to $50,000	15.72	15.73	15.19	15.70	15.35	1.96	1.93	1.57	1.64	1.57
Up to $25,000	29.81	30.01	26.78	26.16	26.73	1.12	1.11	0.88	0.83	0.84
Total	100.00	100.00	100.00	100.00	100.00	100.00	100.00	100.00	100.00	100.00

The following table indicates the condition of our docket with respect to proceedings involving motor carriers under sections 5 and 210a(b) and transfer cases:

	July 1, 1961, to June 30, 1962	July 1, 1962, to June 30, 1963
Finance applications, complaints and investigations under sec. 5:		
Received or instituted	[1] 271	[1] 316
Reopened	24	14
Hearings	139	164
Under submission at end of period	85	51
Applications disposed of, including reopened proceedings:		
By effective recommended order:		
Granted in whole or in part	61	40
Denied	9	8
By report of the Commission or a Division of the Commission:		
Granted in whole or in part	95	58
Denied	30	31
By report of an employee board:		
Granted in whole or in part	104	109
Denied	12	22
Dismissed	29	33
Investigations terminated	18	18
Pending at end of period	272	283
Petitions disposed of	132	122
Rulemaking proceeding under sec. 5(1):		
Terminated by the Commission	0	1
Pending at end of period	1	0
Temporary authority applications under sec. 210a(b):		
Received	119	157
Disposed of:		
Granted in whole or in part	83	107
Denied	35	47
Pending at end of period	8	11
Petitions disposed of	43	44
Applications for transfer or lease of operating rights under sec. 212(b) and sec. 206(a)(6) or (7):		
Received	870	907
Hearings	13	5
Disposed of:		
Granted in whole or in part	686	698
Denied	72	119
Dismissed	77	77
Pending at end of period	188	201
Petitions disposed of	149	160

[1] These figures include for the respective years 13 and 15 proceedings under section 5(7). They do not include 18 and 36 related applications for certificates under section 207, handled concurrently with the section 5 application.

WATER CARRIER AND FREIGHT FORWARDER UNIFICATIONS

In our 76th Annual Report, we indicated that an application by the Weyerhaeuser Company, whose principal business is the growth, processing and sale of forest products, to merge into itself its wholly owned water carrier subsidiary, Weyerhaeuser Steamship Company, was denied and that a petition for reconsideration had been filed. Upon reconsideration, the merger was authorized upon a finding that the benefits to be derived from preservation of the water carrier outweighed the disadvantages.

The merger of the John I. Hay Company, a water carrier with extensive rights along the Illinois waterway and portions of the Mississippi, Ohio, Tennessee, Pearl, and West Pearl Rivers and the Gulf and intracoastal waterways, into A. L. Mechling Barge Lines, Inc., was authorized.

The merger of the Russell Bros. Towing Co., Inc., into McAllister Brothers, Inc., and the acquisition by McAllister Brothers, Inc., of McAllister Lighterage Line, Inc., also were authorized. These carriers operate principally along the eastern seacoast and the Great Lakes areas.

Applications for transfer of three water carrier certificates and two freight forwarder permits were approved during the year. Two applications for the transfer of freight forwarder permits, three applications for the transfer of water carrier certificates and four applications for acquisition of water carriers under section 5(2) were filed during the year.

OPERATING AUTHORITIES

The receipt of applications for motor carrier operating authorities, both permanent and temporary, continues to increase. In this fiscal year the Commission disposed of 12,132 formal and informal matters involving carrier operating rights, with motor carrier applications representing the major portion of our decisional case docket. This enlarging volume of motor carrier filings reflects the growing transportation needs of our expanding national economy. Thus, plans for a new pipeline running through the South and to the East brought a number of applications to provide motor service from the pipeline outlets. The dispersion of long established packing plants at Chicago and other centers to numerous new points in the meat producing areas of the nation also resulted in new demands for motor service. Of significance too has been the need for new motor service created by the expansion of the frozen food industry, particularly in the development of new products derived from potatoes at recently established plants in the Red River Valley, Idaho and Maine potato producing areas.

Other economic sources of new motor carrier applications stem from: (1) the efforts of household goods carriers to expand operations to transport new furniture, office fixtures and similar commodities not encompassed within their existing rights; (2) the importation of frozen meat from South America; (3) the increased agricultural use of fertilizer, herbicides and pesticides; (4) the shift of automobile traffic to rail multilevel car service for distribution from rail terminal points in motor service; (5) a changing pattern of cement distribution based on establishment of storage silos at strategic rail points and water ports, with motor service being utilized for local distribution; (6) production of mobile homes larger than the normal house trailers, necessitating their transportation in towaway for-hire truck service; (7) the growing demand of merchants for transportation of small packages of defined size and weight in retail delivery service; and (8) recent developments in novel types of special motor vehicular equipment designed to meet unique industrial needs.

Few applications proposing regular route passenger service were filed during the year. Requests for authority to conduct special and charter operations in sightseeing and pleasure tours, over irregular routes, formed the bulk of passenger carrier applications. Applications for broker licenses to arrange the same type of tours by bus transportation increased.

Along with the foregoing, the Commission has experienced a concurrent growth in requests for temporary authority to meet promptly the transportation needs of shippers throughout the country. Many of these grants of temporary authority later were followed by applications for permanent authority.

During the autumn of 1962 the Cuban crisis generated a large number of temporary authority filings. The sudden surge of events necessitated immediate and expeditious movement of military personnel, equipment and supplies. In cooperation with the Department of Defense, the Commission issued temporary authority to numerous motor carriers to perform the needed service. A timely and orderly flow of material and personnel, on schedule, resulted.

Enactment of Public Law 87–805 added approximately 3,000 applications to our motor carrier docket. Effective October 15, 1962, this statute repealed the so-called Second Proviso exemption from the motor carrier certificate provisions of the act. Under the Second Proviso exemption, qualified motor common carriers holding appropriate intrastate authority and operating solely within a single State could, under certain conditions, also engage in corresponding motor carrier operations in interstate or foreign commerce without obtaining certificates of public convenience and necessity from this Commission. The new legislation provides for issuance of grandfather certificates of registration to carriers who, on the date of its enactment, were lawfully engaged in operations under the former exemption, and establishes a procedure by which single-State motor common carriers seeking new or additional intrastate operating authority also may obtain, upon a proper showing, a certificate of registration authorizing concomitant interstate operations. The major change thus wrought by Public Law 87–805 is that entry into interstate transportation of this type will, in the future, be based upon an affirmative finding that a public need exists for such interstate services. We received 2,885 grandfather applications for certificates of registration on and before February 12, 1963, the statutory filing deadline. Special rules of practice (49 C.F.R. 1.244) were adopted to govern their handling and disposition. In addition, we issued special rules (49 C.F.R. 1.245) directing the specific procedures to be followed in order to obtain a "non-grandfather" certificate of registration under section 206(a)(6). Although the special rules of practice have been drafted so as to permit all issues to be resolved in the most expeditious manner and, so far as practicable and legally permissible, without formal hearings or other proceedings, we already have encountered a number of technical problems in our administration of the new law. The resolution of these issues and the disposition of the large number of grandfather applications on file with this Commission has resulted in a greatly increased workload for our staff. A summary of actions taken in applications and other proceedings concerning operating authorities, compared to the previous year's receipts and dispositions, follows.

Volume and disposition of cases

Motor carrier	July 1, 1961, through June 30, 1962	July 1, 1962, through June 30, 1963
Applications for permanent common carrier certificates, contract carrier permits, brokers licenses:		
Received	4,199	4,457
Reopened	191	151
Hearings	3,282	3,675
Disposed of, including reopened proceedings:		
Withdrawn or dismissed without report	873	1,041
By effective recommended order	1,813	1,887
By the Commission or a division of the Commission, or Operating Rights Board No. 1, or Operating Rights Review Board	1,666	1,457
Applications granted in whole or in part	2,784	2,657
Applications denied or dismissed in report	695	687
Pending at end of year	2,967	3,190
Petitions disposed of	1,027	934

Complaints, etc.	July 1, 1961, through June 30, 1962	July 1, 1962, through June 30, 1963
Complaints, rulemaking, and revocation proceedings:		
Formal complaints filed, including subnumbers	37	37
Investigations instituted	68	71
Reopened	18	16
Hearings	94	90
Disposed of, including subnumbers and reopened proceedings:		
Dismissed or discontinued	45	29
By effective recommended order	29	21
By the Commission or a division of the Commission	74	44
Pending at end of year	155	185
Petitions disposed of	55	50

Water carrier	July 1, 1961, through June 30, 1962	July 1, 1962, through June 30, 1963
Applications for permanent water carrier operating rights:		
Received	46	31
Reopened	8	0
Hearings	6	16
Disposed of, including reopened proceedings:		
Withdrawn or dismissed without report	13	1
By effective recommended order	7	1
By the Commission or a division of the Commission	41	11
Applications granted in whole or in part	28	11
Applications denied or dismissed in report	20	1
Pending at end of period	22	40
Petitions disposed of	10	1

Freight forwarder	July 1, 1961, through June 30, 1962	July 1, 1962, through June 30, 1963
Applications for freight forwarder operating rights:		
Received	7	10
Reopened	0	3
Hearings	7	4
Disposed of, including reopened proceedings:		
Withdrawn or dismissed without report	3	1
By effective recommended order	4	2
By the Commission or a division of the Commission	7	5
Applications granted in whole or in part	8	4
Applications denied or dismissed in report	3	3
Pending at end of period	18	23
Petitions disposed of	0	8

Volume and disposition of cases—Continued

Alaska-Hawaii "grandfather" applications	July 1, 1961, through June 30, 1962	July 1, 1962, through June 30, 1963
Received	0	0
Reopened	0	2
Hearings held	24	109
Disposed of:		
Dismissed, without report	4	5
By effective recommended order	2	13
By the Commission or a division of the Commission	3	1
Applications granted in whole or in part	4	13
Applications denied or dismissed in report	1	1
Pending at end of year	177	160

Agricultural "grandfather" applications	July 1, 1961, through June 30, 1962	July 1, 1962, through June 30, 1963
Applications for "grandfather" and "interim" motor carrier operating rights: [1]		
Received	1	0
Reopened	12	10
Hearings	6	5
Disposed of, including reopened proceedings:		
Withdrawn or dismissed without report	0	1
By effective recommended order	10	2
By the Commission or a division of the Commission	53	12
Applications granted in whole or in part	50	11
Applications denied or dismissed in report	13	3
Pending at end of year	15	10
Petitions disposed of	58	20

[1] Filed under section 7(c) of the Transportation Act of 1958.

Conversion applications	July 1, 1961, through June 30, 1962	July 1, 1962, through June 30, 1963
Applications for conversion and investigations under section 212(c):		
Received	0	0
Reopened	4	2
Hearings	0	0
Disposed of, including reopened proceedings:		
Withdrawn or dismissed without report	0	0
By effective recommended order	4	1
By the Commission or a division of the Commission	6	1
Applications granted in whole or in part	7	2
Applications denied or dismissed in report	3	0
Pending at end of year	1	1
Petitions disposed of	7	7

"Grandfather" certificates of registration	July 1, 1962, through June 30, 1963
Received	2,888
Disposed of (withdrawn or dismissed)	13
Pending at end of year	2,875

Volume and disposition of cases—Continued

Temporary authority, etc.	July 1, 1961, through June 30, 1962	July 1, 1962, through June 30, 1963
Applications for temporary authority under section 210a(a):		
Received	4,024	4,506
Disposed of	4,005	4,494
Granted in whole or in part	3,337	3,770
Denied	668	724
Pending at end of year	46	58
Petitions disposed of	358	482
Applications to file State certificates:		
Filed	831	222
Disposed of	806	327
Pending at end of year	113	8
Petitions disposed of	6	5
Applications to deviate from regular routes:		
Filed	442	446
Disposed of	420	432
Pending at end of year	75	89
Petitions disposed of	6	7
Proceedings to revoke operating rights without hearing:		
Instituted	691	802
Disposed of	758	811
Pending at end of year	80	71

The regulation of for-hire carriage, in interstate or foreign commerce, has become increasingly complex with the passage of time. Technological developments in manufacturing processes, in packaging, in transportation equipment and facilities, changes in traffic patterns and in distribution centers, coupled with keen competition between various modes of carriage, between carriers by the same mode, and between regulated and nonregulated carriers confuse the regulatory picture. We have gained additional time to consider the more serious problems through the referral of the routine type of case to our Operating Rights Review Board. Established in fiscal year 1962, it disposed of 345 cases during this past year, affording us additional time to consider the more important cases. The success of the Board has been proven by the paucity of petitions objecting to Board action, and the small number of its holdings which have been reversed or modified by Commission action. The "Decision and Order," adopting the decision of hearing officer without the issuance of division or Commission reports, is a procedural technique which also has proven its worth and has afforded us opportunity to give greater attention than would otherwise be possible to operating authority questions which deserve comprehensive study, such as those which appear in the following categories.

AIR-MOTOR TRANSPORTATION

The limits within which for-hire motor transportation of persons or property may be conducted as "incidental-to-aircraft" transportation under the exemption provisions of section 203(b)(7a) of the Interstate Commerce Act continued to occupy our concern. The most significant recent decision in this area was reached in *Hatom Corp. Common Carrier Application*, 91 M.C.C. 725. There, we found that the carriage of passengers between airports in the New York City area and specified Connecticut points located more than 25 miles therefrom was beyond the scope of the "incidental-to-air" exemption, reversing an earlier Division decision that the proposed operation was partially exempt. At the same time, we found that additional consideration should be given to the areas or distances within which motor transportation of persons is "incidental-to-air" within the meaning of that section, and we instituted a rulemaking proceeding in No. MC–C–4000, *Motor Transportation of Passengers Incidental to Transportation by Aircraft.*

The extent to which motor transportation of property falls within the section 203(b)(7a) exemption is the subject of a separate rulemaking proceeding previously instituted in No. MC–C–3437, *Motor Transportation Incidental to Transportation by Aircraft.* Pending final determination in that docket, applications for air freight authority are being treated in accordance with prior decisions, particularly *Kenny Extension—Air Freight,* 61 M.C.C. 587, and *Panther Cartage Co. Extension—Air Freight,* 88 M.C.C. 37.

This is one of the areas in which interagency conferences, mentioned earlier, are in progress. Through such conferences, it is expected that the respective jurisdictions of the Commission and the Civil Aeronautics Board over the motor carriage segments of combined air-motor transportation will be clarified.

ALASKA AND HAWAII

In our last annual report we discussed the decision in *Al Renk & Sons, Inc.—Alaska "Grandfather" Application,* 89 M.C.C. 91, defining standards to be applied in determining the merits of motor carrier applications for Alaska grandfather authority filed under section 206 (a)(5) of the Interstate Commerce Act, as amended July 12, 1960. We construed the amendatory act as intending that Alaskan grandfather applicants be relieved of proving that their operations were as substantial and frequent as those operations which were required to be shown by applicants under previous grandfather legislation. By our order, entered October 25, 1962, we denied petitions for reconsideration of the decision in *Renk,* affirming the conclusions reached therein.

Most of the Alaska motor carrier grandfather applications pending during the reporting year for motor carrier authority to operate within Alaska or between points in Alaska and points in other States, have been the subject of oral hearing. We expect the remainder of the motor carrier grandfather applications to be disposed of within a short time. Still pending are a number of Alaska water carrier grandfather applications, and applications to continue freight forwarder operations (1) within Alaska or between points in Alaska and points in other States, or (2) within Hawaii or between points in Hawaii and points in other States. Of the freight forwarder grandfather applications received, 20 have been heard and are awaiting issuance of reports and recommended orders.

COMMERCIAL ZONES AND TERMINAL AREAS

In our administration of the commercial zone exemption provisions of the act (section 203(b)(8)) we have had occasion in the past year to define or modify a number of areas which are commercially a part of an adjacent municipality. Within these geographical areas, for-hire motor carrier operations, in interstate or foreign commerce, are exempt from the certificate provisions of the act. Also, by general rule, an operating right to serve a particular municipality authorizes service by motor carriers and freight forwarders within the designated commercial zone, subject to specific exceptions. We have prescribed a general population-mileage formula application to all municipalities in the United States. Upon petition, however, consideration is given to authorizing departure from the general formula. In enlarging or refusing to extend zone boundaries we have steadfastly adhered to our position that in the prescription of such a zone we are directing attention to an impersonal situation which exists as an economic fact, and the need for additional service in an extended commercial area or the adequacy of existing transportation services within that area are not material to such a proceeding. Among zones specifically defined during the past year were those for Houston, Tex., and Pueblo, Colo. Existing specific descriptions were modified for Cincinnati and Cleveland, Ohio. We found, too, that enlargement of the St. Louis, Mo.-East St. Louis, Ill., and the Minneapolis-St. Paul, Minn., commercial zones was not warranted. Petitions presently are pending involving Philadelphia, Pa., Detroit, Mich., Chicago, Ill., and Cincinnati, Ohio.

We had occasion also to examine the terminal area limits of a water carrier serving Crescent City, Calif. Pursuant to section 202(c) a motor carrier performing terminal transfer, collection or delivery service for a water carrier is not subject to the certificate provisions of part II of the act but such transportation is considered as though performed by the water carrier. In the case of motor carriers and freight forwarders, the commercial zone definition determines limits of the terminal areas. In the case of a water carrier subject to regulation under part III other factors enter the picture. In *Sause Bros. Ocean Towing Co.* v. *W. R. Chamberlin & Co.*, 91 M.C.C. 199, we found that a contract carrier by water of lumber serving Crescent City could perform terminal operations in a territory much greater in scope than the commercial zone of Crescent City. We considered the sparsely populated nature of the area and the fact that distant lumber producers contributed to the development of the port at Crescent City. We found that, considering the water carrier's line-haul operation, a narrow construction of defendant's terminal area would frustrate lumber producers' access to the port.

CONTRACT CARRIAGE

We indicated last year that following the Supreme Court's decision in *Interstate Commerce Commission* v. *J-T Transport Co.*, 368 U.S. 81 (1961), the Court's interpretation of the statutory criteria which must be considered in an application for motor contract carrier authority was applied specifically in *Moyer Contract Carrier Application*, 88 M.C.C. 767. Petitions in the *Moyer* case have been denied, and its rationale has been followed in subsequent contract carrier applications for motor carrier operating authority.

Other matters arising from the 1957 contract carrier legislation continue to require our attention. We have attempted recently to clarify what constitutes a "limited number of shippers" within the meaning of the statutory definition of a contract carrier contained in section 203(a)(15). Although it has been found to be impossible to arrive at a figure applicable to all situations beyond which a contract carrier may not continue to add contracts, we found in *Umthun Trucking Co. Ext.—Phosphatic Feed Supplements*, 91 M.C.C. 691, that the applicant, upon execution of its seventh contract, reached the stage at which the addition of another shipper would place it in a position of serving more than a limited number of persons. We noted that while the seventh contract would not be necessarily determinative in the operations of other contract carriers, the *Umthun* decision should serve as notice to contract carriers, whose services do not possess a high degree of specialization, that attempts to expand their operations to serve more than six or eight separate shippers will be carefully scrutinized to determine whether they are truly providing service to a "limited number" of shippers.

The meaning and weight to be accorded "accessorial services," in connection with establishing that a proposed service is designed to meet the "distinct need" of a shipper within the statutory definition is another area of complexity. The Supreme Court, in the *J-T Transport* case, pointed out that even though opposing common carriers are able to provide reasonably adequate service, a grant of contract carrier authority may be consistent with the public interest and the National Transportation Policy because the "distinct need" of the supporting shipper might not be as well served by protestants as by applicant. In line with this, in *Griffin Mobile Home Transporting Co. Contr. Car. Applic.*, 91 M.C.C. 801, we granted contract carrier authority where the protesting common carriers would not undertake to provide an "accessorial service," which shippers needed in order to obtain a complete service, and which applicant proposed. Petitions seeking reconsideration or other relief in the *Umthun* and *Griffin* proceedings have been denied.

COORDINATED INTERMODAL SERVICE

As noted in our last report, the continued growth of trailer-on-flatcar or piggyback service led us to institute an investigation proceeding in Ex Parte No. 230, *Substituted Service—Charges and Practices of For-Hire Carriers and Freight Forwarders*. This looks to the prescription of rules encouraging the participation in and expansion of coordinated service by rail, motor and water carriers, express companies, and freight forwarders subject to our jurisdiction. At a prehearing conference in October 1962, proposed rules applicable to the practices and movement of piggyback traffic, essentially distinguishing between that piggyback service which is "joint-intermodal" and that which is an all-rail service, were promulgated by us. About 250 representations have been filed by both shippers and carrier interests, and a hearing examiners' report and recommended order have been issued. The examiners' recommendations and the representations will aid in our endeavor to reach a resolution of the issues presented by the dynamic growth of coordinated motor-rail services.

The development and use of joint-intermodal service in the transportation of new automobiles was described at some length in *National Auto. Transporters Assn.—Declaratory Order*, 91 M.C.C. 395, wherein we held that motor carriers presently authorized to transport new automobiles from points of manufacture or assembly could, under certain circumstances, continue to perform the motor portion of the movement which preceded and followed piggyback or multilevel rail car service without modification of their existing motor carrier operating authorities. In instances in which automobile carriers have suffered a severe loss of traffic by reason of these technological changes, and their existing authorities are not sufficient in scope to provide motor service following a rail movement, we provided a procedure for modification of their certificates or permits which, if the relief sought is granted, will enable them to perform a portion of the motor service which they previously provided from origin to destination in an all-motor service. In response thereto, several petitions for modification of automobile authority have been filed. Several of the conclusions reached were made subject to change or modification which might be reached upon a more complete record in Ex Parte No. 230.

EXPRESS

Historically, the intercity movement of most of the nation's express traffic has been accomplished through the use of passenger train service. In recent years the general diminution in passenger train service has caused the country's largest transporter of express traffic, Railway Express Agency, Incorporated, to file an increasing number of applications seeking authority to operate its own line-haul motor vehicles in the transportation of general commodities moving in express service. In turn, independent motor carriers of ordinary freight have voiced a mounting concern that REA, which is a rail-owned entity, is attempting an unwarranted invasion into the motor carrier field in violation of the policy expressed in section 5(2)(b) of the act. *Railway Exp. Agency, Inc., Extension—Nashua, N.H.*, 91 M.C.C. 311, was chosen as a vehicle to examine the character of the services being provided by REA and to reappraise and restate the requirements and policies we believe should prevail with respect to grants of motor carrier operating rights to REA. The report reviewed the meaning of the REA commodity description, "general commodities moving in express service," and we concluded that there is no present need to redefine the term. We examined the relations to the shipping public of carriers of express and carriers of ordinary freight, and concluded that the two types of services have never been shown to be actually competitive; reviewed the relation of REA's intercity motor operations to REA's status as an express company under the act, as well as the effect of the express company's rail affiliation within the meaning of section 5, and concluded that REA must show the existence of special circumstances in order to obtain operating rights not in the nature of a true express service or to obtain rights totally disassociated from rail service; and reviewed the meaning of various restrictions in REA certificates relative to the performance by it of all-motor service to replace its former use of underlying rail or rail-motor service, and concluded that REA should file petitions, which would be subject to protest by interested persons, to modify its routes to all-motor service. Also we reviewed the performance by REA of pickup and delivery service within terminal areas, and concluded that, because the extent of the terminal areas differs according to whether the intercity connecting service is rail or motor, a proceeding should be instituted to resolve this conflict. While we do not view the report in the *Nashua* case as the final solution to the conflict between REA and its motor common carrier competitors, we do look upon it as an important policy decision in the light of new conditions caused by the gradual disappearance of the expedited passenger operations of the railroads by which express traffic historically moved. The Commission's findings in the *Nashua* decision were recently upheld by a three-judge district court in Massachusetts. It can be expected that its importance to the independent trucking industry will prompt an appeal by them to the United States Supreme Court.

WATER CARRIERS

Water carriers, increasingly, are finding that operations by barge and towboat are more economical than operations by steamship. In No. W–360 (Sub-No. 5), *W. R. Chamberlin & Co. Extension—Tugs and Barges*, decided June 17, 1963, our Operating Rights Review Board found that public convenience and necessity require operation by applicant as common carrier by non-self-propelled vessels with the use of separate towing vessels (barge-towboat operations) in the same area in which it is now authorized to operate by self-propelled vessels (steamships). It was concluded that applicant faces rising costs in maintaining and operating its vessels, inevitable obsolescence thereof and a near impossibility of replacing them with new or used ships. We anticipate the filing of additional applications seeking authority to conduct barge operations in lieu of present steamship operations arising from the efforts by water carriers to reduce operating costs.

The development of new types of barges suitable for the transportation, in bulk, of a more comprehensive range of commodities than formerly possible has raised the question whether bulk water carriers are now engaged in unauthorized transportation of certain commodities under the claim that such transportation is exempt from regulation under section 303(b) of the act. The exemption therein applies solely to the transportation, in bulk, of commodities "which are (in accordance with existing custom of the trade in the handling and transportation of such commodities as of June 1, 1939) loaded and carried without wrappers or containers and received and delivered by the carrier without transportation mark or count." This problem is presently before us in No. W–C–11, *A. L. Mechling Barge Lines, Inc., Investigation of Operations*, which is concerned with the bulk transportation of alumina. The case has engendered considerable interest on the part of water carriers and bulk shippers.

A number of applications were filed in early 1963 which seek common carrier authority to operate as water carriers by barge and towing vessels between points and ports along the Verdigris and Arkansas Rivers from Catoosa, Okla., to the confluence of the Arkansas River with the Mississippi River. These requests for new operating authorities have risen following the approval by Congress of a recommendation by the U.S. Army Corps of Engineers to provide a navigable channel, 9 feet in depth, along the Verdigris River and Arkansas River to Catoosa, Okla. A hearing officer in his report in No. W–1164, *A & O Barge Line, Inc., Common Carrier Application*, which embraces nine applications, found that the proposed waterway project has not been completed. He, accordingly, recommended that the considered applications be dismissed for the reason that they were filed prematurely, subject to the right to refile the applications when the U.S.

Army Corps of Engineers certifies that the considered waterway will be open for navigation within 2 years. These applications are pending before us on exceptions.

Water Carrier Temporary Authorities

Water carriers operating on the inland rivers and canals, Great Lakes or in the coastal trade often are called upon by shippers to provide services beyond the scope of the operating authority they might have under part III of the Interstate Commerce Act. If there is an immediate and urgent need for the service, it is not practical for the carrier to seek permanent authority because of the length of time necessarily required for processing an application or the need may be of a temporary or nonrecurring nature. To meet such a need for service, a carrier may, upon a proper showing, be granted temporary operating authority without hearings or other proceedings. Applications for temporary authority are usually handled to a conclusion within a few days. Activity in connection with applications filed by water carriers under section 311(a) of the Interstate Commerce Act for temporary operating authority continued at about the same level as reported last year.

We received 24 applications of which 16 were granted to some extent. Eight were denied or dismissed. One was pending at the close of the fiscal year.

OTHER IMPORTANT QUESTIONS

The subsequent proceedings all have been designated as cases in which issues of general transportation importance are present.

Accessorial services.—In an application for operating authority, as a common carrier by motor vehicle, to transport bulk liquid fertilizer, *Delaware Exp. Co. Extension—Liquid Fertilizers*, 92 M.C.C. 718 (pending on petition), applicant proposed to furnish the shipper's consignees with mobile storage tanks into which the fertilizer would be unloaded from the line-haul trailer. The opposing motor common carriers were willing to provide only the line-haul service and were not willing to furnish the storage tanks. Applicant's proposal was considered an integral part of the transportation service required by the shipper in instances in which consignees lacked storage facilities. Applicant proposed also to station self-propelled spreader tanks and crews to apply the fertilizer to the soil. This was held to be a nontransportation service and not relevant to the issue of public convenience and necessity.

Broker-passenger.—The extent of a motor carrier protestant's interest in an application for a broker's license to arrange for the transportation of passengers by motor vehicle was considered in *Weidner Travel Bureau, Inc., Broker Application*, 92 M.C.C. 17

(pending on petition). The sole protestant motor carrier alleged that a grant of the broker's license would have an adverse competitive effect upon its operations. No consideration was given to this challenge, the report holding that the services of a broker and a carrier of passengers are complementary rather than competitive.

Substituted motor-for-rail service.—In an application for motor carrier operating authority by a rail subsidiary, *Pacific Motor Trucking Co. Extension—Alternate Route*, 92 M.C.C. 774, (pending on petition) applicant sought authority over a new route, the effect of which would have been to allow it to use piggyback unloading ramps at a point closer to other rail points where it was providing less-than-carload piggyback service.

Protestant motor carriers contested the application as though the proposed change was, in effect, an alternate route, pointing out that it would result in a significant reduction in the combined rail-motor mileage between the termini. The report rejects this characterization of the application, however, noting that the rail carrier affiliate still will serve points on the parent rail carrier's lines; that a rail service comprehending the pickup or delivery of less-than-carload shipments in piggyback service will be provided; and that the traffic to be transported will continue to have a prior or subsequent movement by rail, and move at rail rates on rail billing. The conclusion was reached that applicant had shown it would improve the efficiency of its present service; it would continue to provide a service auxiliary and supplemental to that of the railroad; a grant of authority would not have a materially adverse effect upon the operations of existing independent motor carriers; and it had sustained its statutory burden of proving a need for a substituted-motor-for-rail grant of authority subject to the usual auxiliary-and-supplemental and rail-haul restrictions.

Special equipment.—The use of a particular type of motor vehicle equipment by carriers authorized to transport general commodities, except commodities requiring special equipment, was considered in two important decisions. In *Schreiber Trucking Co., Inc.—Investigation*, 91 M.C.C. 91, we found respondent's use of drop-frame trailers, which are constructed with depressed floors to accommodate commodities whose height prohibited their transportation in ordinary van trailers, i.e., oversized electrical transformers and plate glass, did not violate the exception in its certificate. The drop-frame trailers were found to be ordinary equipment more closely resembling open-top and van-type trailers of the type generally employed by general freight haulers, as contrasted to lowboy trailers used by heavy haulers which are special equipment. Petitions seeking reconsideration and other relief have been denied.

In No. 33554, *Motor Vehicles—Idaho, Nevada, and Utah Origins* (pending on petition), embracing related complaint and investigation proceedings, decided January 24, 1963, the principal issue involved the right of the respondent general commodity carriers, whose authorities excepted the transportation of commodities requiring special equipment, to transport multiple units of automobiles in special automobile "carry-all" equipment accommodating a number of automobiles. Although the transportation of an automobile *per se* does not require special over-the-road equipment, as an automobile can be carried on conventional trucking equipment, we found respondents were not authorized under their existing authority to invade the field of the specialized auto haulers by the use of the auto haulers' special "carry-all" equipment to transport multiple loads of automobiles. Such prohibition applies whether the special "carry-all" equipment used by respondents for multiple loads of automobiles was equipped with a permanent or removable type of superstructure.

NUMBER OF MOTOR CARRIERS AND BROKERS

The following statement shows the number of motor carriers and brokers whose operations are subject to regulation under part II of the act. The statement does not include motor carriers operating exclusively under temporary authority under section 210a(a).

Motor carriers	As of June 30, 1962	As of June 30, 1963
Property carriers:		
Common, issued certificates under sections 206 or 207	11, 611	11, 416
Common, issued certificates under section 212(c)	334	337
Common, issued certificates under section 7(c) Transportation Act of 1958	401	407
Common, issued certificates under section 206(a)(5)	0	10
Common, under 2nd proviso 206(a)(1)	2, 986	2, 981
Contract, issued permits under section 209	2, 356	2, 395
Contract, issued permits under section 7(c) Transportation Act of 1958	26	25
Total property carriers	17, 714	17, 571
Passenger carriers:		
Common, issued certificates under sections 206 or 207	1, 139	1, 134
Common, issued certificates under section 212(c)	1	1
Common, under 2nd proviso 206(a)(1)	100	99
Contract, issued permits under section 209	16	14
Total passenger carriers	1, 256	1, 248
Total motor carriers	18, 970	18, 819
Brokers issued licenses under section 211:		
Property	73	71
Passenger	165	188
Total brokers	238	259

INVENTORY OF MOTOR CARRIER
OPERATING AUTHORITIES

Last year we reported that the program for identifying motor carriers, their routes, the commodities which they are authorized to transport, and other provisions of their operating authorities was brought to current status.

In the past fiscal year, the program was subjected to a series of tests and personnel were trained to extract data from the file. Data not otherwise readily obtainable were made available for use in current Commission operations. Exploratory or pilot studies and procedures were initiated for the purpose of drawing statistical data from the file for research useful in the development of Commission policy, particularly in the area of entry control.

With the installation of the RCA 301 computer equipment, the file is being placed on magnetic tape. For the present, the inventory is used only for Commission purposes and, under certain conditions, for official use by other Government agencies.

RATE PROCEEDINGS AND ACTIVITIES

The Commission has the responsibility to ensure that the public interest is served through provision of reasonable surface transportation rates by regulated carriers. This has become even more complex during this era of intense competition. Our administration of provisions of the act dealing with publication, filing and interpretation of tariffs, suspension of tariffs, and ratemaking in general continue to require concerted attention on the part of both Commissioners and the staff of our Bureau of Traffic.

TARIFFS

Under relevant sections of the act, all carriers subject to the Commission's jurisdiction are required to file with the Commission their rates, fares, charges, and related rules, regulations and practices. Such data must be published, filed and posted by the carriers in the manner prescribed by the Commission. Carriers are prohibited from making any changes in their rates or in the matters mentioned above, except after 30 days' notice to the Commission and the public, unless otherwise authorized by this Commission.

When tariffs are filed they are examined to determine that they give lawful notice of changes and for compliance with other requirements of the law and the Commission.

During the year, 186,633 publications containing newly established or changed freight, express, pipeline, or freight forwarder rates, passenger fares or contract carrier rate schedules were received for examining and filing. The detailed figures follow:

FREIGHT

	Tariffs received
Common carrier:	
Rail	47, 875
Motor	110, 900
Water	2, 244
Pipeline	914
Freight forwarders	10, 413
Total	172, 346

	Schedules received
Contract carrier:	
Motor	2, 569
Water	25
Total	2, 594
Total freight	174, 940

PASSENGER   *Tariffs received*
    Rail _____ 6, 372
    Motor _____ 4, 140
    Water _____ 90

    Total _____ 10, 602

EXPRESS   *Tariffs received*
    Rail _____ 596
    Motor _____ 495

    Total _____ 1, 091

    Total passenger and express_____ 11, 693

    Grand total_____ 186, 633

Of these tariffs and rate schedules, 3,993 were rejected for failure to give the statutory notice or for nonconformity with the Commission's regulations; and 21,249 were criticized for minor irregularities but were accepted for filing since the defects were not sufficient to warrant rejection. Applications requesting permission to change rates or other tariff provisions on less than the 30-day statutory notice, or to depart from the tariff publishing rules, numbered 10,579. With 192 pending on July 1, 1962, the total was 10,771 applications, of which 9,197 were approved, 1,002 denied and 339 withdrawn, leaving 233 pending on July 1, 1963. Also received, examined and criticized were 12,999 powers of attorney, concurrences and revocation notices involving rates and charges. During the year, motor carrier rate data were checked preliminary to issuance of 4,493 new or amended permanent operating certificates and permits, and in connection with 1,362 transfers of operating rights. Similar checks were made in connection with the granting of 4,722 applications for temporary authority.

Motor contract carriers are required to file copies of their contracts with shippers. A total of 5,013 copies of such contracts were filed with the Commission. The act also requires the filing of contracts between freight forwarders and motor common carriers for transportation, and 20,801 such contracts or amendments were received and filed. In our administration of section 22 of the act (derived from the original Act of 1887), which permits free or reduced rates for transportation of property for the United States, State and municipal governments, we processed 21,848 quotations or tenders. All quotations or tenders for U.S. Government transportation are required to be filed with the Commission.

RELEASED RATES

Sections 20(11), 219 and 413 authorize the Commission upon a proper showing to permit carriers to limit their liability for loss or damage. Usually the limitation of liability is accompanied by a consideration to the shippers in the form of reduced rates. Applications for authority under the above sections to establish rates dependent upon declared or agreed value totaled 101. Seventeen were pending on July 1, 1962, for a total of 118, of which 61 were granted, 25 denied, 17 withdrawn, and 15 pending at the end of the year. Twenty-two orders previously entered were rescinded.

SUSPENSIONS

Under provisions of the act, requests may be submitted to the Commission for the suspension and investigation of proposals filed by carriers on rates, fares, charges, and related matters. Requests for suspension, with a few exceptions, are handled by a staff component, the Board of Suspension. Today, as in the past, the suspension procedure in many instances is the testing ground by carriers of new concepts or innovations in ratemaking. Such proposals and their economic impact generate heated interest from competing carriers as well as from shippers or receivers of traffic. Thus it is that our Board of Suspension deals daily, in the public interest with the crucial area of lawfulness of proposals filed with the Commission and against which protests are directed. The action taken initially by the Board, therefore, is vital in terms of the Commission's carrying out its regulatory responsibility in the field of ratemaking.

In the past year, the Board handled 5,130 rate adjustments, covering 8,378 tariff publications, filed by all classes of carriers under our regulation. Protests against these adjustments totaled 5,333, of which 3,853 came from competing carriers, 1,408 from shippers or receivers and 72 from governmental agencies. No protests were directed against 14 adjustments, but the Board considered these on its own motion because of special circumstances.

Reflecting the continuing downward trend in the level of rates considered by the Board, of the 5,130 adjustments 4,484 involved rate reductions. Only 436 were for rate increases. Of the remaining adjustments, 165 covered both increases and reductions while 45 did not have any change in rate levels.

At the suspension level, the action taken on the 5,130 adjustments was as follows:

	Rail	Motor	Water	Frieght forwarder	Express and pipeline	Total	
						Number	Percent
Suspended in full	93	1,672	10	54	3	1,832	35.8
Suspended in part	10	69	1	0	0	80	1.6
Not suspended (permitted to become effective)	767	1,366	103	93	42	2,371	46.1
Otherwise disposed of (schedules rejected, protest withdrawn, protested schedules canceled by carriers, etc.)	126	694	5	21	1	847	16.5
Total	996	3,801	119	168	46	5,130	100.0

As a result of the action taken by the Board initially, 253 petitions were filed seeking relief from the Board's decision to suspend or investigate proposed adjustments; while 688 appeals were filed seeking reconsideration of the Board's decision not to suspend proposed adjustments. A total of 412 investigation and suspension proceedings were discontinued when carriers canceled protested proposals under special permission authority and advised they would not attempt to justify their proposal.

FOURTH SECTION BOARD

Under the provisions of section 4 of the act (derived from the original Act of 1887), it is unlawful for rail and water carriers to charge or receive greater compensation for a shorter haul than for a longer haul over the same line or route, or to charge greater compensation as a through rate than that produced by the sum of separately established rate factors. The Commission may waive these requirements upon the filing of an application for relief by the carriers. The Fourth Section Board handles these requests.

The Board received 587 applications for relief from the long-and-short-haul and aggregate-of-intermediate-rates provisions, an increase of 3 over the previous year. There were 88 pending on July 1, 1962, a decrease of 11 from the previous year. Of these 675 applications, 13 were withdrawn, 17 were denied, 559 were granted in whole or in part, and 86 were pending at yearend. The number of orders entered in response to applications was 602, of which 25 were denial orders, and the remaining 577 were orders granting relief. Petitions received for modification of outstanding orders totaled 40, and 1 was pending on July 1, 1962. Of these 41 petitions, 6 were denied, 34 were granted in whole or in part, and 1 was pending.

INFORMAL RATE CASES AND RELATED WORK

While informal decisions of the Commission or its staff are not binding upon parties to controversies, their persuasive effect in most cases leads the disputants to settle their differences voluntarily, and thus obviates an additional burden on the formal docket. The procedural methods of informal handling are relatively simple, and except for cases involving conferences with the parties themselves, disposition is achieved by correspondence. Through encouragement of the use of informal procedure, rate and transportation disputes between shippers and carriers may be resolved in an inexpensive and timely fashion. Not only are informal resolutions of controversies of economic value to the parties themselves, but this procedure also results in a saving of time and money to the U.S. Government.

We received 1,305 informal complaints against all types of carriers, which was about the same as received the previous year. Dispositions during the year were 1,590, an increase of 506 over the preceding year. The complaints involved allegations of overcharges, unreasonable practices such as misrouting, credit practices of carriers, inquiries as to reduced fares and free transportation of passengers, interpretation of statutory limitation periods, jurisdictional questions, loss and damage claims, and dissatisfaction with carriers' service.

The act provides for an award of damages for violations by railroads, pipelines and water carriers. Often a carrier subject to parts I and III is willing to pay them, or to waive collection of undercharges, in which event a petition for appropriate authority may be filed by the carrier on the special docket in the form prescribed by the Commission. Part I and part III carriers submitted 899 applications, 177 fewer than last year, for authority to pay reparation for alleged unreasonableness of applicable rates or charges. Orders were entered authorizing payment in 714 cases, a decrease of 59 from the previous year. The reparation awarded totaled $993,069.74, or an increase of $65,333.58. The largest single award, embracing 180 cases was one of $41,405.10. Additionally, 393 special docket cases were dismissed or disposed of without orders, an increase of 64 over the previous year. There were 791 requests for photostatic copies and certificates of tariff publications processed during the year, a decrease of 353 from the previous year.

In connection with our continuing program of sampling rail carload waybills, the Bureau of Traffic manually determined the short-line mileages for 29,667 waybills referred to it by our Bureau of Transport Economics and Statistics. These waybills constitute approximately 14 percent of all such waybills filed with the latter Bureau, where the preponderance of them is now processed by electronic means.

FORMAL PROCEEDINGS

Formal proceedings involving rates and practices of the various modes of surface transportation are considered in this section. A summary of reports of special importance issued during the year with a brief statement of the facts and issues involved, has been included to show the broad range of problems presented to the Commission for decision. These proceedings involve intermodal and intramodal competition, complaints by shippers that certain rates place them at a disadvantage in competing with other shippers at a common market, and broad investigations instituted by the Commission on its own motion into various practices of regulated carriers.

Competition continues to intensify as a result of the declining share of traffic transported by common carriers, particularly the railroads.

This is reflected in rate reductions, as each mode seeks to secure an increased share of the available traffic. Such reductions are frequently protested by carriers presently participating in the traffic or by those providing competitive service. The principal argument in protests is that the proposed rates are not compensatory. Our Board of Suspension, described in another section, generally is the body issuing the orders of suspension, which run for seven months. When rate proposals are suspended, a formal proceeding is instituted to determine their lawfulness. They often are bitterly contested, as the introduction into evidence of complex traffic, cost, and other highly technical studies demonstrates. The economic impact of the decisions is widespread, frequently influencing the actions of carriers and shippers not directly affected.

We referred to the creation of the Rates and Practices Review Board, an employee board, in our 76th Annual Report. The Board was established to decide the less complex rate cases, thus permitting Division 2 (our rate Division) and the entire Commission to concentrate on exceptionally difficult proceedings and matters of general transportation importance.

The Board has functioned most successfully; for example, it decided 231 proceedings last year. In only 20 percent of these were petitions filed for reconsideration. Of those, Appellate Division 2 reopened only seven proceedings for reconsideration and two for the purpose of receiving further evidence. Thus, approximately 95 percent of the cases decided by the Board required no further report by the Commission.

The following table summarizes proceedings dealt with by the Bureau of Rates and Practices in 1962 and 1963. It will be noted that 378 motor and 440 rail proceedings were pending at the end of the fiscal year, as compared with 378 and 412 in 1962. The slight increase in rail proceedings is due to an increase in the number of formal complaints filed during the year.

Only those rate cases we consider to be of special importance, decided by report, or pending before us at some stage during the year, are discussed below. In a few instances, the dates mentioned do intrude beyond fiscal 1963, yet circumstances make these cases worthy of some comment.

Summary of rates and practices proceedings, 1962 and 1963

	1962		1963	
	Motor	Rail	Motor	Rail
Pending at beginning of year	424	493	378	412
Instituted, filed and reopened during year:				
Investigations and suspensions	1,468	238	1,292	158
Formal complaints	27	112	27	178
Investigations	99	95	73	82
Ex parte proceedings	1	8	2	10
Fourth section applications		25		17
Section 25 proceedings		22		22
Others [1]	3	2	3	1
Received during year	1,598	502	1,397	468
Total on hand and received	2,022	995	1,775	880
Disposed of during year:				
Investigations and suspensions:				
By report of Commission, Division or Board	194	91	192	53
By effective recommended order	12	3	4	2
Discontinued	1,281	202	1,078	119
Formal Complaints:				
By report of Commission, Division or Board	16	78	11	102
By effective recommended order	10	25	3	17
Dismissed or discontinued	13	19	7	15
Investigations:				
By report of Commission, Division or Board	43	42	49	45
By effective recommended order	31	6	17	9
Discontinued	41	45	31	23
Ex parte proceedings:				
By report of Commission, Division or Board	1	9	1	9
By effective recommended order				1
Discontinued				1
Fourth section applications:				
By report of Commission, Division or Board		9		15
By effective recommended order		13		2
Dismissed or discontinued		11		7
Section 25 proceedings:				
By report of Commission, Division or Board		7		4
By effective recommended order		17		15
Discontinued		1		
Others: [1]				
By report of Commission, Division or Board		2	3	1
By effective recommended order	2			
Dismissed or discontinued		3	1	
Total	1,644	583	1,397	440
Pending at end of year	378	412	378	440
Petitions:				
Pending at beginning of year	33	54	30	56
Received during year:				
Investigation and suspensions	72	60	91	61
Formal complaints	14	126	21	153
Investigations	50	75	46	76
Ex Parte proceedings	3	7	8	6
Fourth section applications		7		4
Section 25 proceedings		2		1
Others [1]		2	1	2
Total	139	279	167	303
Total on hand and received	172	333	197	359
Disposed of during year:				
Investigations and suspensions	78	59	95	62
Formal complaints	13	119	21	158
Investigations	49	80	49	85
Ex parte proceedings	2	5	9	9
Fourth section applications		9		5
Section 25 proceedings		2		
Others [1]		3	1	2
Total	142	277	175	321
Petitions pending at end of year	30	56	22	38

[1] Includes section 5(a) applications, released rate proceedings, freight forwarder complaints, water carrier applications, motor carrier applications, and finance applications involving rate matters and referred to the Bureau for handling and disposition.

As a result of a court decree, we issued a report in *American Barge Line Co.* v. *Alabama G.S.R. Co.*, 316 I.C.C. 759. Its significance stems from our requirement that rail carriers hauling grain from Tennessee and Mississippi River crossings in the South remove the discrimination found to exist where the rates on such grain exceeded the divisions received by the defendants for corresponding service on all-rail grain. Previously, we had required the same proportional rates on ex-barge grain as applied on all-rail grain from river crossings at which proportional rates were established.

In setting rate levels to meet competition, carriers face the problem of creating unlawful conditions insofar as shippers and geographic localities are concerned. We were confronted with this in *Cudahy Packing Co.* v. *Akron C. & Y.R. Co.*, 318 I.C.C. 229. We found that rail rates on fresh meats and packinghouse products from points west of the Mississippi River to official territory were unduly prejudicial to such origins and shippers there located and unduly preferential of origins and shippers on and east of the Mississippi River. We determined that once a complainant has established a prima facie case of undue prejudice and preference, the defendant carrier has the burden of establishing that carrier competition justifies a rate disparity. The degree of motor carrier competition from all points in the origin territory was not the same. We acknowledged that traffic was moving from the prejudiced area and that the aggrieved parties had trade advantages not associated with transportation. A three judge district court in Illinois sustained our action on June 27, 1963.

In *Motor Vehicles—Kansas City to Arkansas, Louisiana, and Texas,* 318 I.C.C. 301, we found that neither the fact nor possibility that motor carriers might lose long-haul traffic to rail piggyback constituted a destructive competitive practice. Piggyback plan III (in which rail carriers provide only flatcars) and plan V (joint motor-rail movement) rates for freight and passenger motor vehicles on a carload basis were thus approved. The piggyback rates approached fully distributed costs, and the overall cost was found lower than for all-motor service. Certain rates published on a per-car basis were found unjust and unreasonable, however. All findings in this case were without prejudice to different conclusions which might arise from Ex Parte No. 230 (see page 71).

Coal from Southern Mines to Tampa and Sutton, Fla., 318 I.C.C. 371, represented an unusual regulatory problem affecting the ability of railroads to compete with private water carriage. Reduced rail rates were proposed on fine coal from mines in Alabama, Kentucky, Tennessee, and Virginia, to Tampa, Fla., to meet unregulated water service to that area. The same water carriers involved also hauled phosphate rock northbound from Florida. The railroads proposed to haul coal southbound in covered hopper cars which otherwise would return empty to Florida after transporting phosphate rock northbound. We concluded that without the proposed rates, the railroads not only would be foreclosed from the coal traffic, but also would face a threat to the retention of northbound movements of phosphate rock. The rates were found compensatory in the peculiar circumstances by excluding from out-of-pocket costs the rate of return on investment of 4 percent provided in the Rail Form A cost formula.

In *Gordons Transports, Inc.*, v. *Strickland Transp. Co.*, 318 I.C.C. 395, opposing lines formed in the transportation industry on almost the entire range of piggyback services. Two railroads and Strickland, a motor common carrier, provided certain rail-motor service involving plan III. They also proposed to provide plan I service (traffic moved at motor rates but using rail services in substitution for the motor movement). While Strickland held operating rights between the points involved, its routes were circuitous and as such were not a cause for alarm for competing carriers. However, with the advent of plan III usage by Strickland, such carriers complained of traffic diversion to Strickland's lines because of the shorter distance covered by the rails between the points. We ruled against the use of plan III by Strickland on the basis of prior Commission decisions that a carrier cannot act as a carrier and shipper at the same time. In addition we condemned plan I usage by Strickland. This significant decision was based on the grounds that use of that plan would render Strickland a competitor with existing motor carriers, whereas it would not be if its motor routes were used. No reasonable relationship existed between the services proposed under plan I to the motor service actually authorized to Strickland. We condemned the proposal. Our conclusions, however, were without prejudice to a possible contrary finding in Ex Parte No. 230 (see page 71). A three judge district court in Texas sustained our action in the *Strickland* decision on July 19, 1963.

To meet market competition in western trunkline territory, eastern railroads sought fourth section relief without the imposition of the usual condition that intermediate rates shall not exceed the lowest combination of rates subject to the act. The condition has been consistently imposed by the Commission for over 50 years. In *Iron and Steel from Official to W.T.L. Territory*, 318 I.C.C. 449, Appellate Division 2 granted the relief, as sought. The background of the condition was reviewed in depth. There was no indication that producers at the intermediate points would be affected. As a practical matter, it was recognized that imposition of the condition would force the carriers either to forego the traffic or reduce the intermediate rates. Both alternatives, however, amounted to a serious revenue loss. But without the condition, the railroads at least had traffic upon which revenues could be earned.

The lawfulness of rates of motor carriers employing owner-operators to perform the line-haul movement was sharply brought into focus in *Iron and Steel Scrap—Conn., Mass. & R.I., to Pa.*, 318 I.C.C. 567. Owner-operators are normally paid a percentage of revenue by the motor carrier. Here an attempt was made to justify rates on the basis that revenue remaining with the carrier covered its costs. Our Bureau of Inquiry and Compliance produced cost evidence making a prima facie case that the rates in issue were less than costs. But the motor carrier overcame this by producing evidence that the revenue retained covered all of its overhead costs by a substantial margin. We concluded that data concerning the costs of individual owner-operators were impossible to verify. We found that when the carrier's retained revenue compensates it for services rendered, the total rate charged will be compensatory, provided the division of revenue accruing to the owner-operators is sufficient to acquire and retain their services. When these criteria were not met, we condemned a rate. *Sheet Steel, Galvanized—St. Louis to Marshalltown, Iowa*, 318 I.C.C. 589.

Upon petition of the Middle Atlantic Conference, a publishing agent for 1,300 motor common carriers, we instituted an investigation into charges for the detention of motor vehicles in middle Atlantic territory and between that territory and New England. We found a chaotic situation. *Detention of Motor Vehicles—Middle Atl. & New England*, 318 I.C.C. 593. We were convinced of the need for a uniform rule, uniformly observed. We also recognized that only through the experience of actual use would we be able to ascertain the value of a uniform rule. We, therefore, prescribed a new rule for a 1-year test period.

Intramodal rail competition is still active. *Baltimore & O.R. Co.* v. *Chicago & E.I.R. Co.*, 318 I.C.C. 771. There, the complainant railroads were seeking a minimum rate order on multiple car ex-river shipments on bituminous coal from Mount Vernon, Ind., to Chicago. Division 2 declined to enter such an order but did determine a lawful rate level which would preserve an alternate route for shippers and which also would permit complainant carriers to maintain their inherent cost advantages. We granted reconsideration of this matter on June 26, 1963. Intramodal rail competition, with rail carriers supporting the Commission's exercise of minimum rate powers is also a dominant feature in two pending grain cases. No. 31874, *Southeastern Assoc. of Railroad and Utilities Commissioners* v. *Atchison, T. & S.F. Ry. Co.*, (the *Southern Governors' Grain Rate* case, mentioned in our 76th Annual Report) and No. 33171, *Omaha Grain Exchange* v. *Chicago, B. & Q. R. Co.* For example, in the *Omaha Grain* case, the lawfulness of the absolute rate-break rule for making rates on grain is in issue. Under that rule, the outbound rates from primary markets can be no lower than proportional rates published from and to the same points. The rule represents an exercise of the Commission's minimum rate authority. And the defendant rail carriers fear that the absence of the absolute rate-break rule would result in destructive intramodal competition.

We noted that Division 2's report in *Reduced Transcontinental Lumber Rates, 1961*, 318 I.C.C. 815, involved an issue of general transportation importance. In that case, the rail carriers reduced rates and increased minimum weights on lumber from Pacific coast origins to eastern destinations. They sought to encourage shippers to load heavier and thus permit more efficient utilization of their equipment. Division 2 approved these rates, which would increase respondent carriers' net revenues substantially without any increase in the volume of traffic. It also found that the dominant motive was not predatory in character and that the reduced rates would not disturb the water carrier protestants' inherent cost advantage.

Confronted with the effect of rates on port interests, Division 2 rendered two significant decisions. In *Export Grain from Texas to Texas Points*, 319 I.C.C. 16, reduced export grain rates to Houston, Galveston, Texas City, and Port Arthur were found unduly preferential of those ports and unduly prejudicial to Corpus Christi, Tex. The rail respondents were given the election of either reducing the rates to all the ports involved or maintaining the existing rate structure. In *Brazos Harbor Nav. Dist.* v. *Abilene & S. Ry. Co.*, 319 I.C.C. 54, Division 2 found certain rates to the port of Freeport, Tex., unlawful. They were found unduly prejudicial to that port and unduly preferential of Houston, Galveston and Texas City, to the extent of the difference in rates. In both cases, the rail carriers involved argued that they did not effectively control the rates. The division found to the contrary and found that the carriers were a common source of the discrimination.

In *Rail-Water, Grain in Bulk, Mo., Ill., and Ind., to Buffalo*, 319 I.C.C. 123, Division 2 approved joint rail-water rates on corn and wheat. The issue of whether or not the rates were changed or initial ones was raised at the hearing. The examiner found the rates to be initial. Division 2 found the issue was not determinative of the case because of the adequacy of the record. Nevertheless, Division 2 held that the rates were changed because they reflect a reduction from the existing combination rates and because that result places the burden of proof upon the parties best able to discharge it. And such a conclusion was found to be consistent with the public interest and the Commission's statutory command for expeditious action. We noted that the case involved an issue of general transportation importance.

Initial rates occur frequently in the motor carrier industry. The Interstate Commerce Act does not specifically place a statutory burden of proof upon the carrier to justify these rates. In *Animal Feed, Miss. and Tenn. to Midwest and Southwest*, 319 I.C.C. 257, we recognized the need to clarify the burden of proof issue. This is particularly necessary because such a determination often is crucial to the outcome of such proceedings. Section 7(c) of the Administrative Procedure Act places the burden on proponents of an order. The right to initiate rates rests with carriers. By publishing rates, carriers become proponents of rates rather than of orders. And, as a practical matter, the rates will stand unless protested. We thus found the burden of proof to rest upon the protestants, for they were the proponents of the order which instituted the proceeding.

After the Supreme Court's decision in *Interstate Commerce Commission* v. *New York, N.H. & H. R. Co.*, 372 U.S. 744 (1963), we issued a report on reconsideration in *Garden Hose & Electric Cable from N.J. or R.I. to Tex.*, 319 I.C.C. 227. In the prior report, 314 I.C.C. 515, a reduced TOFC rate on plastic garden hose was condemned by Division 2 even though it was found to be compensatory. The proposal resulted in a parity of rates, rail vis-a-vis Sea-Land. Sea-Land was found to be the low-cost service, and the proposed rail rate was found to be a destructive competitive practice because rate parity would inhibit Sea-Land's ability to compete and threaten its existence. A lawful level was set at 6 percent above the Sea-Land rate, which action was consistent with *Commodities—Pan-Atlantic S. S. Corp.*, 313 I.C.C. 23. That case was the Commission report from which appeal was taken to the courts.

We affirmed the principle that the destructive competitive cost aspects of a proposal can be determined only if the protestants introduce their costs. Here such costs were not shown. Also, we indicated that service disabilities affirmatively must be shown to be related to competitive ability; that the national defense aspects of the national transportation policy are not self-executing; and that to come within the purview thereof, the assailed rate must be shown to threaten the continued existence of a transportation service uniquely capable of fulfilling a public need. We approved the rate.

In *Sugar, South to Indiana, Ohio River, Intermediate Points*, 319 I.C.C. 782, we reversed a prior report of Division 2, 315 I.C.C. 521. Division 2 had condemned reduced rail and barge rates without prejudice to the establishment of rail rates 10 percent higher than the total costs to the shipper or consignee at the prior barge rates. The Division found that both series of reductions fostered unsound economic conditions in transportation: a rate war and destructive competitive practices. We disagreed. Both series of rates were fully remunerative. We could find no basis for prescribing a differential. By comparing total costs to the shipper via both modes, we concluded that the rail routes, not the barge routes, provided the low-cost service on the involved sugar traffic. We approved both the rail and the barge rates.

Last year, we mentioned Division 2's report in No. 33664, *Loading of Freight by Shippers at Eastern Origins.* On May 6, 1963, we issued a report on reconsideration and reversed Division 2. We approved tariff provisions which extended to shippers the promiscuous loading of freight. The rail carriers' intent was to encourage mutually beneficial loading practices and to encourage the heavier loading of cars. Motor carrier opposition was bottomed on the argument that freight forwarders utilizing all commodity rates would be the primary shippers to benefit from the proposals, and they feared that approval of the practice ultimately would mean losing valuable traffic. We did not find this argument persuasive. Nor were we convinced that the proposals presented a potentially discriminatory situation as found in the prior Division 2 report, 316 I.C.C. 179.

One of the most sharply contested rail cases in recent years was initially decided by Division 2 in *Grain in Multiple-Car Shipments— River Crossings to So.,* 318 I.C.C. 641, the "Big John" case. There, the Southern Railway System proposed severe rate reductions, up to 65 percent, for grain shipped in lots of 5, 10 and 20 jumbo (Big John) hopper cars, each car subject to a minimum load of 90 tons. Other rail lines proposed similar rates for the same aggregate minimum but subject to the minimum of only 50 tons per standard boxcar. While the rates were designed to meet unregulated motor carriage, barge lines were the principal protestants.

These protestants maintained that they had an inherent cost advantage. However, Division 2 disagreed and found that these protestants could only be found to have this advantage if public costs were considered. Such costs were not shown. Thus, overall costs and service advantages were not considered to be relevant. Rates on five-car lots, or 450 tons, were approved, as compensatory and necessary to meet exempt motor transportation. Rates for the other multiple-lot shipments were found not shown to be compensatory or to be competitively necessary. Division 2 also found that the rates proposed for movement in standard equipment were not justified by specific cost evidence. Technological efficiency and managerial initiative were noted in the report as elements to be promoted under the national transportation policy.

By report dated July 1, 1963, we reversed Division 2. We found that public costs were not pertinent in determining which carrier has the inherent cost advantage, that the rates were below a minimum reasonable level, and that the rates were unduly prejudicial to shippers at certain localities and preferential of others. We ordered the rates to be canceled without prejudice to the filing of new schedules reflecting at least an increase of approximately 16 percent in the multiple-car rates presently in effect. This increase would preserve the bargelines' cost advantage on certain port-to-port movements. And it would prevent the rail movement of grain at rates which would not be adequately compensatory if established on nondiscriminatory bases from Tennessee River ports.

The effectiveness of our order was stayed on August 21, 1963, by a district court's temporary restraining order. The stay will remain in effect until a three judge court makes a determination on a complaint assailing our order in this proceeding.

Sheer magnitude of the record and the amount of revenue involved contributed to our problems in deciding *Akron, C. & Y. R. Co.* v. *Atchison, T. & S. F. Ry. Co.*, 321 I.C.C. 17. Eastern, midwestern, and transcontinental lines sought an adjustment in the divisions of joint through rates between points in mountain-Pacific territory and points in the Midwest and East. Evidence adduced at several hearings held over a period of $4\frac{1}{2}$ years finally showed that the western lines received as their share of the revenue about 5 percent more than their share of the cost of service. Revenues exceeded out-of-pocket costs by 57 percent in the West, 43 percent in the Midwest, and 22 percent in the East. It was our conclusion that divisions of the eastern and midwestern carriers should be increased. Primarily, divisions over principal interchange points between East and West were prescribed on a percentage basis; for example, from the east coast to the Pacific coast, the eastern division was raised by 24 percent, and from interior eastern groups to the coast, by 33 percent. Also, scales of divisional factors were prescribed for subdividing the revenue within the East and West resulting from the primary division. Based on traffic studies submitted in these proceedings, upward of 1 billion dollars annual revenue is involved.

In August 1963, a court issued an injunction against our order in this matter, pending final court determination. This, however, was on condition that western railroads would indemnify eastern and midwestern railroads if the Commission's order subsequently prevailed.

We believe a significant step was taken in the area of cost evidence, when we instituted a rulemaking proceeding in No. 34013, *Rules to Govern the Assembling and Presenting of Cost Evidence.* Consideration will be given as to whether the adoption of certain cost formulas developed by our cost finding staff would: (*a*) result in improved quality and reduced quantity of cost evidence; (*b*) eliminate controversy over admissibility of cost data prepared in an approved manner; and (*c*) obviate or at least shorten cross-examination of witnesses on methodology used in preparing cost studies. This rulemaking action is being handled under special rules of procedure which call for the filing of verified statements and reply statements by interested parties.

In 1961, we instituted several rulemaking and related proceedings affecting practices of household goods carriers, Ex Parte No. 19, *Practices of Motor Common Carriers of Household Goods*, et al. After public hearings and issuance of the examiner's recommendations we heard oral argument in May 1963. As instituted, these proceedings cover a broad spectrum of proposals related to the industry's practices, including possible legislative recommendations regarding maximum rates and charges, and the problem of underestimation of charges to the public; extension of credit to shippers; relinquishing household goods at destination to the shippers; and the released rates problem. These proceedings are of utmost importance to the household goods industry inasmuch as practices of the industry have been the target of increasing public criticism and complaint as well as being of deep concern to this Commission.

We mentioned in last year's report that the importance and marked increase in piggyback service prompted us, in June 1962, to institute a rulemaking proceeding in Ex Parte No. 230, *Substituted Service— Charges and Practices of For-Hire Carriers and Freight Forwarders (Piggyback Service)*. This is the most extensive proceeding we have undertaken in the piggyback field. All carriers of property (except pipelines) subject to our jurisdiction were made parties and others interested were invited to participate. It has been handled through a prehearing conference, special rules of procedure, and on the basis of verified statements and other pleadings. Considering the magnitude of the undertaking, we believe it appropriate to note here that the two examiners assigned to this matter served their recommended report August 23, 1963. In it they proposed 23 rules designed to promote coordination of various piggyback services. The matter is now pending on exceptions.

TRAFFIC AND EARNINGS

OPERATING REVENUES

Revenues of eight modes of transportation subject to our regulation rose 1.83 percent in fiscal year 1963, compared with the previous 12 months, to an all-time record of $20.4 billion. Attainment of the new high was directly attributable to the estimated 4.61-percent increase of $366 million for motor carriers of property. The increase in the revenues of this mode was about equal to the increase in the total for the eight modes. Revenues of four other modes were less than in the preceding fiscal year. The increases for pipelines and motor carriers of passengers were $26 and $30 million. Railway Express Agency had about $8 million, or 3 percent, more in revenues than in fiscal year 1962.

Railroads had the smallest percentage decrease but the largest absolute decrease in revenues—$34 million. The Pullman Company and electric railways had decreases of $2 and $4 million, respectively, and carriers by water suffered a decrease of $23 million.

Returns for calendar year 1962 indicate an overall increase of 5.21 percent in revenues for the eight modes, and the total of $20.2 billion was a new high on a calendar year basis. Only two modes had decreases compared with the preceding year, as against four modes on the fiscal year basis mentioned above. Railroads, Railway Express, pipelines, and both types of motor carriers had increases of considerable size in revenues, and the percentage increase for motor carriers of property was 8.96 percent.

Rail revenues in the years covered by the table have been augmented by the reclassification of some electric roads to railroad status. From January 1, 1961, through June 30, 1963, eight electric roads were transferred to the rail or motor category, sold, or abandoned, with a consequent decrease in the electric railroad revenues.

Water carrier revenues, which had risen by 1.24 percent in calendar year 1962 over 1961, had a decline of 5.81 percent on a fiscal year basis. The gains of both motor carrier modes were substantial on either the calendar or fiscal year basis. The long-term upward trend in pipeline (oil) revenues continued and again established new records in calendar year 1962 and fiscal year 1963, the increases being slightly more than 3 percent of the comparable period figures.

Because of duplications resulting from intercompany payments, the revenues of freight forwarders and private car lines have been excluded from the table. The operating revenues of freight forwarders after payments to carriers were $150 million for the calendar year 1962 and $143 million for 1961. Operating revenues of private car lines were $441 million in calendar year 1962 and $435 million in 1961.

Operating revenues [1]

	Year ended Dec. 31, 1961	Year ended December 31, 1962		Year ended June 30, 1962	Year ended June 30, 1963	
		Amount	Percentage change from calendar year 1961		Amount	Percentage change from fiscal year 1962
	Thousands	*Thousands*		*Thousands*	*Thousands*	
Railroad [2]_____	$9,540,266	$9,791,764	+2.64	$9,837,382	$9,803,429	−0.35
Railway Express [3]_____	256,786	270,972	+5.52	263,906	271,829	+3.00
Pullman Co_____	52,349	50,356	−3.81	50,614	48,197	−4.78
Electric railways [4]_____	22,297	21,756	−2.43	22,671	18,237	−19.56
Water lines [5]_____	389,390	394,204	+1.24	401,271	377,968	−5.81
Pipelines (oil)_____	786,718	810,605	+3.04	802,449	828,322	+3.22
Motor carriers of passengers [6]_	689,509	728,905	+5.71	713,679	743,874	+4.23
Motor carriers of property____	7,462,668	8,131,117	+8.96	7,947,741	8,314,148	+4.61
Grand total_____	19,199,983	20,199,679	+5.21	20,039,713	20,406,004	+1.83

[1] Partly estimated.
[2] Includes line-haul and switching and terminal companies; Alaskan and Hawaiian companies are included.
[3] After deducting payments to others for express privileges, $116.4 million in 1961 and $116.9 million in 1962.
[4] Since Jan. 1, 1961, two electric railways have been reclassified as class II line-haul railways, one has been reclassified as a switching and terminal company, one has been reclassified as a motor carrier, one was sold to another railway, and three have been abandoned. The total revenues in 1961 of the eight carriers were $7.4 million. Four of the eight changes occurred in 1961, two in 1962, and two in the first half of 1963. The result is an overstatement of the electric railway decline.
[5] Includes only revenue from domestic traffic of carriers subject to the jurisdiction of the Interstate Commerce Commission.
[6] Does not include motor carrier revenues of electric railways, included under "Electric railways."

TRAFFIC DATA, 1961-62

The reported and estimated freight ton-miles and passenger-miles for 1961 and 1962 of the various types of intercity carriers, both public and private, are shown by the following table. So far as available, estimates of coastwise and intercoastal sea traffic are shown separately in "Sources" of the table.

The estimated increase in ton-miles is based on preliminary data, but the upward direction of the trends is certain. The grand total shows an increase of about 70 billion ton-miles, from 1.3 to nearly 1.4 trillion. The total increase in 1962 is composed of increases of 5.26 percent by rail, 5.99 percent by motor transportation of property, 6.38 percent by water, 1.95 percent by pipelines, and 32.07 percent by airlines. The airlines for the first time accounted for more than a billion ton-miles. Record highs were established by motor carriers of property and by pipelines (oil), while the rails showed the first year-to-year increase since 1959 as well as the highest level since 1957. The pipeline (oil) ton-miles exceeded the previous high of 233.2 billion in 1961 by 4.6 billion. The pipeline data are restricted to oil and products thereof, and do not include the 108-mile movement by pipeline of coal in Ohio [2] and of gilsonite (72 miles) in Utah, which together amounted to about 200 million ton-miles per year, nor the movements of natural gas or water. The movements of natural gas are discussed below

[2] It has been reported that new low volume rates for coal may result in the closing of the Ohio slurry pipeline.

under long-term trends of ton-miles.   Also omitted from pipeline data are relatively short movements of limestone and other materials. Waterborne ton-miles increased in most areas over the 1961 level.

Total intercity passenger-miles reached a new high in 1962, largely by increases in traffic by private automobile and air, as in 1961, but in this instance also by a small increase by bus.   Railroad passenger traffic again declined, continuing the long-term trend.   Water carrier passenger-miles accounted for a relatively small part of the total, as in the past.

The inclusion in the table of Alaskan and Hawaiian data has little effect on the comparability of the data with ton- and passenger-miles of previous years.   Water traffic coverage is unchanged.   The pipeline (oil) data are changed very little because of the small amount of mileage of pipe involved.   The rail and highway additions have had little influence on trends.   Only in the air data has the inclusion of the two newest States been of importance.   Data for 1959, 1960, and 1961 in the 75th and 76th Annual Reports are on a basis corresponding to those used for this table.   However, bus passenger-mile data are on a preliminary basis only and are not comparable to data shown in reports for years prior to 1957.

Volume of intercity traffic, public and private, by kinds of transportation [1]

Agency	Ton-miles				Passenger-miles			
	1961	1962	Percentage of grand total		1961	1962	Percentage of grand total	
			1961	1962			1961	1962
	Millions	*Millions*			*Millions*	*Millions*		
1. Railroads and electric railways, including express and mail	566, 997	599, 977	42. 96	43. 04	20, 527	20, 181	2. 67	2. 52
2. Motor vehicles: [2]								
Motor carriers of passengers					19, 703	21, 279	2. 56	2. 66
Private automobile					692, 000	719, 680	89. 97	89. 81
Motor transportation of property	313, 141	331, 900	23. 60	23. 81				
Total motor vehicle	313, 141	331, 900	23. 60	23. 81	711, 703	740, 959	92. 53	92. 46
3. Inland waterways, including Great Lakes	209, 706	223, 089	15. 80	16. 00	2, 345	2, 736	0. 30	0. 34
4. Pipelines (oil) [3]	233, 172	237, 723	17. 57	17. 05				
5. Airways (domestic revenue and pleasure and business flying, including express and mail)	895	1, 182	0. 067	0. 085	34, 599	37, 491	4. 50	4. 68
Grand total	1, 326, 911	1, 393, 871	100. 00	100. 00	769, 174	801, 367	100. 00	100. 00

[1] Some revisions have been made in the data presented in the 76th Annual Report, and parts of the 1961 and 1962 data are still preliminary.
[2] Schoolbus data are excluded.
[3] Includes refined products and crude oil, with an allowance for gathering lines.
Sources: (Paragraphs below are numbered to correspond with items in table):

1. Reports to the Interstate Commerce Commission. Electric railway ton-miles and passenger-miles estimated on the basis of revenue. Does not include nonrevenue ton-miles which amounted to 15,561 million in 1961 and 15,743 million in 1962 for class I railroads.
2. Highway ton-miles estimated on the basis of Bureau of Public Roads data for main and local rural roads, mileages of routes and vehicles in urban and rural areas, and on Department of Agriculture data on farm consumption. Alaska and Hawaii are included.

INTERCITY TON-MILES OF FEDERALLY REGULATED AND OTHER CARRIERS, 1961

Beginning with data for 1961, it has been possible to allocate the ton-miles shown in the table at page 74 between water carriers which are federally regulated and those which are not. This allocation is according to the status of the carrier and not the traffic; i.e., legally exempt traffic carried by water carriers which have authority issued by the Interstate Commerce Commission is included as traffic in the federally regulated carrier category. The allocation is based on tons of traffic by ports of origin and destination, as reported to the Board of Engineers for Rivers and Harbors.[3] Of the 209.706 billion ton-miles of 1961 waterway traffic shown in the table on page 74, 38.327 billion, or 18.3 percent, were by carriers subject to the Commission's regulation. These waterborne ton-miles by Commission-regulated carriers include traffic within the territorial waters of the United States, but do not include that part of coastwise, intercoastal, and noncontiguous traffic on the high seas. Traffic from or to U.S. ports destined to or from a foreign port is included to the extent that it is carried in U.S. waters. A part of this "foreign" traffic is handled by carriers subject to Federal Maritime Commission regulation, but a division of such traffic between regulated and unregulated portions is not available and all such traffic has been assigned to the unregulated group.

For all coastwise traffic, out of a total of 312.000 billion ton-miles, 33.217 were by Interstate Commerce Commission regulated carriers and 278.782 by others; this includes ton-miles both in U.S. waters and on deep water.

Thus, including coastwise and intercoastal deep-sea and all other intercity traffic, 59.8 percent of all traffic moves by federally regulated carriers; with the omission of deep-sea traffic—68.9 percent. The range in portions regulated runs from 18.3 percent of the waterborne traffic, as shown in the table on page 74, or 14.9 percent of all water-

---

Passenger-miles in private automobiles estimated on basis of data from the Bureau of Public Roads on rural and intercity travel and from average load data. Motor carrier passenger-miles based on Public Roads and Interstate Commerce Commission data. As processing of certain data is not complete, highway ton-mile and private automobile passenger-mile estimates herein for 1962 should be regarded as preliminary. Because of changes in base beginning with 1957 estimates for motor carriers of passengers for 1957–61 published in the 73rd, 74th, 75th, and 76th Annual Reports, the above estimates for 1961 and 1962 are not comparable with estimates published for prior years. Private automobile data above and in *Transport Economics*, August 1962, for 1956–60 are comparable with previously published data for 1949–56, *Intercity Passenger Miles, 1949–1956*, Statement No. 580.

3. Ton-mile data are from Corps of Engineers, U.S. Army. Data for 1962 are preliminary estimates. Does not include most coastwise and intercoastal ton-miles, 317.4 billion ton-miles in 1961, as estimated in the Bureau of Transport Economics and Statistics *Deep-Sea Domestic Waterborne Traffic, 1956–1961*. Some duplication exists between these and the figures in the table. The data presented in the 76th Annual Report have been revised. Figures in the table include Alaskan and Hawaiian but not deep-sea ton-miles.

4. Interstate Commerce Commission, Bureau of Mines, and other data.

5. Based on Civil Aeronautics Board statistics, Federal Aviation Agency surveys, and other data. Covers domestic except movements over international waters or foreign countries. These figures, as they include, for example, Alaskan and Hawaiian, are not comparable with data in annual reports prior to the 75th.

[3] Supplement 2 to part 5, *Waterborne Commerce of the United States, 1961*, Department of the Army, Corps of Engineers.

borne traffic including deep sea, to 100 percent for the railroads, regulated by this Commission, and 100 percent of the ton-miles shown for air, regulated by the Civil Aeronautics Board. Some 33.4 percent of the intercity highway ton-miles and 86.1 percent of the pipeline (oil) ton-miles were by Interstate Commerce Commission regulated carriers.

LONG-TERM TRENDS: TON-MILES, 1939–62; PASSENGER-MILES, 1949–62; AND REVENUES, 1947–62

The distribution and trends of three transportation factors—ton-miles for the period 1939–62, passenger-miles for 1949–62, and revenues for 1947–62—by kinds of carriers are shown in the charts which follow.

Because coverage is not available for the entire period for the deep-sea coastwise and intercoastal domestic operators, and for deep-sea service to Alaska and Hawaii from the 48 contiguous States, a separate chart is provided comparing these carriers with those operating on the Mississippi River system and a third group operating on the Great Lakes. The first group is included in the ton-miles in the table at page 74 only to the extent that those ton-miles are produced in U.S. waters. The estimates of deep-sea ton-miles were computed from data supplied by the U.S. Maritime Administration.

The shipping lines carry a limited number of commodities in large volume. Oil is of major importance in the deep-sea trade, ore and coal are important on the Great Lakes, and the commodities which comprise the majority of the traffic on the Mississippi are coal, petroleum, sulphur, grains, and iron and products. Trends have been relatively smooth except on the Great Lakes.

Another chart compares the Federal Reserve Board index of industrial production, the index of gross national product less services, and an index of intercity ton-miles. All series are based on the year 1939. The index of gross national product less services is based on constant dollars, hence is comparable with the physical volumes of the other two indexes. Based on these indexes, the trends are roughly similar except that industrial production has tended to rise faster in recent years. The industrial production index does not include imports and agricultural products which are included in national product, and in ton-miles when transported.

While ton-miles are not affected by a number of factors of economic importance, such as reliability, speed, and consist of traffic, the ton-mile unit provides a constant physical measure over a period, regardless of changes in other elements. Rail, pipeline, and highway ton-miles are actual. Waterborne ton-miles are derived by multiplying the tons in the shipments by miles between origins and destinations for the channels reported used. Air ton-miles are tons multiplied by the great circle distance between origin and destination. Movements from the direct line to avoid storms or for other reasons are not reflected in waterborne and air ton-mile data.

While there have been fluctuations over the years covered, the ton-mile totals of each of the various groups show reasonably well defined trends. Rail ton-miles increased rapidly after 1939 under preparedness and war pressures to a peak in 1944 and thereafter fluctuated generally downward, with a decreasing share in the total. The 1962 rail total was higher than in the last 4 years, but lower than in the 3 preceding years, lower than in a number of the immediate post-war years, and well below the wartime peaks. Motor vehicle, pipeline (oil), and air ton-miles reached record levels in 1962. Motor-vehicle, inland waterway, including the Great Lakes, pipeline (oil), and air ton-miles have shown generally upward trends, although with some fluctuations, wide in the case of the waterways.

The pipeline (oil) ton-miles understate the total from all pipeline movements as they do not include the movements of natural gas or the movements of water in the great aqueducts supplying cities, irrigation projects, etc. The increase in importance of natural gas has been particularly noteworthy. At the turn of the century, in 1900, natural gas (wet) contributed only 3.2 percent of the production from mineral energy fuels and energy from water power produced in the United States, in terms of British thermal units, while bituminous coal, lignite, and anthracite contributed 88.9 percent. Preliminary percentages for 1962 are 34.1 and 26.2.[4] Natural gas energy in 1900 equaled one twenty-seventh of the energy supplied by coal production; in 1962, it exceeded coal energy by 30 percent. Total energy produced in 1962, measured in British thermal units, was more than five times the 1900 level, and natural gas energy increased from 3 to 34 percent of total production.

The wide variance in gas pressures in pipelines and the problems involved in securing an equivalent transportation measure for the movement of this natural gas, together with lack of quantity, origin, and destination data, have precluded estimates of gas pipeline ton-miles. Inclusion of natural gas movements in intercity ton-mile estimates, if available, would further dwindle the railroad share of intercity traffic and lessen the proportionate gains by other modes.

Passenger-miles data include intercity private automobile passenger-miles on a comparative basis throughout the period. The private automobile continued to dominate the field of intercity passenger transportation by accounting for about nine-tenths of the intercity total by all modes. As the grand total has risen year after year, it is evident that the travel market is expanding, but the railroads in

---

[4] Supplement Table 2, *Mineral Industry Surveys,* Petroleum Statement, Monthly, March 11, 1963, Bureau of Mines, Department of the Interior.

particular have not been able to maintain their share. Bus data for 1957–62 are not comparable with data for the period 1949–56.

In 1962, as in previous years, the trend in for-hire passenger transport has continued toward the use of the less expensive means within an agency of transport. Difficulties exist in measuring the effect of these economy fares since, for example, first-class air travel under some of the "family" and "wife at half fare" plans results in cheaper travel than by coach.[5] However, in scheduled air service, the coach and economy service passenger-miles in 1961 overtook the first-class passenger-miles, and in rail service the declines over the period have been greater in parlor and sleeping car service than in coach other than commutation.

If for-hire carriers could make service sufficiently attractive to bring some private automobile passenger-miles into the for-hire category, increases would be possible from diversion of a small percentage of the private automobile total. With almost 90 percent of passenger-miles moving by private automobiles, a diversion of slightly over 2 percent to the for-hire carriers would increase their traffic by 20 percent. The practicability of a diversion cannot be judged. Although some attempts have shown promising results, in other instances diverted traffic was not retained for any extended time.

Considerable variation exists in the post-1947 upward trend of operating revenues of Commission-regulated carriers. Motor carriers of property have shown the greatest increases. Since 1947, their operating revenues have more than tripled. The pipelines (oil) have more than doubled their revenues in the same period. The water lines showed a 63.2-percent increase in 1962 over 1947. Motor carriers of passengers have had a 36-percent increase in the same period. The railroads have not shown increases comparable with those of the other carriers. Revenues of electric railroads, particularly in recent years, have been reduced by transfers to the railroad group, and by abandonments. In 1952, there were 45 electric railway carriers with $81 million in railway operating revenues; in 1962, there were 18 with $22 million. Recent abandonments included one of the largest of the carriers, the Chicago, North Shore & Milwaukee.

The two companies connected most closely with rail operations, Railway Express and Pullman, in recent years have been well below their 1947 revenue levels although the Express Company in some of the later years has shown a degree of recovery. The decline in parlor and sleeping car passenger-miles has been only partially compensated by increased rates and, therefore, first-class service revenues remain in a declining state.

---

[5] The Civil Aeronautics Board entered into an investigation of fares of this type after the close of the 1963 fiscal year.

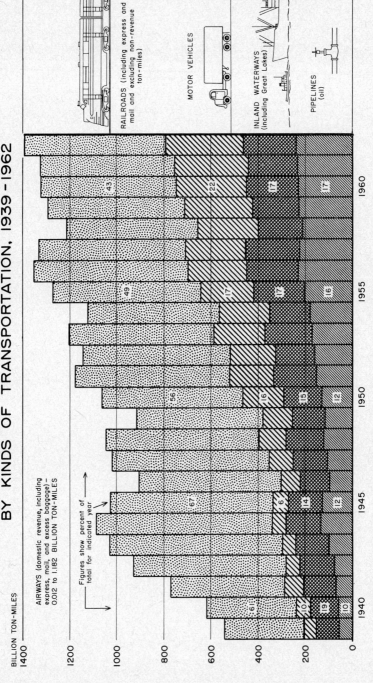

INTERCITY TON-MILES, PUBLIC AND PRIVATE, BY KINDS OF TRANSPORTATION, 1939-1962

Source: 1939-1959, I.C.C., Bureau of Transport Economics and Statistics, Intercity Ton-Miles, 1939-1959, Statement No. 6103; 1960-1961, Annual Report of the Interstate Commerce Commission; 1962, staff estimates.

INTERCITY PASSENGER-MILES, 1949-1962

TOTAL INTERCITY PASSENGER-MILES

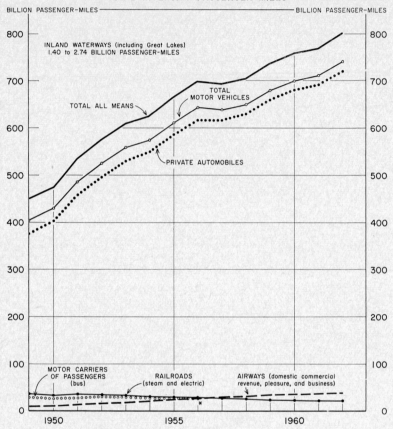

BILLION PASSENGER-MILES ————————— BILLION PASSENGER-MILES

INLAND WATERWAYS (including Great Lakes)
1.40 to 2.74 BILLION PASSENGER-MILES

TOTAL ALL MEANS

TOTAL
MOTOR VEHICLES

PRIVATE AUTOMOBILES

MOTOR CARRIERS
OF PASSENGERS
(bus)

RAILROADS
(steam and electric)

AIRWAYS (domestic commercial
revenue, pleasure, and business)

REVENUE INTERCITY PASSENGER-MILES

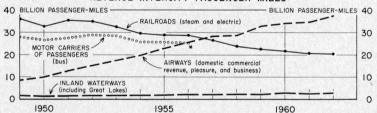

BILLION PASSENGER-MILES ————————— BILLION PASSENGER-MILES

RAILROADS (steam and electric)

MOTOR CARRIERS
OF PASSENGERS
(bus)

AIRWAYS (domestic commercial
revenue, pleasure, and business)

INLAND WATERWAYS
(including Great Lakes)

* Data for 1957-1962 on motor carriers not comparable because of change in base.
Source: 1949-1956, I.C.C., Bureau of Transport Economics and Statistics, Intercity Passenger-Miles, 1949-1956,
Statement No. 580; 1957-1961, Annual Reports of the Interstate Commerce Commission;
1962, staff estimates.

OPERATING REVENUES,[1] BY TRANSPORT AGENCY
1947 – 1962

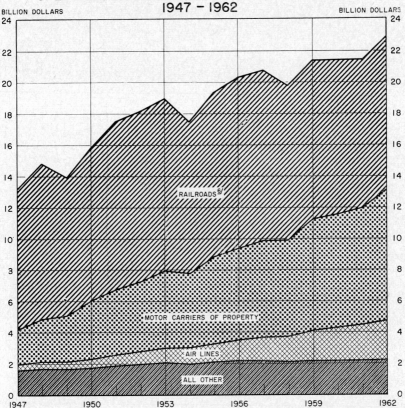

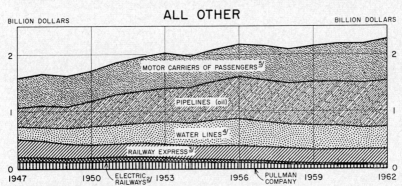

[1] Partly estimated.
[2] Shifts of carriers from electric to line-haul railway classification and partial and complete abandonments have affected the decline by an indeterminate amount.
[3] After deducting payments to others for express privileges.
[4] Includes only revenues from domestic traffic of carriers subject to the jurisdiction of the Interstate Commerce Commission.
[5] Does not include motor carrier revenues of electric railways, included under electric railways.
[6] Includes switching and terminal companies.

SOURCES : 1947–61 Annual Reports of the Interstate Commerce Commission ; revised motor carrier revenues, 1947–56, I.C.C., Bureau of Transport Economics and Statistics, *Statistics of Class I, II, and III Motor Carriers, 1939–1956*, Statement No. 589 ; and 1962, staff estimates. Air data from Civil Aeronautics Board ; data cover operating revenues in domestic revenue operations only, including Alaskan but not oversea, and do include the local Hawaiian line within those islands. Inclusion of Alaskan revenues makes no perceptible difference in the chart.

INDEXES OF OPERATING REVENUES,[1/] BY TRANSPORT AGENCY, 1947 – 1962

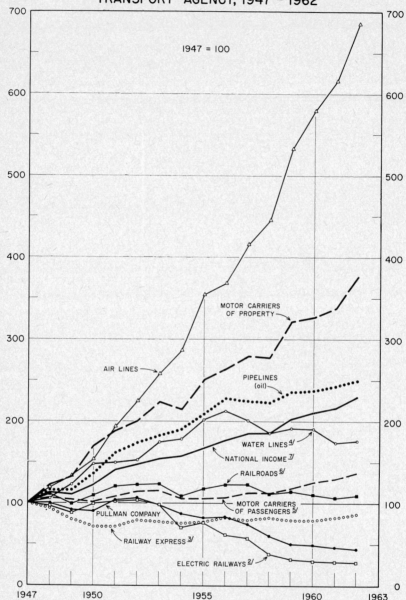

1947 = 100

MOTOR CARRIERS OF PROPERTY

AIR LINES

PIPELINES (oil)

WATER LINES [4/]

NATIONAL INCOME [7/]

RAILROADS [6/]

MOTOR CARRIERS OF PASSENGERS [5/]

PULLMAN COMPANY

RAILWAY EXPRESS [3/]

ELECTRIC RAILWAYS [2/]

[1] Partly estimated.
[2] Shifts of carriers from electric to line-haul railway classification and partial and complete abandonments have affected the decline by an indeterminate amount.
[3] After deducting payments to others for express privileges.
[4] Includes only revenues from domestic traffic of carriers subject to the jurisdiction of the Interstate Commerce Commission.
[5] Does not include motor carrier revenues of electric railways, included under electric railways.
[6] Includes switching and terminal companies.
[7] Revised national income. Source: U.S. Department of Commerce, *Survey of Current Business*, July 1963.

SOURCES: 1947–61, Annual Reports of the Interstate Commerce Commission; revised motor carrier revenues, 1947–56, I.C.C. Bureau of Transport Economics and Statistics, *Statistics*

GREAT LAKES, MISSISSIPPI RIVER, AND DOMESTIC DEEP SEA TON-MILES, 1955-1961

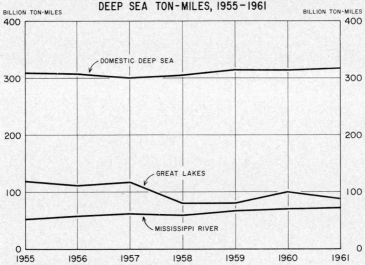

Source: Office of Engineers, Maritime Administration, and Interstate Commerce Commission.

INDEXES OF INTERCITY TON-MILES, INDUSTRIAL PRODUCTION, AND GROSS NATIONAL PRODUCT (LESS SERVICES) 1939-1962

Source: Federal Reserve Board, Office of Business Economics, and Interstate Commerce Commission.

of Class I, II, and III Motor Carriers, 1939–1956, Statement No. 589; and 1962, staff estimates. Air data from Civil Aeronautics Board; data cover operating revenues in domestic revenue operations only, including Alaskan but not oversea, and do include the local Hawaiian line within those islands. Inclusion of Alaskan data makes no perceptible difference in the chart.

Airline domestic revenues and national income are also shown in the chart of operating revenue indexes. The air carrier index rose 80 percent more than the index for motor carriers of property, the surface carriers with the greatest rate of increase. However, the motor carriers of property and the oil pipelines, as well as the airlines, show increases above those in national income; all other transportation series are below that level. The indexes are computed in current dollars.

EMPLOYMENT TRENDS, 1950–62

The first chart which follows shows total employment in line-haul railroad transportation and certain allied services, local and suburban transportation, motor freight transportation and storage, intercity and rural buslines, and common carrier air transportation. The basic data have been converted to indexes and are shown in an accompanying chart in that form, using the year 1950 as the base. To permit comparison of transportation and industrial trends, an index for total nonagricultural employment is included.

In 1962, changes were relatively small with a continuation of the decline in railroad employment and slight increases for motor freight transportation, intercity and rural buslines, and air. The transfer of some local and suburban buslines to government authority operation accounts for part of the decrease in employment in this category, the employees being shown in the "Government" category after the transfer.

Recent trends have been in accord with the long-term trends—downward for railroads and an easing of declining employment for buslines. Employment in motor freight transportation and storage and in air transportation common carrier groups increased somewhat faster in previous years than total nonagricultural employment. Employment figures for pipelines, not including natural gas, have been available only since 1956. While there was an increase in 1957, employment has shown a continuous year-by-year decline for the period 1957–62. These pipelines are not represented on the charts.

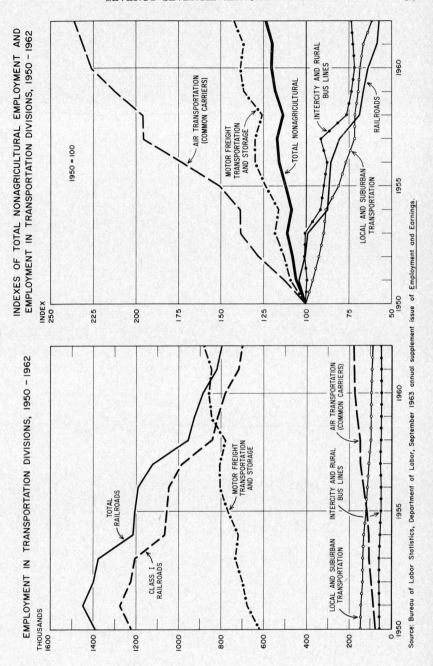

INDEXES OF TOTAL NONAGRICULTURAL EMPLOYMENT AND EMPLOYMENT IN TRANSPORTATION DIVISIONS, 1950 - 1962

EMPLOYMENT IN TRANSPORTATION DIVISIONS, 1950 - 1962

Source: Bureau of Labor Statistics, Department of Labor, September 1963 annual supplement issue of Employment and Earnings.

CLASS I LINE-HAUL RAILROADS

Following the 1963 first quarter decline of $48 million in operating revenues from the first quarter of 1962, class I line-haul railroads increased second quarter revenues by $60 million over revenues of the second quarter of the preceding year. Improved general business activity and greater freight movements accounted for total operating revenues of $4.715 billion, for the first half of 1963, or 0.02 percent above the $4.704 billion for the same period of 1962. Decreases in all operating expenses, except transportation costs and general expenses, reduced total operating expense by 0.08 percent. First half 1963 expenses declined to $3.684 billion from $3.713 billion in the first half of 1962. As a result, the operating ratio declined from 78.9 percent to 78.1 percent. Revenue, other income, and expense data are given in table A of appendix H for calendar years 1961 and 1962, and for the first 6 months of 1962 and 1963.

Comparative operating statistics for the same periods are shown in table B of appendix H. Freight operations produced the following changes in first half 1963: Miles of road declined from 217,000 to 215,937; average haul (miles per revenue ton per road) increased to 268.0 from 262.1 miles; loaded car miles increased 1 percent and empty car miles increased 1.5 percent; gross ton miles per train-hour rose to 68,863 from 67,091, an increase of 2.6 percent; percentage of freight locomotives which were unserviceable increased from 6.8 to 7.1; and, interrupting a long-term trend, freight cars unserviceable declined from 7.5 percent to 7.3 percent of the car fleet.

Geographically, operating revenues indicate best results for the southern district; the 1963 6-month total exceeded that for the previous year by 1.4 percent; western district revenues increased by 0.7 percent, while the eastern district had a decline of 1.1 percent in this item. Although most prevalent in the eastern district, decreases in revenues were experienced by individual roads in all districts, when compared with the first half of 1962.

Review of the above operating statistics for recent years indicate generally an improvement in railroad efficiency. The average rail haul has increased steadily. "Loaded car miles" and "Empty car miles" have decreased, indicating the use of equipment of larger capacity (since tons of revenue freight reported have declined less rapidly) and better use of equipment capacity. "Gross ton miles per train hour" have been increasing constantly, and relatively fewer freight locomotives were reported as unserviceable than in earlier years. On the other hand, unserviceable freight car percentages have shown a continuously upward trend.

Passenger service in the first 6 months of 1963 showed no significant changes. Miles of road operated decreased to 85,042 from 86,070; passengers carried decreased by 1 percent; revenue per passenger per mile increased 2.5 percent to 3.26 cents (3.18 in 1962); and the average journey per passenger per road declined slightly from 59.9 miles in 1962 to 47.5 miles.

Both "Passenger miles operated" and "Passengers carried" have been declining in recent years. "Revenues per passenger per mile" have been increasing, as the roads have attempted to recover rising costs of service. The length of the "Average journey per passenger per road" has tended to fluctuate.

The passenger deficit for class I line-haul railroads was $394.3 million in calendar 1962 as against $408.2 million in calendar 1961, a reduction of 3.4 percent.

Current figures for railroad employment are shown in table C of the same appendix. Changes in the latest 6-month period included a decline in all groups of employees; and total employment was down from 706,277 to 674,620, or 4.5 percent. The reduction of railroad employment was contrary to employment trends in the other service industries generally.

The selected balance sheet and income accounts included in the two tables in this section recapitulate the quarterly reports at the end of the fiscal year, and provide comparable information for recent years. The current assets to current liabilities ratio (excluding materials and supplies) interrupted a decline of recent years and increased to 1.31 from 1.20 in 1962. The cash position ratio (including short-term investments) also improved, rising to 0.82 from 0.74 in the previous year. In the condensed income account, cost of materials, depreciation, and other expenses (except wages and salaries) increased 1.4 percent or $47.0 million over the preceding fiscal year as a result, primarily, of increases in the depreciation account due to new Internal Revenue guidelines. For the same period, taxes (income, profit, and payroll) showed a substantial drop for the 1962 period, decreasing 18.7 percent, or $195 million, reflecting (1) elimination of the passenger excise tax; (2) the tax-credit adjustment; and (3) some reduction in local (State and county) impositions.

Additional statistical summaries for the latest 11-year period concerning class I line-haul railroads are presented in tables III, VI, VII, VIII, IX, and XI of appendix G.

Current assets and current liabilities, class I line-haul railroads as of June 30

Item	1960	1961		1962 [1]		1963	
	Amount	Amount	Percent change from 1960	Amount	Percent change from 1960	Amount	Percent change from 1960
	Millions	*Millions*		*Millions*		*Millions*	
Total current assets_____	$3,053	$2,741	−10.2	$2,879	−5.7	$3,082	+0.9
Cash and temporary cash investments_____	1,553	1,313	−15.5	1,458	−6.1	1,631	+5.0
Materials and supplies_____	600	528	−12.0	501	−16.5	474	−21.0
Total current liabilities_____	1,839	1,896	+3.1	1,983	+7.8	1,991	+8.3
Net working capital:							
Including materials and supplies_____	1,214	845	−30.4	896	−26.2	1,091	−10.1
Excluding materials and supplies_____	614	317	−48.4	395	−35.7	617	+0.5
Ratios							
Current assets to current liabilities:							
Including materials and supplies_____	1.66	1.45	_____	1.45	_____	1.55	_____
Excluding materials and supplies_____	1.33	1.17	_____	1.20	_____	1.31	_____
Cash and temporary cash investments to current liabilities_____	0.84	0.69	_____	0.74	_____	0.82	_____

[1] Revised.

Condensed income account—class I line-haul railroads

Item	Calendar year				12 months ended with June 30, 1963
	1959	1960	1961	1962	
	Millions	*Millions*	*Millions*	*Millions*	*Millions*
Revenue and other income_____	$10,140	$9,861	$9,511	$9,765	$9,784
Cost of materials, depreciations, and other expenses, except wages and salaries_____	3,270	3,271	3,235	3,357	3,411
Taxes, including income, profits, and payroll_____	1,048	999	991	905	846
Total deductions_____	4,318	4,270	4,226	4,262	4,257
Remainder for employees and investors_____	5,822	5,591	5,285	5,503	5,527
Wages and salaries [1]_____	4,760	4,661	4,425	4,452	4,384
Investors' share:					
Rent for leased roads [2]_____	54	51	48	47	46
Interest on obligations_____	369	367	364	357	[3] 358
Other deductions [4]_____	62	67	66	76	79
For dividends and surplus_____	577	445	382	571	660
Total_____	1,062	930	860	1,051	1,143
Percent wages and salaries_____	81.8	83.4	83.7	80.9	79.3
Percent investors' share_____	18.2	16.6	16.3	19.1	20.7

[1] Chargeable to operating expenses and not including the following amounts of payroll taxes, in millions: 12 months ended June 30, 1963, $374; year 1962, $382; 1961, $364; 1960, $394; and 1959, $374.
[2] Represents largely intercompany payments among railroads in the form of interest and dividends.
[3] Partly estimated.
[4] Miscellaneous deductions from income applicable to "other income" shown, contingent charges (capital and other funds), and amortization of discount on funded debt.

PRIVATE CAR LINES

A total of 177 private car lines owning 10 or more cars filed reports for 1962. Of these, 27 had 1,000 or more cars each. Operating revenues for the year totaled $441.3 million, an increase of 1.3 percent over 1961.

These firms, holding a net investment in transportation property of $1,368.1 million, owned or controlled 325,189 cars at the end of 1962, an increase of 2,616 over the preceding year. Of this number, 80,625 were refrigerator cars, 128,368 petroleum tank cars, 27,783 other tank cars, and 88,413 other type cars, including box, gondola, open-top hopper, and T.O.F.C. During 1962 the category, "other type cars," increased by 3,004 cars, the largest numerical change of any category.

Eight railroad-owned or railroad-controlled refrigerator car lines operated about 78 percent of all privately owned refrigerator cars at the end of 1962. These 8 lines possessed 63,172 such cars, an increase of 1,256 over the year before, and 1,337 "other" cars. The cars owned by these companies produced 2,136.3 million car-miles or 39 percent of the total of 5,496.6 million car-miles recorded for all private car lines. The railroad-affiliated companies' operating revenues of $140.3 million in 1962 were up 1.7 percent from 1961, and their net investment in property and equipment, $320.9 million, represented an increase of 3.3 percent. These companies produced 31.8 percent of total private car line revenues, and they accounted for 23.5 percent of the total net investment.

MOTOR CARRIERS OF PROPERTY

Increases in operating revenues and tons of revenue freight accrued to class I motor carriers of property in the first half of 1963, compared with a year earlier. Total operating revenues increased from $2.6 to $2.9 billion, or 10.8 percent. Tons of revenue freight carried were 166.9 million or 7.1 percent above the 155.9 million for the 6 months in 1962. All districts reported increases in operating revenues: western—15.8 percent, southern—10.9 percent, and eastern—10.6 percent. Total operating expenses increased concomitantly, arising from $2.5 to $2.8 billion, resulting in an increase in the operating ratio from 95.8 to 96.4 percent.

Contrasting the operations of all intercity class I motor carriers for the calendar years 1961 and 1962, operating revenues for 954 reporting companies increased 9.6 percent to an all-time high of $5.37 billion from the $4.90 billion in the earlier year. The record figure was achieved despite adverse effects of the longshoremen's strike in the final quarter of 1962. Total operating expenses increased from $4.70 billion to $5.14 billion reflecting a slight improvement in the operating ratio, which declined from 95.9 percent to 95.7 percent. Net income of these carriers rose sharply in the first quarter of 1962, after a deficit in the like quarter in the previous year. The rising trend continued throughout the year to a total net income of $109.4 million, an increase of 21.5 percent over the $90.1 million for 1961. Additional data are presented in table E of appendix H.

District and regional data for property carriers reflect some further contrasts. Eastern district revenues increased by $246.9 million, or 9.8 percent over 1961. The western district showed a gain in revenues of $129.1 million, or 7.9 percent; while the southern region had increased revenues of $95.1 million, or 12.7 percent. Operating ratios placed the southern region in top position with 94.6 percent, followed by the western district, 95.7 percent, and eastern, 96.1 percent.

Motor carriers of general freight, comprising the largest operating group, had a revenue increase of $309.8 million or 9 percent over 1961, to $3.75 billion. Although expenses advanced with expanding operations, the operating ratio was down to 95.5 percent compared with 95.7 percent for the previous year. Income rose accordingly with an overall gain of $14.6 million or 22.7 percent. The improvement can be partially accounted for by the fact that operations in the first quarter of 1961 resulted in a deficit.

Income of the special commodity carriers rose to $24.7 million in 1962 and was 13.7 percent above the previous year. Revenues increased 10.6 percent in 1962, somewhat more significantly than those for the general freight carriers, and amounted to $1.41 billion against $1.28 billion for 1961. Operating expenses decreased and the operating ratio for this group declined to 96.5 percent from 96.7 percent in the previous year.

Operating revenues of contract carriers, which are less sensitive to short-term changes in production, increased by 14.1 percent over 1961, advancing from $180.9 million to $206.3 million. Total income, however, increased to $5.5 million, or by 45 percent. Despite pressure of expenses incurred to handle the increased volume, the operating ratio declined slightly from the 1961 figure of 95.3 percent, it being 94.7 percent.

Local carriers had the least relative change in revenues, increasing to $334.2 million, or by 8 percent, from the 1961 total of $309.4 million. Net profits, however, declined to $4.89 million as contrasted with $4.93 million in 1961, or 0.08 percent. While the eastern district had a net income of $0.9 million, the western district and southern region had deficit operations.

The relative importance of the various groups of class I motor carriers of property with respect to selected operating data for calendar years 1952 and 1962 are shown below:

Item	Carriers of general commodities		Carriers of special commodities		Local carriers		Contract carriers	
	1952	1962	1952	1962	1952	1962	1952	1962
	Percent of total	Percent of total	Percent of total	Percent of total	Percent of total	Percent of total	Percent of total	Percent of total
Number of carriers represented_____	46.2	52.6	26.0	33.6	17.0	8.2	10.8	5.6
Operating revenues_____	63.4	65.8	22.6	24.7	8.1	3.6	5.9	5.9
Operating expenses_____	64.3	65.5	23.0	24.9	7.4	3.6	5.3	6.0
Net income (after taxes)_____	60.0	69.3	23.4	21.6	11.2	4.8	5.4	4.3
Truck and tractor miles operated____	57.2	55.4	32.6	37.1	1.7	1.4	8.5	6.1
Tons of revenue freight transported__	47.0	52.9	36.9	40.0	4.0	1.7	12.1	5.4

A composite picture of classes I, II and III motor carriers of property shows total revenues of $8.13 billion in calendar 1962, an increase of 8.96 percent over the $7.46 billion in 1961.

MOTOR CARRIERS OF PASSENGERS

Total operating revenue in 1962 for 208 class I motor carriers of passengers rose 7.3 percent over 1961 to $657.9 million while operating expenses increased only 5.6 percent to $577.2 million, improving the operating ratio from 89.1 to 87.7 percent, according to quarterly reports of the carriers. The total number of revenue passengers carried declined 1.9 percent to 715.7 million.

Intercity carriers.—The 140 intercity carriers of passengers were responsible for most of the industry gains. Total operating revenues for this group rose to $524.6 million in 1962, up 8.7 percent, and the number of passengers carried increased 0.6 percent to 227.1 million. Results by type of services were as follows: intercity service—number of passengers up 1.3 percent, revenues up 8.6 percent to $401.5 million; local and suburban service—number of passengers down 1.3 percent, revenues up 3.4 percent to $23.7 million; charter or special service— number of passengers down 0.3 percent, revenues up 8.4 percent to $41.4 million; other services provided revenues of $58.0 million, up 12.4 percent from 1962.[6] Expenses increased at a slower pace giving an operating ratio of 85.2 percent in 1962 compared to 86.9 percent in 1961. Net income after tax increased 31.1 percent to $42.6 million.

Each of the nine motor carrier regions showed good gains in revenue in 1962 over 1961 although two areas, New England and central regions, carried 3 percent and 8.6 percent fewer passengers, respectively. Midwestern region had the greatest percentage increase in revenues—

---

[6] Includes revenues from package express service discussed in detail under "Small Shipments" section in Service and Facilities chapter.

up 19.6 percent to $18.8 million on a 14.9-percent increase in the number of passengers carried. The least increase in revenues was in the Rocky Mountain region where a 2.3-percent increase in the number of passengers carried provided total operating revenue of $8.1 million, up 4.5 percent.

For the first half of 1963 increases of 4.7 percent from the 1962 period in both revenues and expenses of intercity motor carriers of passengers left the operating ratio unchanged at 91.4 percent. Total revenues for the group were $316 million and total expenses $288.8 million. These results were achieved despite a decrease in number of passengers carried in local service of 10 million, or 4 percent, to 240.6 million. However, the number of passengers carried in intercity and in charter services increased 5.6 percent and 7.6 percent, respectively, to 83.6 million and 25.4 million.

Local carriers.—This group of 68 carriers did not fare as well as intercity carriers as revenue for 1962 increased 2.1 percent to $133.2 million while expenses at $130.1 million were up 2.4 percent. As a result, the operating ratio worsened slightly to 97.6 from 97.3 percent in 1961. Net income after taxes, however, increased 5.1 percent to $2.6 million. Local and suburban service showed a decline in the number of passengers carried to 442.9 million, down 3.6 percent, and passengers carried in intercity service decreased to 14.7 million, down 1.1 percent. Charter and special services passengers increased 5 percent to 21 million. The total number of passengers carried declined 3 percent to 488.6 million.

Reports are received from local service class I motor carriers of passengers for only seven of the nine geographic regions, and, of these, two of the areas showed declines in total operating revenues for 1962. Revenue fell 27.3 percent in the southwestern region to $544,935 as the number of passengers carried was down 8.6 percent to 1.7 million. Pacific region carriers reported a decline of 6.3 percent and 18.7 percent to $2.9 million and 2.1 million for revenues and passengers, respectively. The greatest percentage increase in revenues occurred in the southern region where revenues of $11.3 million were up 6.9 percent from 1961 while the number of passengers carried rose 0.3 percent to 46.2 million. The southern region was the only area to report an increase in the number of passengers carried.

WATER CARRIERS

Preliminary data compiled from annual reports of 198 inland and coastal water carriers indicate total operating revenues rose 3.3 percent from $270.8 million in 1961 to $279.7 million in 1962. The class A carriers' contribution to total revenues declined slightly to 87.1 percent even though revenues increased $5.4 million to $243.6 million, a 2.3 percent rise. Class B carrier revenues in 1962 were $8.9 million, up 10.2 percent over 1961, and their share of total revenues increased to 3.2 from 3 percent. Class C carriers again slightly increased their share of total revenues—to 9.7 percent, $27.3 million, in 1962, from 9.1 percent, $23.6 million, in 1961, representing a 10.8-percent revenue increase.

Inland and coastal carriers.—Class A and class B carriers received $252.5 million, or 90.3 percent of total revenues; expenses rose to $226.3 million in 1962, and the operating ratio improved slightly to 89.64 percent from 90.42 percent in 1961.

Of the four active navigation areas, only the Great Lakes Area continued to experience the general decline of 1961, as revenues fell 8.7 percent to $34.3 million in 1962. The greatest percentage gain was registered on the Pacific coast as revenues rose 7.8 percent to $43.7 million, while carriers on the Atlantic and gulf coasts reported revenues of $50 million, an increase of 1.1 percent. Carriers on the Mississippi River and tributaries received $124.5 million, up 4.9 percent over 1961, representing 49.4 percent of total revenues for all areas.

Analysis of revenues of class A and class B carriers by type of service shows passenger revenues increased 11.1 percent in 1962 to $8.9 million from $8 million in 1961. Pacific coast carriers' passenger revenues increased $1.5 million to $2.9 million in 1962 as passenger service accounted for nearly half of the total revenues of the area. It should be noted that Canadian Pacific Railway Company vessels earned $2.3 million of Pacific coast passenger revenues and that the $1.3 million increase registered by this company in 1962 offset a more than $500,000 decline in passenger revenues for Atlantic and gulf coast and Great Lakes carriers. The number of revenue passengers carried in all areas increased 7.6 percent to 2.9 million in 1962. The service generally consisted of ferry operations and excursion trips.

A 4.5 million ton increase in freight carried by the Mississippi River group and a 0.7 million ton increase on the Pacific coast was more than sufficient to offset losses in tonnage in the Atlantic and gulf and the Great Lakes areas with the result that tonnage for all areas rose 3.1 percent to 104.9 million. Freight loadings declined 12.3 percent to 8.2 million tons for the Atlantic and gulf coast carriers, and Great Lakes tonnage at 21.8 million was down 2.7 percent. The increase for Mississippi River carriers was 8.4 percent to bring the total tonnage to 58.3 million, while carriers on the Pacific coast increased their tonnage to 16.6 million, or 4.2 percent over 1961.

The increased freight tonnage in 1962 was not reflected in total freight revenues as revenues fell to $172.2 million, off 0.6 percent, continuing the 1960–61 decline. Increased revenues of 2.8 percent to $100 million and 1 percent to $23.8 million in the Mississippi and

Pacific coast areas, respectively, failed to counter declines of 5 percent and 9.4 percent in the Atlantic-gulf and the Great Lakes groups, respectively, where revenues were $19.6 million and $28.8 million in 1962.

For the first half of 1963 freight revenues of class A and class B inland and coastal water carriers declined 8.1 percent to $117.7 million from the 1962 total. Revenues of the Atlantic and gulf coasts and intercoastal carriers fell 20.8 percent and 21.7 percent to $22.3 million and $20.7 million, respectively; minor increases were recorded by Mississippi River and Pacific coast carriers and there was a small decrease in Great Lakes trade. Passenger revenues of all areas, at $2.1 million, were down 14.6 percent as revenues of Pacific coast carriers fell 62.1 percent to $238,338, and those of Great Lakes carriers at $463,166 were down 15.6 percent. Atlantic and gulf coasts, Mississippi River, and intercoastal carriers received revenues of $671,632, up 15.3 percent, $561,144, up 4.7 percent, and $134,764, up 19.1 percent, respectively.

Maritime carriers.—The total operating revenue from foreign and domestic service of 23 maritime carriers reporting to the Commission in 1962 rose 24.5 percent over 1961 to $628.5 million. Six Atlantic and gulf coast carriers reported revenues of $74.3 million, 33 percent above 1961. Revenues of four Pacific coast carriers were $24.8 million, up 4.2 percent, and intercoastal carrier revenues, accounting for 84.2 percent of total maritime carrier revenues, were up 24.6 percent over 1961 to $529.4 million.

Analysis of maritime carrier reports by type of domestic operation service (excludes foreign operations) shows declines in both passenger and freight revenues as well as in traffic handled. Coastal and intercoastal passenger revenue fell 6.4 percent from 1961 to $661,526 in 1962 with only intercoastal carriers reporting passenger service in 1962. Freight revenues declined 4.1 percent for all areas to $101 million in 1962, the decrease stemming solely from intercoastal carriers, for which revenues of $42.1 million were down $12.4 million or 22.7 percent from 1961. Atlantic and gulf coasts carriers and Pacific coast carriers reported increased revenues for 1962 of 21.0 and 8.7 percent to $35.5 million and $23.4 million, respectively. Revenue tons carried in all areas declined 6 percent to 4.1 million tons, with only the Atlantic and gulf group showing an increase for 1962 over 1961 as tonnage on these coasts at 1.7 million was up 6.7 percent. The Pacific coast and intercoastal groups reported decreased freight in 1962 of 10.3 percent and 14.5 percent, or 632,012 tons and 1.8 million tons, respectively.

FREIGHT FORWARDERS

During the year 1962, the Commission received reports from 87 freight forwarders, 1 less than in 1961. As in 1960 and 1961, there were

64 class A forwarders, with revenues of $100,000 or more; they accounted for 99.7 percent of total freight forwarder revenues of $470.3 million, which total was an increase of 4.8 percent over 1961. The three largest forwarders accounted for 45 percent of the total revenue, a decrease of 1.7 percentage points.

Class A freight forwarders handled 21.7 million shipments in 1962, a decline of 16.5 percent from the previous year. However, total weight of shipments rose 7.5 percent to 4.3 million tons and average weight per shipment increased from 308 pounds to 397 pounds. The sharp increase in average weight probably reflects the establishment by forwarders of volume rates for shipments of 10,000 pounds or more.

Among class A companies, transportation revenues increased 4.9 percent to $464.6 million and incidental revenues decreased 9.8 percent to $4.2 million. Net income after income taxes increased 11.1 percent to $6.8 million.

Operating expenses of class A forwarders amounted to $136.8 million in 1962, a rise of 3.7 percent. Transportation purchased (not considered an operating expense) rose 4.6 percent to $318.4 million. Payments were distributed as follows: railroad transportation, $179.7 million, 56.4 percent of the total purchased; motor carrier transportation, $68.7 million, 21.6 percent; pickup, delivery and transfer service, $66.6 million, 20.9 percent; water transportation, $1.4 million, 0.5 percent; and other services, $2.1 million, 0.6 percent. For 1961 the railroad, motor carrier, and pickup-and-delivery expenses represented 58.8, 20.0, and 20.0 percent, respectively, of the total transportation purchased. While the railroad share of the total declined 2.4 percentage points, 1961 to 1962, there was a slight increase in the amount of the payments to the railroads; payments to motor carriers increased 12.7 percent.

For the first half of 1963, revenues, expenses, and transportation purchased on the part of class A forwarders showed little change from the like period in 1962. For 57 forwarders reporting in 1962 and 1963, revenues declined 0.4 percent to $225.8 million, operating expenses increased 2.4 percent to $68.2 million, and purchased transportation declined 1.4 percent to $153 million. Net income after taxes showed a reduction of 17.4 percent to $3.1 million.

OIL PIPELINES

Consistent with the general increase in economic activity, oil pipelines increased product throughput (number of barrels of oil originated and received from connections) by 4 percent in the first half of 1963. The quantity was 2.6 billion barrels versus 2.5 billion in 1962. Operating revenues also increased—to $396.2 million from $379.5 million, or 4.4 percent.

For the full year 1962, pipeline companies handled 5.1 billion barrels of crude and refined products combined against 4.9 billion in 1961. Transportation revenues for this service increased 3 percent from $786.7 million to $810.6 million. The operating ratio declined in the three successive years 1960, 1961, and 1962, being, respectively, 54.2, 53.4, and 52.6 percent.

Additional comparable data on the pipelines for the latest 3 calendar years for which statistics are available are included in table J of appendix H.

TAXES

Class I line-haul railroad tax accruals of $905 million in 1962 were 8.7 percent less than those for 1961, with increases in some and decreases in other types of taxes making up the total. Payments under the Railroad Retirement Act increased 5.2 percent to $246 million and those under the Unemployment Insurance Act rose 4.4 percent to $135.8 million, the latter increase representing, in part, a temporary increase from 3.75 to 4 percent in the unemployment insurance rate. Average monthly employment declined 4.5 percent, from 715,000 in November 1961, to 683,000 in the same month of 1962.

Total Federal income tax accruals for 1962 of $156.8 million were 35.3 percent less than for 1961. Factors in this decline included a statutory change under which the railroads are permitted to deduct a tax credit of up to 7 percent of the cost of new capital expenditures, and the establishment by the Internal Revenue Service of depreciation allowances more liberal than those formerly permitted. Other accrued taxes in 1962 were $366.5 million, a 4.7-percent decrease from 1961.

For class I intercity motor carriers of property, 1962 Federal income taxes of $70 million represented a decrease of 2.8 percent from 1961. For operating taxes and licenses the increase was 11.9 percent to $333.9 million. These carriers also secured significant tax savings from the tax credit and changes in depreciation guidelines.

For class I intercity carriers of passengers, the Federal income tax increase, 1961 to 1962, was 20.4 percent to a total of $33.1 million while operating taxes and licenses increased 5.1 percent to $39.4 million.

In 1962, class A and class B water carriers accrued $9.7 million in income taxes and $4 million in other taxes due. These amounts represented a decrease of 15.9 percent and an increase of 11.2 percent, respectively, from 1961.

Income and excess profits tax accruals from operations of oil pipelines amounted to $115.3 million in 1962, an increase of 3.5 percent over 1961. Other tax accruals totaled $41.9 million, an increase of 2.4 percent above the previous year.

A comparison of carriers representing various modes of transportation in terms of the share of each of total 1962 operating revenues, net investment at the close of 1961, income and excess profits taxes, and other tax accruals for 1962, is shown below.

Revenues, net investment, and taxes—1962 [1]

(*Thousands*)

Kind of carrier	Operating revenues	Net investment in carrier operating property and equipment, Dec. 31, 1961	Taxes	
			Income and excess profits	All other
Class I line-haul railroads_____	[2] $9,439,895	$22,790,552	[3] $156,786	$748,258
Motors carriers of property (class I intercity)[4]__	5,373,749	743,544	[5] 69,996	333,948
Motor carriers of passengers (class I intercity)[6]_	524,639	219,213	[5] 33,132	39,427
Water carriers (class A and class B)_____	[7] 252,465	191,916	[5] 9,748	4,119
Oil pipelines_____	810,605	1,977,713	[5] 115,284	41,928
Total_____	16,401,353	25,922,938	384,946	1,167,680
	Percentage distribution [8]			
Class I line-haul railroads_____	57.6	87.9	40.7	64.1
Motor carriers of property_____	32.8	2.9	18.2	28.6
Motor carriers of passengers_____	3.2	.8	8.6	3.4
Water carriers_____	1.5	.7	2.5	.4
Oil pipelines_____	4.9	7.6	30.0	3.6
Total_____	100.0	100.0	100.0	100.0

[1] Net investment in carrier property and equipment at the close of the preceding year.
[2] Railway operating revenues.
[3] U.S. Government income and excess profits taxes only.
[4] From Quarterly Report Q-800.
[5] U.S. and State taxes combined.
[6] From Quarterly Report Q-750.
[7] Total water-line operating revenues.
[8] Owing to rounding, some columns may not add to 100.

SERVICE AND FACILITIES

INTERMODAL COORDINATION OF FREIGHT SERVICE

Further progress was made toward achievement of a standardized system for the expeditious and economical interchange of containerized freight among the several modes of transport, and for its movement on a through bill of lading at a single-factor rate. Of particular significance were improvements in physical facilities for intermodal interchange of highway trailer vans and other types of containers, including temporary storage incident to such exchange, and the establishment of a number of cooperative arrangements between pairs of individual carriers of different modes.

As an example of the utilization of coordinated service the U.S. Post Office Department recently inaugurated regularly scheduled train-trailership-truck mail service to points in Central America.

Rail-Highway Service

Optimism in regard to the future of piggyback (trailer-on-flatcar or T.O.F.C.) service was reflected by a number of events during the reporting year. Railroads continued, at considerable cost, to modify existing structures and other facilities to permit clearance of piggyback and multilevel automobile rack loads. Several railroads inaugurated, completed, or were in the process of carrying out systemwide plans for the enlargement of tunnels, lowering of tracks, or the removal of various kinds of obstructions to such traffic. Designers of highway trailers placed increased emphasis upon equipment features primarily of importance in piggyback service.

Table A below shows continued increases for all districts in the number of rail cars loaded with T.O.F.C. traffic during calendar 1962 and during the first half of 1963. T.O.F.C. loadings in the southern district showed the largest percentage increase for the past 3 years.

The weekly average of 13,585 T.O.F.C. loadings for 1962 was 19.5 percent above 1961, and 27.5 percent greater than the 1960 average, although only 6 carriers were added to the reporting group since 1960. The 13.4-percent increase in loadings in the first half of 1963, over the comparable period in 1962, and the increase in weekly carloading averages, suggest a sizable increase in total carloadings for the full 1963 year.

TABLE A.—*Trailer-on-flatcar loadings* [1] *by districts, 1960–63*

	Calendar year—						First half of—			
	1960		1961		1962		1962		1963	
	Cars	Percent	Cars	Percent	Cars	Percent	Cars	Percent	Cars	Percent
Cars loaded:										
Eastern district	251,523	45.4	286,625	48.5	351,217	49.7	171,586	49.7	179,705	46.0
Southern district	33,412	6.0	50,729	8.6	83,406	11.8	38,196	11.1	60,669	15.5
Western district	269,180	48.6	253,892	42.9	271,818	38.5	135,032	39.2	150,744	38.5
Total	554,115	100.0	591,246	100.0	706,441	100.0	344,814	100.0	391,118	100.0
Percent increase from the previous period:										
Eastern district		26.7		13.9		22.5		30.5		4.7
Southern district		209.9		51.8		64.4		69.4		58.8
Western district		30.7		d 5.7		7.1		2.3		11.6
Total		33.5		6.7		19.5		20.5		13.4
Weekly average	10,656		11,370		13,585		13,262		15,043	
Maximum week	12,224		13,498		15,996		15,196		17,052	
Number of reporting railroads	55		58		61		60		61	

[1] Includes gondola cars and flatcars loaded with van containers (without trailer chassis and wheels).
d Decrease.

Source: Association of American Railroads.

The number of class I line-haul railroads participating in T.O.F.C. tariffs increased from 57 in 1958 to 100 in 1963. For railroads other than class I, the number participating, which rose from 31 to 131 in the period 1959–62, fell to 93 in 1963. It appears that service proposed by some smaller roads in the prior period for the movement of T.O.F.C. traffic, failed to attract the traffic.

Table B below shows the number of railroad cars equipped for T.O.F.C. service on June 30 for the years 1959 through 1963, and the percentage increase, as compared in each case with the previous year.

TABLE B.—*Flatcars equipped for trailer-on-flatcar (piggyback) service, 1959–63* [1]

	As of June 30—									
	1959		1960		1961		1962		1963	
	Number	Percent	Number	Percent	Number	Percent	Number	Percent	Number	Percent
Railroad owned	4,571	66.9	6,106	56.3	6,630	54.5	6,718	47.0	6,312	37.8
Privately owned [2]	2,264	33.1	4,740	43.7	5,527	45.5	7,563	53.0	10,396	62.2
Total	6,835	100.0	10,846	100.0	12,157	100.0	14,281	100.0	16,708	100.0
Percent increase over previous year		63.1		58.7		12.1		17.5		17.0

[1] Includes some gondola cars and flatcars for carrying van containers (without trailer chassis and wheels).
[2] Includes cars owned by pools which are in whole or in part owned by railroads.

There were various other indications of the growth of piggyback service. These included announcements by carriers, shippers, and equipment manufacturers.   It was estimated that there were in 1963 approximately 25,000 trailers directly involved in piggyback service, and that based on the current rate of growth, there will be a demand for more than 50,000 new units by 1968.   The increasing availability of plan V (joint through rail-motor rates, service, and billing) also may be a significant factor in further expansion of piggyback service. For example, a major eastern district railroad announced plan V service involving a fleet of 750 trailers and some 20 participating motor carriers serving 30 States, the District of Columbia, and Canada.   A western trunk-line railroad announced in March the extension of plan V service to customers in a 20-State area, with participation by 200 motor carriers in the coordinated service.

From the standpoint of equipment replacement, it is expected that depreciation guidelines for railroad rolling stock, published by the Internal Revenue Service in 1962, will result in replacement of converted equipment with cars designed specifically for T.O.F.C. use.

Land-Water Service

Construction of new containerships and conversion of older ships to handle containerized freight continued to provide increased capacity in coastwise and intercoastal freight service during the fiscal year.

Late in September 1962, Sea-Land Service, Inc., initiated containership service between the east and west coasts using three converted 630-foot tanker ships, each with the capacity of 476 35-foot highway trailers.

Freight service to islands within the Hawaiian chain has been extended by the use of barges adapted for the interchange of containers between ships and barges.   Experimentation with both self-propelled barges and automated barges for use in this service is now underway.

Efforts to develop an "ocean-truck" through bill of lading have resulted in the establishment by one carrier of a new "Thru Export-Import-Bill-of-Lading Service" to the Far East.   The service provides for motor carrier responsibility from origin to destination. Also, a freight forwarder and a container firm joined services to provide for through movement of small shipments from points within the United States to European destinations.

Air-Surface Service

In efforts to provide door-to-door service on a single bill of lading, several coordinated air-land services have been inaugurated during the past year.   Examples of the services now offered through such airline-motor carrier joint agreements are: (*a*) a through bill of lading and "name-the-day" "air van" service, recently announced by a major air cargo carrier and six large van lines; and (*b*) a program offering door-to-door service on a single bill of lading, initiated by another major air-cargo carrier in cooperation with more than 60 motor carriers. The plan, known as "Skyroad," is designed to serve some 1,500 cities. Also, many motor carriers now have agreements with the largest American transoceanic airline to furnish destination service on jet-transported cargos.

The continued development of jet cargo aircraft, helicopter facilities and services, containerization, and other technological innovations within the airline industry will undoubtedly make possible additional intermodal coordinated freight service programs.

Containerization

Containerization continues to be a primary subject of research efforts directed toward coordination of transportation services. Industry, Government, and private institutions continue to support standardization within the container fabrication industry. Significant advances have been made toward standardization of containers utilized in domestic freight movements. As mentioned in our previous annual reports, the American Standards Association has approved specifications for the standardization of containers to be used in domestic traffic. These standards are expected to provide guidelines for the design of containers which will meet the requirements of both transportation and shipping interests and to contribute substantially to an efficient, coordinated transportation system.

While formal efforts to reach agreement on standardization have been in progress for some time, many containers continue to be designed and constructed to meet particular needs of shippers. It was recently reported that there are approximately 30,000 to 40,000 van containers, more than 250,000 cargo containers, and a much larger but undetermined number of pallet containers in service today.[7] The report also states that slightly less than 3,000 van containers were produced annually during the period 1958 through 1961 but that production of these units increased significantly in 1962 when more than 7,000 were built.

As to the future, the report foresees an estimated 288,000 van containers in use by 1970 and it estimates that by 1975 there will be more than 675,000 units in service.

A significant step toward acceptance of international standards for van containers was taken by the delegates to Technical Committee 104 of the International Organization for Standardization in accepting specifications (subject to formal approval) for 10- and 20-foot van-type freight containers.

---

[7] *Containerization, The outlook for shipping containers,* Transportation and Defense Section Commercial Research Division, U.S. Steel Corp., June 1963.

Introduced during the year was a container known as the "Inver-tainer." The design, similar to that of a blunt-nosed projectile with tail fins, is 5 feet long and 7 feet wide, with 4-foot sides. Since the design provides for gravity filling and discharge, the primary use of the container would be in the movement of bulk commodities. It is suggested by the designer that several of the "Invertainers" can be fitted together to form the secondary floor of a truck trailer, rail car, or larger container upon which mixed cargo can be loaded.

In addition to several new and promising concepts introduced dur-ing the fiscal year, numerous unique or experimental containerized freight movements were carried out through shipper-carrier coordi-nation during the year. A complete potash plant was moved in 53 containers and cases from an east coast port to the Port of Haifa, Israel; and a "container" moved 36,000 pounds of Florida grapefruit to Basel, Switzerland. The self-contained refrigeration unit made the 4,000-mile, 19-day trip utilizing rail, water, and motor carriers. In still another innovation, the superior speed of passenger over freight locomotives was used by a major railroad to furnish motive power for freight trains consisting of conventional rail cars, contain-ers, and piggyback trailers, all refrigerated to protect the lading.

SMALL SHIPMENTS

For movement of small shipments over longer distances generally, there is no alternative but to use regulated carriers or the postal service. During 1962 and 1963, increases were sought in charges for this type of service due to higher costs of providing the various services. For example, in 1962 express charges were increased and, in 1963 proposals were renewed for increases in parcel post charges. During the same period, there have been diverse trends in small ship-ments volume and in revenues reported by carriers.

REA Express, which had shown a small decline in shipments, 1960 to 1961, reported a 1962 increase of 1.3 percent to 66.9 million ship-ments. Revenues, with the further benefit of the rate increase, in-creased 4.2 percent to $382.6 million.

"Express privilege" payments to carriers employed, while increas-ing by 0.4 percent to $116.9 million for 1962, showed continued development of trends evident in the preceding year. In terms of the total payments, the rail shares for 1961 and 1962 were 76.8 and 73.9 percent, respectively; those to air carriers 20.7 and 23.5 percent; and those to motor carriers, 2.1 percent for both years. Express privilege payments to water and other carriers were approximately 0.5 percent of the total payments in the respective years.

The amount paid to railroads in 1962 was $86.4 million, a decline of 3.4 percent, while payments to air and motor carriers increased 13.9 and 4.3 percent to $27.5 million and $2.5 million, respectively. The declining payments to railroads reflect in considerable measure REA's freedom, under its 1959 agreement with the railroads, to route traffic by whatever means it chooses, as well as continued reductions in passenger train operations.

Parcel post service, with an average weight of 5.9 pounds per piece in fiscal 1962, as well as in the previous year, is relatively well known to the general public, in comparison with other small-shipment services. Declines of limited extent in revenues, number, and total weight of mailings in fiscal 1962 continued trends noted for the previous year. For zone-rated parcel post, fiscal 1962 revenues decreased 0.5 percent to $572.6 million, the number of mailings 1 percent to 792.3 million, and the weight 0.4 percent to 4,705 million pounds.

The Post Office Department renewed its request to the Commission, for consent to an increase of approximately 13 percent in rates on fourth-class mail, and the matter is under consideration in Docket No. 33750, *Reformation of Rates and Other Conditions of Mailability of Fourth-Class Mail.* The Post Office request was made following the approval of Public Law 88–51, June 29, 1963, which suspends for 3 years the statutory requirements relating to a 4-percent spread between parcel post revenues and costs.

Shipments handled by 64 freight forwarders with revenues of $100,000 or more numbered 21.7 million in 1962, a decrease of 16.5 percent from the previous year. Total weight of shipments rose 7.5 percent to 4.3 million tons and average weight per shipment increased from 308 pounds to 397 pounds, possibly reflecting "volume shipments" of 10,000 pounds or more. The total shipments yielded revenues of $464.6 million, an increase of 4.9 percent.

Less-than-carload shipments of the railroads, as in previous years, continued to decline. The 1962 tonnage, 2.2 million tons, was 15.6 percent less than the 1961 figure, while revenue declined 20.4 percent to $99.7 million.

For class I motor carriers of general commodities, less-than-truckload shipments, viz., up to 10,000 pounds, showed in 1962 increases of 4.6, 8.8, and 11.1 percent, respectively, to 230.9 million shipments, 63.2 million tons, and $2,380.2 million of revenue. Average weight per shipment showed a 4.2-percent increase from 526 to 548 pounds.

Increased costs, principally at terminals, for handling less-than-truckload traffic resulted in numerous requests for increased minimum charges or for increases in rates, by surcharge or otherwise, on such traffic. While costs have likewise increased for handling truckload traffic, they have not been as severe as for less-than-truckload traffic.

Motor carriers of passengers continued their promotion in the package express area. The 1962 revenues of class I passenger carriers, from this source, increased over 1961 by 14.3 percent, to a total of $41.9

million. This increase was close to a percentage point more than the 13.4-percent increase, 1960 to 1961.

RAILROADS

In administering car service provisions of the act, without directly participating in actual railroad management or administration, the Commission has responsibility for encouraging railroad efficiency through improved utilization and operation of the nation's freight car fleet. The Commission undertakes to regulate car service throughout the United States by maintaining in the field representatives with practical railroad operating knowledge, to assist the railroads in obtaining optimum distribution and use of the available freight car supply. Discussions of railroad construction and abandonment activities and discontinuance of passenger train operations are included in the chapter on Finance Proceedings (page 31).

Regulation of the railroad industry in fiscal year 1963 was attended by introduction of various new concepts by carriers, such as the high volume transportation performance of integral trains. Repetitive problems were no less disruptive because of lack of novelty. A progressively decreasing car supply was aggravated by two major railroad work stoppages and a longshoremen's strike. A serious interruption in the nation's railroad industry occurred in the costly 30-day strike and paralysis of operations of the Chicago and North Western Railway. Problems connected with the handling of traffic destined to industries located on the carrier's lines were alleviated somewhat by the issuance of Taylor's ICC Order No. 147, which authorized this carrier and its connections to divert and reroute traffic over any available route.

Because of an impending work stoppage on the Florida East Coast Railway Company, Taylor's ICC Order No. 150, effective January 21, 1963, authorized the carrier and its connections to reroute traffic over any available route. The strike of nonoperating employees of the Florida East Coast Railway Company became effective January 23, 1963. With supervisory personnel performing operating functions, the carrier has been able to provide much of its normal transport capability.

During periods of work stoppage, which in cases of major lines affect large geographical areas and wide segments of the population, 46 strategically located field offices provided the Commission with an immediate and up-to-date evaluation of the situation. By assisting carriers in disposing of railroad cars immobilized by the strike and redirecting a normal pattern of traffic into and out of the affected area, the Commission lessens the economic impact of stoppages.

A longshoremen's strike would have had a side effect by immobilizing rail cars, but this was averted by early issuance of an embargo.

However, with resumption of activities at the ports and a stepped-up grain-loading program by the Commodity Credit Corporation, severe boxcar shortages developed in many parts of the country. Field staff personnel were assigned to areas most affected and provided direct assistance and guidance to railroad management to help alleviate the critical condition.

Today's commerce is fast-paced, more sophisticated and more complicated than ever before; and for this reason, shipper demands for customer-oriented special equipment have resulted in an increase in ownership of specially equipped boxcars, covered hoppers, and heavy-duty flat cars for trailer-on-flatcar service, together with bilevel and trilevel rack cars for new automobiles. At the same time a decrease in the ownership of the conventional type equipment continues.

American railroads, during the recent past, have moved forward with the theory and policy of "flexibility promotes efficiency." This progressive thinking has brought about continued innovations in operational improvements, which have caused a period of rapid technological change.

Prompted by the economics of commerce, integral trains and unitized trains have been introduced into modern high-volume transport. These concepts of transportation offer a high utilization ratio of rail car fleets and offer a mass production approach for transportation.

A "unitized train" is usually one of a specified number of cars shuttling back and forth between production point and volume consumer, such as a coal mine-utility operation. Cars are assigned usually to this service exclusively. It is operated on rigid schedules, and costs substantially less to operate.

The "integral train" concept envisions the handling of volume traffic moved in lightweight cars equipped with unloading devices, which permits expeditious handling by the shipper and the receiver.

From the standpoint of car service, these concepts of transportation offer high utilization ratios of rail car fleets. In the coal industry it is visualized that an average coal car making 75,000 ton-miles per year could be increased to 600,000 or 750,000 ton-miles per year.

Eighty-five and 100-ton hopper cars are being placed in operation in the coal industry. This large capacity offers increased car service utility to the extent that power plants are now being designed to burn coal near power-consuming areas, rather than at mine-mouth locations.

Transportation officials see no reason why other bulk cargoes and even merchandise trains cannot similarly move in unit or integral trains. Other commodities might include grain, sugar, iron ore, aluminum and copper ores, petroleum products, and chemicals.

A recent survey of train operations indicates that there has been a decided swing to high-speed service (50 miles per hour and over), including trailer-on-flatcar operations now provided by most railroads.

This year, as in the past, the Commission played a key role in the task of moving the nation's combined winter and spring wheat crops. During the harvest seasons the primary assignment of many field agents was to provide day-to-day promotion of efficiency and economy in "car service," defined as the "general service of a railroad in distributing and handling cars." Their efforts were equally beneficial to railroads, shippers and receivers, and milling and grain trade groups. No single commodity exerts such a tremendous strain on the nation's boxcar supply as movement of the annual grain crops. Beginning in May with the winter wheat crop in Texas, the harvest advances steadily northward through Oklahoma, Kansas, Nebraska, and eastern Colorado; then into the Northwestern spring wheat area (Minnesota, the Dakotas and Montana), ending in late fall in the Far Northwest States. Adding to the railroads' problem of supplying cars for the movement of this vast tonnage of grain is the U.S. Department of Agriculture's Commodity Credit Corporation's year-round grain program—the relocation of old grain stocks from country storage and elevators to storage outside the principal producing areas, along with their sustained export movement. The shipments in this government relocation program, simultaneously with the annual harvest, place a severe strain upon the available boxcar supply.

The increased use of laborsaving machinery, particularly the use of combine fleets, has stepped up the harvest so that in some areas it is only 15 to 20 days in length. As a result, millions of bushels of wheat are offered for shipment, causing an enormous demand for rail cars to load and move the grain promptly.

Because of the low percentage of home cars on western grain loading roads, the Commission issued Service Order No. 943, effective May 8, 1963, applicable to plain boxcars with doors less than 8 feet wide of nine railroads involved in handling the winter wheat harvest. This order provided for the loading of western ownerships, named in the orders, to the owners, via the owners, to a junction with the owners, or to certain States in which they operate. In the absence of such loading, cars were to be moved home empty.

This order resulted in expeditious return of cars to the western roads and improved their car supply to the extent that the order was vacated June 19, 1963, at the request of the beneficiary roads.

In preparation for this gigantic assignment, our car service agents, well in advance of the grain harvest, surveyed the grain-loading railroads to ascertain the status of assembling, conditioning and storing of suitable boxcars. We determined the availability of man and motive power and mill, elevator and terminal market facilities. Any obstacle to prompt movement, release or disposition of grain cars was given remedial attention immediately to provide the country elevators with an adequate boxcar supply and to prevent terminal congestion.

In the 1962 fall harvest a generally satisfactory boxcar supply enabled carriers to handle all the grain for which storage space was available in the subterminal and terminal markets. Shipper complaints on car supply or related activities were at a minimum.

Our car service activities also extend to encouraging better utilization of cars used for other volume commodity movements, such as seasonal increased loadings involving agricultural products, building and construction materials, forest and lumber products, and heavy fruit and vegetable movements.

For a number of years we have been greatly concerned with the diminishing supply of freight cars and the critical shortages that have occurred during periods of peak loadings. Freight car ownership (See table A) on June 30, 1963, was the lowest ever recorded.

TABLE A.—*Ownership of freight-carrying cars in the United States as of June 30 of the last two fiscal years was as follows:*

	1962	1963
Class I railroad ownership	1, 582, 103	1, 529, 947
Class I railroad controlled refrigerator cars	60, 271	59, 107
Private car owners (exclusive of railroad controlled refrigerator cars)	262, 302	260, 680
Class II and all switching and terminal railroads	31, 899	31, 908
Electric railroads	1, 611	1, 593
Grand total all freight-carrying cars in United States	1, 938, 186	1, 883, 235

Foremost among the factors contributing to the recurring shortages are an inadequate car ownership, a relatively high percentage of unserviceable or bad-order cars, and the inefficient utilization of existing equipment. This year, as in the past 8 years, we are recommending legislation to amend section 1(14) of the act. This would authorize the Commission to determine whether per diem charges for the use of railroad freight cars should be computed on the basis of cost of ownership and maintenance, value of use, or upon such other basis or combination of bases to provide reasonable compensation to the owner, contribute to sound car service practices, and encourage the acquisition of an adequate national fleet of freight cars.

This recommended amendment would provide the carriers with an economic incentive to procure and maintain their fair share of a national car supply and assist substantially the Commission in its efforts to alleviate the crippling economic effects of freight car shortages.

During the past year the Commission exercised its emergency power in issuing service orders designed to promote car service in the interest of the public and the commerce of the people. Service orders are the medium by which the Commission may require the carriers to change their published rules and regulations. Also, when emergencies exist, railroads may be ordered to perform certain beneficial functions or to prohibit practices which in the Commission's opinion are detrimental to efficient car handling.

These orders are titled "Taylor's Order No. ——" issued by C. W. Taylor, Director of the Bureau of Safety and Service, as Agent of the Interstate Commerce Commission and vested with authority to authorize diversion and rerouting of loaded and empty cars in emergency situations.

The number of service orders issued and served on the railroads during the past year totaled 6, including 3 revised orders. Also 9 amendments to service orders (not including 14 Taylor Orders and amendments thereto issued under Revised Service Order 562) were issued during the past year.

In addition, a total of 39 permits were issued by the Commission's Permit Agent under Service Orders 939 and 943 and served on interested carriers.

During the year ended June 30, 1963, three service orders were vacated or expired by date limitation. As of the same date seven service orders were in effect.

The past year was one of extremely heavy boxcar demands, with substantial shortages of high-grade and special-size equipment reported during most of the period. The wide-door 40-foot car and all types of 50-foot plain boxcars were in short supply throughout the year. Demands for this equipment are increasing steadily as a result of mechanized loading and unloading, increased palletization of loads, and the need for greater capacity to accommodate larger loads moving under higher minima. While there has been an increase in ownership of the above types of equipment, demands for cars of these sizes are expected to exceed the available supply. Recognizing that the supply of serviceable boxcars is totally inadequate to supply the needs of the shippers, the Commission's Service Order No. 939 (covering the utilization of 50-foot plain boxcars and 40-foot plain boxcars with door openings that are 8 feet wide or more) continues in effect in an effort to relocate cars to owners' rails and to areas where the demand is greatest.

While average gross-ton miles per train-hour rose from 36,954 during World War II to 67,491 in 1962 and average train-miles per train-hour increased from 15.7 to 20, utilization of equipment as expressed in turnaround time in days increased from 13.67 days in 1947 to 19.24 days in 1962. Utilization of equipment has been further impaired by the decrease in car-miles per freight car-day, loaded or empty, both serviceable and unserviceable, from a World War II high of 50.6 miles to 42.8 miles during 1962. Hours per day of cars moving in trains decreased from 3.33 to 2.34; thus cars were standing or moving in terminals an average of 21.66 hours daily, or over 90 percent of the time.

The effectiveness of achieving proper utilization of equipment has been strongly influenced by the trend to provide specialized equipment and use it in assigned service (one-way loads) for large shippers; and by a corresponding decline in ownership of the types of equipment used in general service.

That this condition will continue and become more critical is reflected in orders for 8,121 new boxcars on June 30, 1963, of which only 1,682 or 20.7 percent were for plain 50-foot boxcars. The decrease in plain boxcar ownership is resulting in chronic car supply problems. For the first time since fiscal 1956, boxcar shortages were reported throughout the year. As a result of the heavy movement of grain, daily shortages of 11,229 plain boxcars were reported during the week ending March 30, 1963. This was the highest daily shortage of plain boxcars reported since October 29, 1955, when the daily shortage was reported as 12,491 cars. This shortage was further aggravated by the decrease in ownership of 105,145 cars. (See tables B and C, and charts on page 111.)

TABLE B.—*Ownership, serviceable ownership and turnaround time (in days), class I railroads*

	As of July 1—			
	1948	1953	1958	1963
Ownership				
Plain box	679, 242	678, 378	681, 259	555, 430
Equipped box	49, 276	51, 784	50, 029	68, 660
Total box	728, 518	730, 162	731, 288	624, 090
Refrigerators	104, 904	100, 807	96, 511	90, 495
Gondolas	308, 918	295, 244	282, 730	245, 057
Hoppers	545, 239	560, 972	524, 904	437, 102
Covered hoppers	14, 793	31, 814	56, 870	71, 267
Flat	50, 739	46, 768	49, 983	54, 820
Others	78, 622	83, 646	81, 433	66, 223
Total cars	1, 831, 733	1, 849, 413	1, 823, 719	1, 589, 054
Serviceable cars				
Plain box	649, 236	645, 675	638, 382	509, 443
Equipped box	45, 534	47, 952	46, 581	65, 145
Total box	694, 860	693, 627	684. 963	574, 588
Refrigerators	98, 005	95, 747	89, 877	86, 262
Gondolas	291, 357	276, 826	252, 545	215, 360
Hoppers	521, 178	531, 762	478, 386	408, 002
Covered hopppers	14, 577	31, 301	55, 697	69, 742
Flat	47, 920	44, 528	47, 653	52, 457
Others	74, 157	79, 854	77, 813	63, 384
Total cars	1, 742, 054	1, 753, 645	1, 686, 934	1, 469, 795

	Calendar year—			
	1947	1952	1957	1962
Turnaround time—days				
Box	12. 74	15. 52	17. 64	19. 41
Refrigerators	22. 11	26. 83	29. 92	30. 81
Gondolas	14. 33	15. 51	17. 18	22. 24
Hoppers	13. 10	15. 23	14. 62	16. 41
Covered hoppers	(1)	15. 44	18. 47	21. 46
Flat	16. 79	22. 52	21. 27	13. 64
Total cars	13. 67	16. 33	17. 43	19. 24

1 In 1947 covered hopper cars were included in hopper car ownership.

TABLE C.—*Cars installed, retired and ordered, fiscal years 1948, 1953, 1958, 1963*

	1948	1953	1958	1963
Cars installed				
Box	41, 071	18, 456	20, 291	10, 076
Refrigerator	9, 189	3, 723	3, 031	5, 914
Gondola	6, 767	12, 086	15, 090	594
Hopper	36, 023	23, 111	25, 016	6, 541
Covered hopper	1, 705	3, 943	6, 713	4, 319
Flat	(1)	813	892	2, 454
Other	1, 275	1, 809	1, 680	574
Total cars	96, 030	63, 941	72, 713	30, 472
Cars retired				
Box	35, 648	23, 088	21, 076	36, 267
Refrigerator	9, 263	2, 120	5, 952	3, 085
Gondola	20, 649	12, 613	9, 876	8, 489
Hopper	11, 454	20, 801	17, 540	29, 251
Covered hopper	182	38	2—1	181
Flat	(1)	1, 707	1, 092	1, 286
Other	4, 469	2—933	3, 481	5, 233
Total cars	81, 665	59, 434	59, 016	83, 792
Cars ordered				
Box	28, 745	8, 987	4, 418	14, 051
Refrigerator	6, 851	2, 577	996	7, 574
Gondola	18, 680	6, 149	4, 893	423
Hopper	48, 751	6, 400	2, 491	5, 139
Covered hopper	(3)	(3)	1, 905	5, 926
Flat	3, 106	1, 604	549	6, 770
Other	7, 097	4, 395	2, 128	7, 044
Total cars	113, 230	30, 112	17, 380	46, 927

[1] Included in "Other."
[2] Negative retirement indicates increase in ownership in excess of new installations resulting from reclassification, transfer or purchase or loss of used equipment, etc.
[3] Covered hoppers included in "Hopper."

MOTOR CARRIERS

Motor Carriers of Property

Unlawful transporation, including unlawful transportation of motor vehicles by the driveaway method, and motor carriers operating beyond the scope of their certificates and permits continues to be a major problem. Unquestionably, the source of this problem lies with those shippers who supply the freight to the unlawful operators in return for cheaper transportation at the expense of supporting a sound regulated transportation industry adequate to meet the needs of commerce and the national defense. We have been and continue to be heavily engaged in investigations of unlawful practices. While complete data as to the extent of unlawful operations is not easily ascertained, those which come to our attention more than consume our manpower capabilities in terms of time, and time operates to the advantage of the unlawful operator. Obstacles to establishing proof of violations largely govern the "time" or duration of an investigation. Complexities of different modus operandi used to defeat regulation and which must be clearly unfolded serve to prolong many investigations. Schemes, devices and clever techniques often impede the investigation and the investigator must use ingenuity to counter these efforts in order to successfully conclude an investigation. We

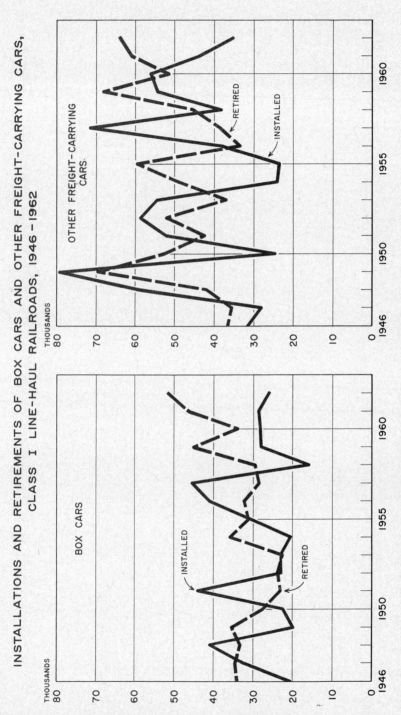

INSTALLATIONS AND RETIREMENTS OF BOX CARS AND OTHER FREIGHT-CARRYING CARS, CLASS I LINE-HAUL RAILROADS, 1946-1962

Source: I.C.C., Bureau of Transport Economics and Statistics, Transport Statistics in the United States.

believe progress is being made. The courts have decided favorably some important cases and we have issued cease and desist orders to a number of respondents engaged in unlawful transportation activities. These court decisions serve to strengthen our enforcement arm. Our enforcement investigations looking to court action or proceedings before us reached an all-time high this year. Some cases of particular interest are reported in the chapter on Enforcement and Compliance.

In June 1963, the ICC participated with State officials in a road check to obtain information on unlawful motor transportation. Federal and State personnel jointly manning check points established in 40 States stopped trucks around the clock for 7 consecutive days. ICC staff working alone manned check points in three additional States.

Based on information developed from this road check, the Commission estimates that unlawful motor transportation may represent between $500 and $600 million annually in lost revenues to regulated carriers. This estimate takes into account Commission experience that warning of road checks spreads rapidly and unlawful operators either "hole-up," use alternate roads to bypass check points, or delay moving until conclusion of the checks.

Our highway road checks of driver and vehicle safety condition have been a dominating factor in bringing about improved vehicle inspection and maintenance by motor carriers. Effective September 5, 1962, we prescribed regulation [49 C.F.R. § 195.13] by which drivers found to have been on duty or to have driven or operated immediately prior to examination by our motor carrier field staff longer than the time permitted by our maximum hours of service regulations may be notified and declared "out of service" until such drivers can return to duty in compliance with these regulations. Provision for declaring imminently hazardous vehicles "out of service" has been in effect for a number of years. The recent rule is aimed at the driver. Road checks conducted during the 1962 calendar year produced evidence that the trend toward improved carrier vehicle maintenance, interrupted by less favorable findings in 1961, had been resumed.

Between September 5, 1962, and June 30, 1963, 264 drivers were declared "out of service" because of violation of our maximum hours of service regulations.

We lack sufficient field personnel to perform the desired level of effective enforcement of the act and regulations compatible with preserving a safe and economically sound motor carrier transportation service. Despite progress that has and is being made, we feel that without adequate field personnel commensurate with the problems, our regulatory efforts must be considered at best as "catching the few"; and we hope "scaring the many."

During the year we received more than 10,000 oral or written complaints, largely concerning claims for loss or damage to goods transported and because of delays in delivery of goods. Many of these alleged inability to obtain any communication from the carrier in response to the complaint. Others came to us following unsatisfactory negotiations with the carrier. These complaints were received for the most part from the smaller shippers and particularly the individual shipper of household goods. We are without jurisdiction over the settlement of claims for the loss and damage of goods. As a matter of policy, however, we transmit complaints which we receive to the carriers for their consideration.

We are aware that the industry performs satisfactory services seldom evidenced to us by shipper commendation, nonetheless our complaint experience bespeaks a need for betterment of shipper relations by more expeditious claims processing.

Motor Carriers of Passengers

This year has been characterized by an expansion of long-distance through bus service and increased patronage of express passenger service between metropolitan areas. While new and improved highways have provided much of the impetus for this expansion, air conditioning and washroom facilities have tended to make such service more attractive. Other innovations such as telephones for the use of passengers as well as for assistance in making connections with other buses, continue to be made. In addition to passenger transportation, buses are carrying substantial amounts of package express and mail, providing prompt delivery to small communities in particular.

Charter and special service travel continue to be an important source of revenue to the industry. In this connection, there is a growing problem in the loss of charter business by authorized carriers to unauthorized operators who "lease" equipment to clubs and other organizations for use in interstate passenger transportation. The industry is cooperating with our field staff as we continue to investigate these unlawful practices.

We received complaints alleging violation of our regulations governing discrimination in operations of interstate motor carriers of passengers, but the number was small in comparison to the overall volume of complaints received. However, because of their nature, investigation is difficult and time consuming. For the most part, carriers have been fully cooperative in correcting conditions within their control. Enforcement action of particular interest is discussed in the chapter on Enforcement and Compliance.

Passenger safety continues to be a major factor in our regulatory role. Our program of safety inspection of passenger carrier buses at bus terminals is designed to uncover, and enable carriers to correct defects or deficiencies before buses are dispatched. Special attention is currently being given to drivers and vehicles used to transport migrant workers, made subject to regulation by amendment to the act in 1956 [49 U.S.C. 304(a)(3a)]. During the latter half of the year, we inaugurated a widespread program to determine compliance with our safety regulations [49 C.F.R. Part 198] by carriers of migrant workers by motor vehicle. Arrangements were made for voluntary presentation of vehicles for inspection at some points. However, many of the carriers failed to participate. In addition to the voluntary program, special and routine road checks were held throughout the States to determine safety compliance by these carriers. Inspections disclosed a need for greatly improved compliance with our driver physical examination requirements. While newer vehicles were in fair compliance with our parts and accessories requirements, older vehicles fall short of reasonable compliance standards since worn parts and inoperative accessories are not repaired or replaced. Investigations further disclosed a predominant trend toward migrant worker transportation by modes not subject to our safety regulation; i.e., by passenger automobile or station wagon and of a migrant worker transporting himself or his immediate family. The trend away from the use of vehicles subject to our vehicle and driver safety regulations is due, in part, to the cost of complying with the safety regulations and to the necessity of paying State taxes imposed upon commercial type vehicles. We shall continue to give our attention to investigations of migrant worker transportation.

Motor Carrier Field Work

A numerical summary of our motor carrier field work in safety, enforcement, operating authority, rates and tariffs, insurance, and account matters for the past 2 years follows. Fewer property carrying vehicles were inspected for safety condition this year than last because of our road checks focused upon determination of unlawful transportation operations in lieu of safety checks. The regulation relating to drivers declared "out of service" did not become effective until September 5, 1962.

Motor carrier field work

	July 1, 1961, through June 30, 1962	July 1, 1962, through June 30, 1963
Safety:		
Investigations and reports on:		
Overall safety compliance	6,243	6,324
Explosives or dangerous articles compliance	182	197
Safety condition of property vehicles	45,732	39,468
Safety condition of buses	3,537	3,072
Vehicles declared "out-of-service"	7,844	6,268
Hours of service compliance	445	532
Drivers declared "out-of-service"		264
Road observation violations	9,439	7,519
Accident investigations including supplementary	857	776
Safety conferences	1,361	1,483
Road checks	5,070	5,706
Service of safety regulations on private and exempt carriers	7,972	8,100
Other safety matters handled	9,854	10,914
Enforcement:		
Complaints received	4,795	5,064
Investigations and reports on:		
Alleged violations complained of	4,957	5,251
Suspected unlawful transportation developed on road checks	6,122	5,389
Possible criminal, civil or Commission proceedings	1,141	1,256
Overall economic regulation compliance	1,855	1,726
Loss, damage, service, etc., complaints handled	9,938	10,568
Court or Commission proceedings appearances	328	307
Other enforcement matters handled	6,578	6,670
Operating authority:		
Investigations and reports on applications for:		
Permanent operating authority	299	208
Temporary operating authority	4,084	4,719
State certificate filings	373	2,085
Revocation of authority or dismissal of application	470	512
Transfer of operating authority	813	804
Authorization to temporarily operate properties sought to be acquired	108	135
Consolidation, merger, purchase, control, etc	66	90
Other operating authority matters handled	14,044	15,587
Rates and tariffs:		
Investigation and reports on overall rate and tariff compliance	455	514
Assistance in preparation special permission applications, tariffs and schedules, adoption notices and supplements, concurrences and powers of attorney, and revocation of concurrences and powers of attorney	1,328	1,534
Examination of tariffs and schedules	1,683	2,046
Tariff and rate interpretations	2,972	3,385
Other rate and tariff matters handled	4,992	4,917
Insurance:		
Investigations and reports on insurance compliance	3,605	3,829
Other insurance matters handled	2,606	2,077
Reports:		
Investigations and reports on:		
Change in classification for accounting regulation purposes	22	29
Delinquent accounting reports	2,878	2,548
Other accounting matters handled	1,368	1,303

WATER CARRIERS

Strenuous competitive forces and increasing port and vessel operating costs have been instrumental in encouraging water carriers to initiate economies through improved methods. A carrier which had been providing intercoastal service between Elizabeth, N.J., and Los Angeles and Oakland, Calif., with conventional breakbulk cargo ships has substituted three 630-foot containerships with intercoastal sailings every 14 days in each direction. Each of these ships has capacity for carrying 476 35-foot highway trailer van bodies. Loading and unloading with ships' gantry cranes can be accomplished in 12 hours, a fraction of the time required for working a conventional breakbulk

type ship. Losses resulting from damage and pilferage have been substantially reduced. During the year it also extended its intercoastal
operation by providing service between Oakland and Portland, Oreg.
Service between these west coast ports is performed with a roll-on-roll-
off type oceangoing barge capable of carrying about sixty-five 35-foot
trailers. This service also is provided on a 14-day frequency to con-
nect with the intercoastal sailings at Oakland. Service to inland
points is accomplished at all ports by participation in through routes
and joint rates with motor carriers and railroads, making available a
through service for carrying shipments in the same container from
consignor to consignee. The carrier also provides regularly scheduled
coastwise service between Atlantic and Gulf of Mexico ports with
smaller containerships.

Other carriers in the intercoastal trade have continued to provide
general cargo service in connection with other operations in which
they are engaged. One of these carriers, now merged with its parent
corporation which is in the lumber business, carries substantial quan-
tities of lumber eastbound. Another is affiliated with a large steel
company which ships its products westbound. Three other common
carriers provide a limited intercoastal service as an adjunct to their
worldwide shipping operations. But one of the regular carriers in the
intercoastal trade, which suspended operations in 1961 and put its five
ships in worldwide tramp trading, has sold the last of its vessels.

The nuclear-powered freighter, NS *Savannah*, has been plagued
with labor difficulties and provided a very limited passenger-freight
intercoastal service. It accomplished one intercoastal voyage from
Atlantic coast ports to the west coast and returned to Galveston, Tex.
We authorized a coastwise trip from Texas to Massachusetts but, due
to further labor strife, the ship was immobilized at Galveston at the
close of this report year.

On the Atlantic coast, railroad competition has forced discontinuance of a New York-Savannah containership run by one of the two
remaining common carriers offering steamship service. The vessel
thus relieved has been placed in the New York-Puerto Rico trade.
Trailer-on-flatcar (T.O.F.C.) service offered by the railroads from
the Northeast to the South and Southwest has introduced strong
competition for the two Atlantic-Gulf common carriers.

A Pacific coastwise carrier operating self-propelled vessels in the
lumber trade lost one of its ships on the Oregon coast. It now provides
a substituted tug-and-barge operation under temporary authority and
is seeking permanent authority for this operation. Shortages of long-
shoreman labor gangs at California ports have been less prevalent than
in the past. One of the coastwise carriers which had planned to

institute a containership service late in 1962 between California and Washington ports has now abandoned or suspended such plans.

Completion of Ice Harbor Dam on the lower Snake River in Washington has extended the Columbia River waterway system and considerably enlarged the territory into which bargelines can provide service. Construction of dams on the Columbia River system has enabled the lines to operate with more barges in a single tow. The carriers are acquiring barges of greater carrying capacity and larger and more powerful towing vessels. One of the carriers is acquiring three 250-foot combination barges capable of carrying 450,000 gallons of petroleum or 82,500 bushels of grain. The barges are equipped with screw conveyors and high-capacity pumps for speedy discharge of either dry or liquid cargo.

On the Mississippi River system, bargelines also are continuing to acquire large and more powerful equipment. Severe weather and ice conditions slowed operations during the 1962–63 winter particularly on the middle Mississippi River and on all of the Ohio River and the Illinois Waterway. Service on the Mississippi River above Cairo, Ill., was further complicated by low water during the winter months, caused partly by the impounding of water in upper Missouri River reservoirs for electric power purposes. This condition limited the operations of larger vessels to ports below Memphis, Tenn., and Cairo, while smaller vessels and tows performed service above those ports. The dockworkers' strike at Atlantic and Gulf ports also resulted in tying up a substantial number of barges at Gulf ports.

Except for the transportation of bulk commodities, there is very little common carrier service performed between ports on the Great Lakes. One of the smaller regulated steamship operators which resumed service in 1961 after a period of several years' inactivity has again suspended operations. Another carrier, which has engaged in passenger cruise service for half a century, sold one of its two remaining ships after operating unprofitably during 4 of the past 6 years. The vessel sold is now being operated in Canadian service. The movement of export grain directly from Duluth, Minn., by foreign-flag vessels has had an adverse effect upon the movement of grain by the domestic fleet. The importation of ore and the operation of petroleum pipelines also are reducing the traffic which was formerly carried by the Great Lakes fleets.

The New York State Barge Canal System ended the 1962 season with a significant increase in tonnage after a 7-year downward trend. A navigational project for lowering lock sills was completed for the 1963 season. It is expected that the additional foot of depth will result in a 10-percent improvement in operating efficiency by enabling carriers to load at or near barge capacities.

A further increase in the construction of waterside plant facilities has been noted. This increased activity is attributed by the tug-and-barge industry to a desire by shippers to utilize barge transportation for the movement of their bulk commodities.

FREIGHT FORWARDERS

Freight forwarders have built or are occupying new and improved terminals at a number of locations throughout the country. Many are advantageously utilizing T.O.F.C. service which is being offered to a greater extent by the railroads. The availability of T.O.F.C. service also has invoked a greater interest in the control of freight forwarders by motor carriers. Somewhat more than one-fourth of the freight forwarders, handling about one-half of the total freight forwarder tonnage, are controlled by or under common control with motor carriers. We have no jurisdiction over such acquisitions of control of freight forwarders, but we have recommended to the Congress that all acquisitions of control, mergers, consolidations or unifications involving freight forwarders be placed under section 5 of the act which would require that certain findings of consistency with the public interest be made before such actions could be approved.

OIL PIPELINES

Progress continued in all segments of the industry: physical plant, operations, income, and technical development. This is graphically illustrated in several tables and charts in the chapter on Traffic and Earnings. Complementing these data are some changes in physical plant that expand the picture. In the 10 years since 1952, barrels of oil products received into the system rose 46.5 percent or 1.6 billion barrels. In 1952, each pipeline-mile carried an average of 25.5 thousand barrels of product. Ten years later the average was 32.1 thousand. Although pipeline mileage increased 15 percent, carrying capacity apparently increased 26 percent, indicating more intensive use of facilities and/or introduction of larger capacity pipe. Pipeline mileage grew much more rapidly in product pipelines than in gathering lines, reflecting the reaction to the leveling of demand for crude oil, absence of growth in refinery capacity, and more intensive use of existing lines to meet short-term fluctuations in crude oil demand. Product pipeline growth has continued its rapid pace by reason of substitution of pipelines for other modes of transportation.

Comparison of data in the *Triennial Report on Crude Oil and Product Pipelines* of the Bureau of Mines dated January 1, 1962, with the Commission's figures on regulated pipeline carriers for the same period, reveals the following:

	Bureau of Mines	I.C.C.
	Miles of pipelines	*Miles of pipelines*
Crude	70,355	62,251
Product	53,200	41,830
Gathering	76,988	49,656
Total	200,543	153,737

Although unregulated pipeline miles were 23.3 percent of the total, ton-mile statistics indicate that only 13.9 percent of the traffic was unregulated in 1961.

Certain technical developments in pipeline operation and construction achieved operational status during the year. Utilization of computers to control the movement of products in pipelines had been achieved previously; currently, usage of computers to design fully automated pipeline systems is a workable objective. Mobile pipe mills, which fabricate pipe on the right-of-way as needed, are operational for a limited range of pipe size. Equipment for a greater range, including sizes smaller and larger than the 6- to 10-inch pipe now produced, have been designed or are planned. These developments complement the semiautomatic and automatic welding techniques recently developed and previously reported.

One of the most significant economic changes in pipelines during the year was the report of the proposed "moth-balling" of the coal-slurry pipeline operated between the mines at Cadiz, Ohio, and an electric utility plant in Cleveland. Discontinuance of the use of this pipeline is dependent upon the level of rates established by the competing railroads.

LABOR-MANAGEMENT RELATIONS

In 1962 there were four fewer work stoppages affecting surface transportation companies [8] than in the preceding year but the average dispute embraced more workers and persisted for a longer period of time.[9] Approximately 114,500 workers, an increase of 17,500 over 1961, were idled by 141 work interruptions. As a result an estimated 1,303,000 man-days were lost during 1962, an increase of more than 90 percent over 1961. Each of the three segments of the surface transportation industry disrupted by work stoppages recorded sharp rises in idle man-days.

---

[8] Includes railroad transportation, motor freight transportation and warehousing, water transportation, and pipeline transportation. Excludes local and suburban transit, interurban passenger transportation, and transportation services.

[9] According to data furnished by the Division of Wages and Industrial Relations, Bureau of Labor Statistics, U.S. Department of Labor.

The most serious and complex labor-management conflicts in the water transportation and railroad segments were concerned with problems of job security. Wage increases and related fringe benefits were usually the most prominent issues contested in labor disputes in the motor freight transportation and warehousing area. For the second straight year oil pipelines were the only part of the surface transportation industry not troubled by a work cessation resulting from labor-management discord.

Although water carriers accounted for only one-quarter of the number of work stoppages in 1962, they employed 65 percent of the workers inactivated by labor-management conflicts and experienced the loss of almost as many man-days as both railroads and motor freight carriers combined. Thirty-five work interruptions involving 74,600 employees caused the loss of 646,000 man-days to the water carrier industry. These figures represent increases over the comparable 1961 data. The single largest labor dispute involved about 50,000 members of the International Longshoremen's Association serving the east and the gulf coasts. This work stoppage, initiated on October 1, was temporarily halted on October 5 by court injunction sought by the President under the provisions of the Taft-Hartley Act, ordering union members to return to their jobs. The work stoppage was resumed on December 23 after the expiration of the 80-day "cooling off" period and continued through January 25, 1963, when a 2-year contract was signed. This agreement, in addition to granting increases in wages and fringe benefits, provides for a suspension of the issue of size of work gangs pending the completion of a study currently being made by the Department of Labor of manpower utilization and job security in the longshoring industry.

During 1962 railroads were involved in only 4 work interruptions covering 15,700 employees. Both of these totals were considerably less than comparable figures for the previous year. However, since the durations of the work stoppages were more prolonged in 1962 than in 1961, the number of idle man-days in the railroad industry increased from 169,000 to 391,000. Approximately 15,000 railroad workers were idled for 30 days during August and September 1962, by a dispute between the Chicago and North Western Railway Company and the railroad telegraphers union. Work was resumed without a settlement and the issues were submitted to an Arbitration Board. Basically, the Board ruled that management should retain "the initiative" in determining which jobs are to be abolished, but must give both employees and the unions 90 days' notice before eliminating jobs. This arbitration award subsequently served as a model for a job stabilization agreement reached between the New York Central Railroad and the railroad telegraphers union.

There was no significant change in the number of work stoppages suffered by motor freight and warehousing companies in 1962 as compared to 1961. On the other hand, the 24,200 workers involved and the 226,000 man-days lost as a result of the 102 labor disputes represented increases of 62 and 74 percent, respectively.

In July 1962 the Nation's railroads announced their intention to put into effect on August 16, rules changes based upon recommendations made by the Presidential Railroad Commission in February 1962. The unions immediately sought an injunction in a Federal district court to prevent the introduction of these rules changes. This court and the appellate court held that the railroads could initiate the changes; however, temporary injunctions were issued which preserved the existing situation pending further appeal. In March 1963, the Supreme Court upheld the decisions of the two lower courts. The railroads then scheduled layoffs for about 37,000 firemen on April 8, but, on April 3, the President, under the provisions of the Railway Labor Act, appointed an Emergency Board to mediate the work rules dispute. Negotiations following the recommendations of the Emergency Board led to another impasse. Again, the railroads announced they would impose changes in the controversial work rules. The date was originally set for July 1, but at the personal request of the President, the deadline was extended to July 11, 1963.[10]

---

[10] The effective date was further postponed to July 29 and again to August 29. Congress passed a bill August 28 providing for a seven-man compulsory arbitration board, with the President to appoint three if the railroads and the unions could not agree on the neutral members, the board to act upon a limited number of issues and its findings to be binding for a 2-year period. The President appointed the neutral members on September 5. The arbitration board on November 26 made its award on the fireman and crew consist issues, to be effective January 25, 1964. Generally, the award provided for reduction in the number of firemen through attrition; the crew consist issue was remanded to the local properties for negotiations but guidelines were set to govern the size of train crews until local agreements are made.

MOBILIZATION PLANNING FOR DEFENSE

Our mobilization planning and defense readiness capability increased markedly during the year both in Washington and more importantly at the regional, State and field office levels. Our plans and programs are interrelated with those of other Federal agencies with responsibility for, and interest in, transportation planning and with State plans. We have proceeded on a close Federal-State cooperation concept in developing plans for the modes of transportation subject to ICC jurisdiction. Our policy of developing practical, workable and unclassified plans has resulted in programs acceptable to the transport industry. This in turn has resulted in wide dissemination of these plans by and through the industry.

These plans and programs, subject to overall policy direction and central program control by the Office of Emergency Planning, set out broad action guidelines as well as concepts for substantive organizational development.

Representation has been provided on several interagency committees and boards at the national level; and we have continued to furnish regional support as necessary, and liaison representation to the National Resources Evaluation Center.

Our three-man Mobilization Staff, under the direction of the Chairman, provides general guidance and assistance in coordinating preparedness planning and related activities. In fulfilling its emergency preparedness functions, the Commission has relied on its established offices and bureaus and its field organization. The bureaus have utilized their field representatives and the executive reservists to form a decentralized emergency organization to carry out the programs initiated at the national and regional levels.

The domestic surface transportation industry is linked to the Commission's programs by the appointment of transportation officials to the Commission's Unit of the National Defense Executive Reserve. The following table shows the status of the Commission's Unit of the National Defense Executive Reserve as of June 30, 1962, and June 30, 1963, and indicates the progress made in developing the standby organization.

ICC Executive Reserve Program

NDER group	1962			1963		
	On rolls	Additional nominees	Total	On rolls	Additional nominees	Total
Rail	304	114	418	426	69	495
Motor	44		44	123	78	201
Water	10	15	25	38	16	54
Other	14		14	14		14
	372	129	501	601	163	764

Railroads

Rail emergency mobilization planning has been substantially advanced by the establishment of an emergency rail organization geared to meet national civil defense emergencies. In this emergency group a regional senior and alternate senior rail reservist have been designated for each of the eight Office of Emergency Planning regions. These designees participated in the selection of key executives in order to provide a Senior State Executive Rail Reservist for each State in the region. Liaison with State officials has been established by these reservists. Qualified operating personnel have also been designated to serve at principal railroad terminals and gateways to provide leadership in the local areas. The regional senior reservist and his alternate, the State reservists, and the terminal representatives located in a number of important terminals in the United States, provide the nucleus of a vital organization which, if necessary, can direct railroad rehabilitation and continued operation in an emergency. Our field personnel continue to work closely with regional and State level reservists in developing and maintaining the reserve organization.

Regional Rail Communications Reservists were selected, and met in Washington, D.C., on May 27, 1963, for orientation and examination of existing Federal emergency communications plans. These reservists will assist the Regional Senior Rail Reservists in ascertaining existing telecommunications capability; will maintain familiarity with industry and Federal emergency communications plans as they would affect railroad operations during emergency periods; and will advise on communications problems during a national emergency. Regional training and orientation meetings for rail reservists were conducted in three Office of Emergency Planning Regions, and State level rail reservist meetings were held in five States.

During the year procedures were drafted for permitting orderly movement by rail in and out of port areas during an emergency, and are now under review. Such procedures are necessary to help prevent congestion in port areas, and to coordinate railroad transportation with ocean shipping in periods of national emergency.

Motor Carriers

Progress in motor carrier emergency mobilization planning is typi-fied by the formation of joint ICC-State Emergency Motor Transport Boards. The emergency boards have been formed and are functioning on a standby basis in 46 States and the District of Columbia. Forma-tion of boards in the remaining States in the near future is anticipated.

The boards will centralize ICC and State regulatory authority over motor transport during an emergency period. Thus the motor trans-port industry need look to only one source for assistance and guidance. Each board is composed of an ICC representative, a State representa-tive, and a motor transport industry representative. The chairman of the board has been designated upon recommendation of the board members and appointment by the Governor of the State, with the concurrence of the Chairman of the Commission. Four motor carrier executive reservists in each State have been selected to assist the ICC board member, and they will provide expertise in for-hire carriage of property and passengers, private motor carriage, and motor vehicle maintenance.

A publication entitled "Motor Transport Emergency Preparedness" was developed during the year. An initial printing of 250,000 copies was received in June. The publication outlines actions which should be taken by motor transport companies for the continuity of manage-ment and protection of facilities and physical plant in a national emergency. It also contains emergency instructions for drivers and explains the Emergency Motor Transport Board program. Distribu-tion is being accomplished through the boards.

Inland Water Carriers

Inland water carrier emergency mobilization planning is also progressing. A standby emergency organization composed of Re-gional Senior Inland Waterway Executive Reservists and alternates, responsible for specific coastal or inland waterway systems, with desig-nated water carrier reservists assigned to selected water carrier termi-nal points, has been programed on an eight-region basis.

A basic inventory of inland waterway terminals and vessels was completed. Data cards and inventory listings were provided to the National Resources Evaluation Center for inclusion in the NREC Sys-tem. The inventory provides data, heretofore not available to mobili-zation planners, on some 500 inland waterway terminals, their loca-tion and capacity, and data on inland water craft which normally utilize the terminals. This information, combined with a previously recorded Inland Waterways-Locks and Dams category, will provide a more refined capability to perform damage assessment and situation evaluation under emergency conditions.

General Preparedness Activities

The Cuban situation in the fall of 1962 afforded a realistic opportunity to test the Commission's emergency readiness capability. Steps had been taken some months prior to the incident in designating emergency mobilization personnel, in Washington and in the field, to carry out emergency responsibilities. The Commission's plans were reviewed and quickly revised where necessary. The ICC Transport Mobilization Orders were ready to be placed in effect should the need have arisen. The ICC Unit of the National Defense Executive Reserve was prepared, and could have been activated if required. A review of the agency's readiness at an Office of Emergency Planning Special Facilities Branch site, and at the Commission's alternate headquarters site, were made coincidental with the crisis. Regional representatives of the Commission met with the OEP regional boards and reviewed field emergency readiness. The Commission was ready to proceed with further emergency actions on short notice.

To keep Executive Reservists and the Commission's field staff abreast of planning concepts and to provide national policy guidance, we have distributed approximately twelve hundred (1200) copies of our Emergency Planning and Operations Manual to reservists and staff members with mobilization planning or emergency assignments. Semiannual rosters of membership, information bulletins and other material also have been furnished to the reservists.

During the fiscal year the Commission revised its internal Cascade Alerting System, and assigned a roster of duty officers to acknowledge any warning from the Office of Civil Defense on a round-the-clock basis, and to disseminate the warning to predesignated officials. A draft document of Commission emergency functions to be performed during a period of national emergency has been prepared to specify those activities which must be continued by the Commission in an extreme emergency situation.

A teletype set (receiving only) has been installed in the ICC Building by the Office of Emergency Planning. This places the Commission on a Defense Coordination Teletypewriter Network (DEFCORD), to receive emergency planning information and guidance from OEP rapidly and simultaneously with other Federal agencies. The receiving set is activated automatically from a remote sending point. It is tested at least once daily. The system is, however, capable of providing authenticated printed instructions on a 24-hour basis.

In cooperation with the Office of Emergency Planning and the Office of Emergency Transportation, the first phase of a supply-requirements study on transportation needs was completed in December. Phase I of the study was concerned with supply requirements during a 3-year period prior to outbreak of conventional war. A preliminary analysis of controlled materials requirements and cost levels of construction and maintenance programs for the domestic surface transport modes was developed and submitted. Further study will be undertaken to develop estimated supply requirements for a post nuclear attack period.

We participated in the joint military-civilian exercise (Spade Fork) at the national level in cooperation with other agencies. Our emergency preparedness measures were tested in assumed pre-attack and post attack situations, and the exercise proved helpful in enabling us to analyze problems or incidents of an interagency nature.

At the request of the Office of Emergency Planning, and within the guidelines furnished by that office and the Office of Emergency Transportation, we assisted in developing the transportation portion of sample organization and operations plans for States. The sample plans are to serve as guides to the States in developing their programs and to assure coordination with Federal plans and policies.

We continued our emphasis on emergency preparedness and non-classified readiness programs. Many of these activities have been carried on in accordance with written agreements between the Commission and the Office of Emergency Planning and with funds delegated from that agency. OEP originally transferred $86,000 to the Commission for fiscal year 1963. Late in the fiscal year, additional funds were transferred to cover the expanding cost of these efforts. The total amount made available by OEP for fiscal year 1963 was $100,900.

PROMOTION OF SAFETY

RAILROADS

The Commission's administration of railroad safety laws has been confronted by and been responsive to numerous significant changes in rail transportation. Control of train movements by signal indications through traffic control systems has expanded, resulting in more efficient track utilization. Today a single track often functions in place of a double track or replaces a multiple-track operation. Train communication systems, including radio and inductive systems, have been widely adopted and have contributed to the safety of both road and yard operations.

During this period of technological progress, the Commission's authority in the field of railroad signaling was broadened by amendment to the Transportation Act of 1920. As contained in section 25 of the act, authority is extended to all types of railroad signals, including interlockings and train and traffic control systems. Enactment of the Power Brake Law of 1958 also added to the Commission's duties and responsibilities in matters of railroad safety. These actions by the Congress are strengthening the continuity of the Commission's long record of promoting the safety of employees and travelers upon railroads, under laws dating back to the original Federal Safety Appliance Act of March 2, 1893.

The Section of Railroad Safety and the Section of Locomotive Inspection in the Bureau of Safety and Service administer the railroad safety program. Detailed reports on railroad safety [11] and locomotive inspection [12] matters are published as separate documents.

Number of Persons Killed and Injured

Accidents involving railroad operation (train, train-service, and non-train accidents) resulted in 2,038 persons killed and 26,104 injured during fiscal year 1963,[13] compared with 2,088 killed and 27,506 injured in 1962.

---

[11] Report of the Section of Railroad Safety, Bureau of Safety and Service, to the Interstate Commerce Commission.

[12] Fifty-Second Annual Report of the Director of Locomotive Inspection to the Interstate Commerce Commission.

[13] Preliminary figures used for first 6 months of 1963.

Fatalities from train, train-service, and non-train accidents for the first 6 months of 1963, compared with the corresponding period in 1962, are shown in the following table:

Classification of persons	Number of persons killed	
	Jan.–June 1962	Jan.–June 1963 [1]
Trespassers	302	253
Employees on duty	85	85
Passengers on trains	4	3
Others (chiefly highway-rail crossing accidents)	598	580
Total	989	921

[1] Preliminary figures used for first 6 months of 1963.

Investigation of Accidents

The following table shows data for serious train accidents investigated during the past 5 years under the Accident Reports Act. In each case, a report was published setting forth the facts and the Commission's findings and recommendations.

Year ended June 30—	Number of accidents investigated			Persons	
	Collisions	Derailments	Total	Killed	Injured
1959	35	14	49	100	945
1960	29	14	43	68	726
1961	21	11	32	42	983
1962	21	8	29	57	641
1963	24	16	40	61	1,215

Accident Reports Act

Railroad accidents resulting in injury to persons or property damage are reported in accordance with the Accident Reports Act and related Commission rules. Accident and casualty records were examined to determine compliance with the reporting rules, as follows:

	Year ended June 30—	
	1962	1963
Regular inspections of accident records	361	349
Number of railroads examined	351	331
Number of complaints investigated	8	14
Number of infractions disclosed	42	16
Number of accident and casualty files examined	21,600	21,846

Accidents at Rail-Highway Grade Crossings

There were 3,149 accidents at rail-highway grade crossings in 1962, resulting in the death of 1,241 persons and the injury of 3,192. Automobiles, buses and trucks were involved in 2,920 of these accidents, in which 1,122 persons were killed and 3,075 were injured. In 57 of these accidents, derailment of trains resulted in 36 fatalities and 68 injured. Casualties to rail passengers and employees in train and rail-highway grade crossing accidents totaled 18 killed and 189 injured. These statistics do not include accidents at grade crossings in which trains were not involved.

Accidents at highway grade crossings, year ended December 31

Accidents and casualties	1960			1961			1962		
	Number	Number of persons		Number	Number of persons		Number	Number of persons	
		Killed	Injured		Killed	Injured		Killed	Injured
Accidents at highway grade crossings	3,195	1,364	3,424	3,204	1,291	3,514	3,149	1,241	3,192
Accidents at highway grade crossings involving motor vehicles [1]	2,966	1,254	3,277	2,914	1,168	3,288	2,920	1,122	3,075
Derailments of trains at highway grade crossings involving motor vehicles	70	48	161	54	25	182	57	36	68
Miscellaneous train accidents as a result of collisions between trains and motor vehicles	92	77	94	164	96	89	199	106	106
Railroad casualties:									
Passengers		14	129		1	154		1	73
Employees on duty		11	86		9	133		17	116
Total		25	215		10	287		18	189

[1] Passenger automobiles, buses, and trucks.

The Commission continued its investigation, in docket No. 33440, *Prevention of Rail-Highway Grade Crossing Accidents Involving Railway Trains and Motor Vehicles*. This proceeding was instituted by the Commission, on its own motion, February 6, 1961. Extensive public hearings have been held for the purpose of determining what further safety requirements can or should be made, within the authority of this Commission; what additional legislation may be necessary, and for the further purpose of focusing public attention on the gravity of the safety problem occasioned by collisions at railroad crossings between railway trains and motor vehicles.

Safety Appliances

We are concerned with the increasing laxity in the equipment maintenance practices of the railroads, as evidenced by the mounting percentage of defective units noted by field agents. In addition, a persistently high level of improper train brake tests are reported. The Commission has processed and investigated a large number of complaints in the safety appliance area during the year. These matters are handled directly with the railroads concerned in an attempt, through voluntary compliance, to keep the level of defective units of equipment and improper tests as low as possible. Court action, however, often is necessary.

The following table shows the results of safety appliance inspections made by the Commission, with corresponding data for the preceding year:

Item	Year ended June 30—	
	1962	1963
Freight cars inspected	1,416,097	1,282,431
Percentage defective	5.9	6.3
Passenger cars inspected	35,963	29,988
Percentage defective	6.2	5.0
Locomotive units inspected	110,007	93,205
Percentage defective	0.8	1.0
Number of defects per 1,000 cars and locomotives inspected	62.24	66.53

Car Construction Problems

The development and manufacture of large dimension freight cars for specialized purposes continued to increase. Most of these cars are so large they come very close to line clearance tolerances established by the Association of American Railroads. Our field agents and technical staff at Washington, continually confer with the car manufacturers on clearance problems posed by the safety appliance locations on oversize cars.

To protect the safety of employees and travelers on the railroads some modifications in location of safety appliances are necessary, insofar as construction of the car will permit. Most of these modifications are worked out through ICC-industry studies and conferences often held at the car building plant.

Signal Devices and Communications Systems

According to reports submitted by the carriers, the following block-signal systems, interlocking, and automatic train-stop, train-control, and cab-signal devices were in use on January 1, 1963:

Type of signal protection	Plants	Miles of—		Locomotives
		Road	Track	
Block-signal systems:				
Automatic		81,184.0	106,695.4	
Nonautomatic		21,956.3	22,356.4	
Total		103,140.3	129,051.8	
Corresponding totals, Jan. 1, 1962		104,540.8	131,176.7	
Interlocking	3,776			
Automatic train-stop, train-control, and cab-signal devices:				
Train-stop		9,082.1	13,444.7	4,802
Train-control		1,018.0	1,936.9	1,002
Cab-signal		4,033.1	8,492.9	3,588
Total	3,776	14,133.2	23,874.5	9,392
Corresponding totals, Jan. 1, 1962	3,939	14,158.7	24,511.9	9,434

As of January 1, 1963, train communication systems were in use on 198 railroads, of which 79 had both line-of-road and yard and terminal installations in service, 61 line-of-road installations only, and 58 yard and terminal installations only. Line-of-road installations were in service for operation over a total of 141,725 miles of road, and there were 1,030 yard and terminal installations. There were 27,392 wayside stations and mobile units, such as locomotives, cabooses, passenger and other cars provided with train communication equipment, and 8,164 portable two-way radio sets in service.

Detailed information concerning these installations is contained in the annual statistics bulletin, published separately.

In the year ended June 30, 1963, 218 applications were filed for modifications of block-signal systems and interlockings. At the beginning of the year, action was pending on 46 applications previously filed. During the year 209 applications were acted upon, and action was pending on 55 at the close of the year. Public hearings were held on 33 applications.

Thirty applications were filed for modifications or relief from the Commission's signal requirements. At the beginning of the year action was pending on six such applications. Of this total, 26 were acted upon, and action was pending on 10 at the close of the year. Public hearings were held on three applications for relief from the requirements of the rules.

In the year ended June 30, 1963, 26 complaints were received in connection with alleged violations of the rules, standards and instructions. At the beginning of the year, action was pending on seven complaints previously filed. During the year investigations were completed on 29 and action was pending on 4 at the end of the year.

During the year ended June 30, 1963, 4,245 systems were inspected, which was 262 less than the number inspected the previous year. This was because of vacancies in the signal inspection forces due to retirements and illness during the year, equivalent to 6 percent of the inspection force.

The Commission closely follows technological developments in the railway signaling and communications fields to keep abreast of problems arising in connection with administration of section 25 of the Interstate Commerce Act.

The Commission at present has proceedings in progress in Ex Parte No. 171, *Rules, Standards, and Instructions for Signal Systems*, considering the proposed revision of 27 sections of the Rules, Standards and Instructions. Some of the proposed revisions are desired because of technological progress in the railway signaling field while other revisions are for the purpose of clarifying the present rules.

A recent development in the use of electronics in the field of railway signaling is being followed closely by the field staff and departmental technicians of the Commission. It concerns the application of so-called solid state techniques for the operation of traffic control systems and remote controlled interlockings. Briefly, transistor and semi-conductor devices are used to turn on and off electric currents in pre-determined code patterns, something formerly accomplished by relays.

At the receiving station, the solid state devices respond to the coded information to cause switches and signals at the controlled location to set up a desired route. However, the safety of operation still depends on conventional field equipment. In one foreign country at least one railroad has installed an interlocking using solid state elements in place of relays in connection with various interlocking functions.

Development work by manufacturers indicates that in time solid state elements may become sufficiently advanced to replace gravity type relays for safe use in circuits. When this occurs, the solid state elements will be carefully studied to insure that they provide an ac-ceptable degree of safety.

Installation of solid state automatic switching in connection with a retarder classification yard now under construction is contemplated by one railroad. Solid state electronic elements are used in the transmission of information and data involved in recently developed automatic car-identification systems also, and at least one such elec-tronic system has been used successfully by an eastern railroad.

Explosives and Other Dangerous Articles—Regulations

Aggressive competition in both domestic and international trade channels has produced extensive activity with respect to packaging and transportation of goods classed as "dangerous" in the Commission's regulations. The methods of packaging are under constant review and development by shippers faced with economic problems in meet-ing existing requirements, the impact of foreign commerce, product purity, and safety. Both commercial and military organizations con-tinue to devise new varieties of materials as well as to increase the volume of shipments. This has resulted in an unprecedented demand for supplemental regulations or interim authority to provide a means of shipment. In this regard, a total of 404 amendments to the regula-tions and 907 Special Permits were issued to keep pace with needs.

Regulatory groups such as States; bridge, tunnel and turnpike authorities; firefighting organizations; and others have been unusually active in discussing, formulating or requesting extensive changes in regulations. Particular interest has centered on improving the mark-ing of shipments or vehicles to provide better controls and to avoid or minimize accidents.

International regulatory groups and agencies also have been advancing regulations for all modes of transport. These activities have direct bearing on practices in this country and will command even greater attention in coming months to insure that reasonable uniformity in regulations will be established. Every effort is made to cooperate with domestic and international groups in order to reduce the complications which arise when the proposals of so many sources must be given consideration. Requests of other nations for qualifying their containers or packaging methods under the Commission's regulations are increasing.

The space, rocket and missile programs have required concerted attention as movements of essential items increased substantially. Because of the variety of rocket fuels and methods of containment, handling, or precaution involved, it was necessary for the Commission to deal with such matters continuously to resolve problems arising from the unusual character of the materials and methods of transport.

Extensive revisions in tank car and tank truck specifications as well as complete rearrangement of regulations pertaining to gases and development of new regulations for radioactive material are in final stages of study and will be considered for adoption in a short time.

Observations by the field staff to determine degree of compliance with the regulations resulted in a total of 1,593 reports of inspections and reports of 2,498 violations.

Hours of Service of Employees

The Commission's field agents, on both a regular and unexpected basis, continually inspect and analyze the hours of service conditions on the various railroads, as required by the Hours of Service law. As a result of our activities, the number of violations has remained at a low level during the past decade.

The following table shows statistics relating to the hours of service of railroad operating employees:

	Year ended June 30—	
	1962	1963
Railroads reporting instances of excess service	112	117
Instances of excess service reported	2,548	2,890
Instances of excess service investigated	1,767	1,671
Examination of hours of service records	781	777
Completed investigations of complaints	62	94
Violations involved in regular inspections	63	49
Violations involved in special investigations	97	109

ACTIVITIES RELATED TO CONDITION OF LOCOMOTIVES [14]

Inspection of Locomotives

In accordance with the provisions of the Locomotive Inspection Act, the Commission establishes and approves certain design standards for the construction of locomotives, together with rules and regulations to govern inspection and testing of locomotives used on common carrier railroads. These standards, rules and regulations are designed for the purpose of promoting the safety of employees and travelers and, as indicated in the accompanying chart, have resulted in a very significant reduction in the number of accidents and casualties.

New type locomotives introduced during recent years have continued the trend toward higher horsepower per unit and use of newly developed power and control components. This has resulted in longer runs, greater utilization, and in many cases less frequent shopping of locomotives. Thus, it is even more imperative now that the utmost care be used in making the prescribed inspections and tests to assure a continued high level of safe locomotive operation.

The following table shows the scope of inspection activities for a period of 6 years:

Reports and inspections—steam locomotives, locomotive units other than steam, and multiple-operated electric locomotive units

	Year ended June 30—					
	1958	1959	1960	1961	1962	1963
Number of locomotives for which reports were filed	36,905	36,069	35,645	35,074	34,789	34,473
Number inspected	95,593	105,347	108,629	98,332	94,592	79,781
Number found defective	8,394	10,912	11,126	9,399	9,050	8,497
Percent of inspected found defective	8.8	10.4	10.2	9.6	9.6	10.7
Number ordered out of service	395	648	531	504	488	420
Number of defects found	21,532	32,330	32,830	28,308	26,032	25,718

On June 30, 1963, there were 65 fewer steam locomotives for which carriers filed reports than there were on June 30, 1962. The number of locomotive units other than steam and multiple-operated electric locomotive units for which reports were filed during this period decreased by 251.

In compliance with the Rules and Instructions for Inspection and Testing of Locomotives, 2 specifications were submitted by carriers for steam locomotives; 1,073 specifications and 1,179 alteration reports were received for locomotives other than steam; 56 specifications and 117 alteration reports for heating boilers mounted in locomotive

[14] Locomotive Inspection activities are shown in detail in the report of the Director of Locomotive Inspection, published separately.

units; and 18 specifications for multiple-operated electric locomotive units were submitted by carriers.

Inspection and repair reports for steam locomotives filed with district inspectors during the year totaled 2,669; for locomotives other than steam, 383,518; and for multiple operated electric locomotive units, 29,850.

No formal appeals from decisions of district inspectors were filed by the carriers.

Accidents and Their Investigation

The Locomotive Inspection Act requires that all accidents caused by the failure of any part of a locomotive which results in serious injury or death to one or more persons be promptly reported by the operating carrier to the Director of Locomotive Inspection. All such accidents are carefully investigated by our District Inspectors and detailed reports submitted to the Director of Locomotive Inspection.

Seventy-one accidents resulting in 98 injuries were reported and investigated. Two of these accidents involving seven injuries occurred during the previous year but were reported too late to be included in the last annual report.

No fatalities resulted from failure of parts or appurtenances of locomotives during the year. However, there was an increase of 4 accidents and 25 injuries over the previous year. The following table shows the number of accidents and casualties for a period of 6 years:

Accidents and casualties caused by failure of some part or appurtenance of steam locomotives, locomotive units other than steam, and multiple-operated electric locative units

	Year ended June 30—					
	1958	1959	1960	1961	1962	1963
Number of accidents	72	66	50	71	67	
Percent increase or decrease from previous year	4.0	8.3	24.2	[1]42.0	5.6	[1]5.9
Number of persons killed	0	0	0	0	0	0
Percent increase or decrease from previous year	0	0	0	0	0	0
Number of persons injured	86	90	81	77	73	98
Percent increase or decrease from previous year	4.4	[1]4.7	10.0	4.9	5.2	[1]34.2

[1] Increase.

Of the 71 accidents in 1963, 17 were caused by the defective condition of floors, steps and passageways of diesel-electric locomotives. Fourteen of the 17 resulted from accumulations of oil on walking surfaces of the locomotives, an increase of 10 compared with the preceding year. Six accidents were caused by defective condition of cab seats, compared with 15 in the previous year.

The following chart shows the relation of defective locomotives to accidents and casualties resulting from locomotive failures.

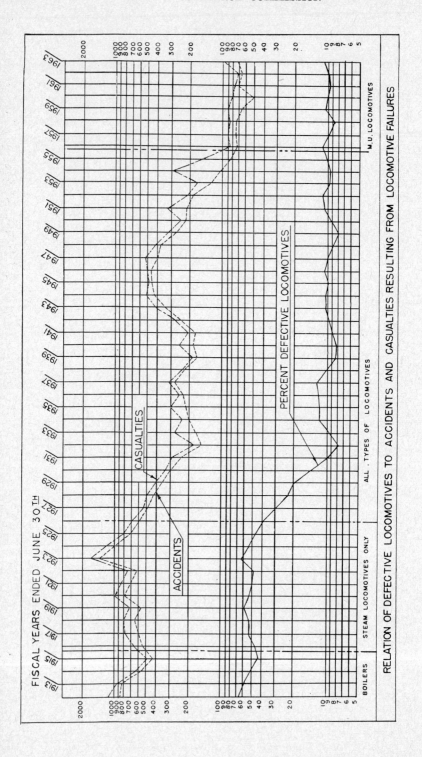

RELATION OF DEFECTIVE LOCOMOTIVES TO ACCIDENTS AND CASUALTIES RESULTING FROM LOCOMOTIVE FAILURES

MOTOR CARRIERS

The President in April of 1963 called on all agencies of Government and all citizens to increase their efforts to reverse the sharply increasing trend of street and highway accidents which caused nearly 41,000 deaths during 1962.

During 1962 motor carriers required to report accidents to the Commission had 1,811 fatalities. While this annual total has been exceeded 3 times, the number of deaths reported by motor carriers of property established a new high of 1,705 in 1962. This was an increase of 24 percent above the number reported by property carriers in 1961 and was 13 percent higher than the 1,504 annual average for the 5 years ended with 1961. Intercity miles operated by property carriers in 1962 was 6.7 percent higher than in 1961.

By contrast, motor carriers of passengers reported 123 fatalities in 1962, as compared with 122 reported in 1961 and 18.5 percent below the annual average of 151 fatalities occurring in bus operations for the 5 years ended with 1961.

The high total of fatalities involving property carriers in 1962 reflects the worsening trend of recent years. In our 72d Annual Report, we showed that motor carriers of property filing operating statistics with the Commission had in the 5-year period ended with 1957, increased their intercity miles above the previous 5 years by 41.6 percent but had experienced 0.7 percent fewer fatalities in the later period. In the 5 years ended with 1962, motor carriers of property operated 8.3 percent more miles than in the 5 years ended with 1957 but experienced 8.9 percent more fatalities than in the previous period.

Now that the ever increasing number of motor vehicles moving on the highways of the country has risen to 79 million, operators of interstate commercial vehicles are confronted with an accelerating exposure to accidents. In addition, the expansion of improved roadway mileage has resulted in higher speeds. Many State weight limits have been liberalized. Vehicles of interstate carriers are larger, more powerful, and travel at higher speeds for longer distances.

To cope with this trend, we made several major safety regulation changes. In 1956, we tightened our regulations relating to brake performance. In 1960, we added rules for vehicle lighting, adopting for the first time a mandate for flashing signal lamps to identify a disabled vehicle or a vehicle otherwise stopped and creating a hazard. Last year, we completely revamped the maximum hours of service regulations, imposing for the first time a daily limit of on duty hours beyond which a driver may not lawfully drive. This revision also incorporated a provision to enable our staff to remove drivers from service if they operate beyond maximum limits. We revised our motor carrier accident reporting regulations, effective January 1, 1963, eliminating the requirements for the reporting of certain matters now considered inconsequential, but extending the requirements to provide for reporting of accidents involving vehicles operating within commercial zones. Also, we now require the maintenance of accident registers by all carriers, including private carriers, engaged in interstate operation.

While we have materially strengthened our motor carrier safety regulations in recent years, less time of our field staff has been devoted to supervision of motor carrier safety because of greater attention being focused on curbing unlawful motor transport. Enforcement actions concluded in the courts involving safety violations in this fiscal year were 31.7 percent less than 2 years ago.

The large number of firms conducting motor carrier operations, and the limitation of our relatively small safety staff, make it necessary for us to rely heavily upon educational efforts and spot check inspections to further the promotion of safety activities by motor carriers. The estimated number of motor carriers subject to our jurisdiction and the number of vehicles operated by such carriers are as follows:

Type of carrier	Number of interstate carriers (approximately)	Number of vehicles (approximately)
Authorized for hire	18,587	923,725
Private	82,152	771,864
Exempt for hire (203(b))	33,609	200,040
Public Law 522	686	4,312
Migrant workers	6,320	8,138
Total	141,354	1,908,079

Our safety responsibility extends to a large number of carriers not subject to economic regulation. Except for certain requirements relating to insurance and filing designation of agents which apply to Public Law 522 carriers (those operating from a foreign country to the same or another foreign country through the United States), we have no jurisdiction except as to safety matters over the estimated 120,000 interstate carriers in the groups listed above which are other than authorized for-hire carriers. The latter group, which operates nearly one-half the total number of vehicles, are those we can most readily supervise because we are constantly aware of who they are and their location. The private carriers and carriers of exempt commodities, not only are more numerous but also, on the average, operate less than 10 vehicles each. Therefore, from the standpoint of practicability, we endeavor to enforce our safety requirements through our road-check inspection activities, through accident investigations of the more serious accidents, and by communication with such carriers through industry organizations and trade publications.

On June 30, 1963, our records showed we had served copies of regulations on 60,271 private carriers of property, 24,530 carriers of exempt commodities, 508 Public Law 522 carriers, and 132 carriers of migrant workers.

Our road-check program was carried on in all sections of the country, including service areas on the major turnpikes. Thorough inspections were made of 39,189 property-carrying vehicles, compared with 45,714 vehicles in fiscal 1962. These vehicles were composed of 70,919 units (power unit or trailer) of which 6,530 or 9.2 percent were removed from service.

One of our principal educational efforts consists of publishing accident investigation reports listing accident causes and recommendations for preventive measures. Ten accidents occurring in nine States were the subject of published reports, one of which was a formal proceeding, Ex Parte No. MC–63, with hearings before a Commissioner. In addition, our staff participated in three formal ex parte proceedings which involved collisions between railroad trains and motor vehicles transporting flammable liquid.

We published an analysis of mechanical-defect accidents reported during 1959, 1960 and 1961, to emphasize the principal causes of accidents in which vehicle component failures were a factor.

The 10 accidents selected for published reports, other than the grade crossing cases, were part of 317 serious accidents investigated by our staff. One common carrier of passengers, five common carriers of property and four private carriers of property were involved.

In five of the ten cases covered by published reports, driver deficiencies were major causative factors. These included one case of epilepsy, and others involving use of alcohol and drugs by the commercial drivers.

In three cases, poorly maintained vehicles were principally responsible, although in one of these the driver was operating during the period of a suspended license and otherwise had a very poor record. Two cases resulted from fire and explosion in the transportation of dangerous commodities.

In each of the three formal investigations of grade crossing accidents, private carriers of property were the operators of the motor vehicles which were transporting flammable gases and liquids. Only one of the three motor vehicles was moving in interstate service.

We have continued the policy of limiting certificates relating to the transportation of explosives and certain other hazardous materials to a period of 5 years to permit a periodic review of the safety record of the carriers holding such certificates. For the first time, we denied an extension of such a certificate because of the unsatisfactory safety and accident record of the holder. We have continued to furnish the Department of Defense reports concerning the safety record of carriers transporting explosives for the military services. During the year, ten carriers were removed from the approved list of that Department on the basis of information furnished by us.

Of 2,004 applications for temporary authority, 155 applications were denied because of an unsatisfactory safety record, and 111 others were granted for a limited period of time to permit further examination of the carriers' safety practices.

During 1962, we inspected 2,183 buses operated by authorized carriers of passengers. Of these 1,137 were free from any mechanical deficiency; 127 were found to have 4 or more defects per vehicle, and 25 buses were in such seriously deficient condition they were removed from service at the point of inspection. Of this number, 21 were removed because of brake deficiencies, 1 because of a steering defect, 1 because of a hazardous tire condition, 1 because of a fuel system deficiency, and 1 because of a suspension system defect.

During 1962, we made inspections of 76 vehicles transporting migrant workers. Twelve were found to be without mechanical defect, 40 had 4 or more defects per vehicle, and 2 were ordered out of service because of hazardous mechanical conditions.

Since the effective date of the new hours of service regulations, September 5, 1962, to the end of the fiscal year, 182 drivers were ordered out of service because of driving beyond the limits of the hours of service regulations.

Accident Record

Although we have had safety responsibility for private carriers of property, for-hire carriers of exempt commodities, and certain other classes of carriers for a number of years, we have not required reporting of accidents from any of these groups except carriers of exempt commodities and some foreign carriers operating over highways in the United States. Beginning January 1, 1963, all carriers are now required to maintain accident registers to enable us, to the extent we are able to inspect carriers' records, to determine accident trends. However, we are able to gauge accident experience principally on the basis of accident reports filed by common and contract carriers, and by special investigation of the more serious accidents which come to our notice.

We made special investigations of 317 serious accidents, compared with 356 in the preceding year. The 317 cases investigated involved a total of 397 commercial vehicles. Thirty-four of these were buses and 363 were property carrying trucks and combination vehicles. The property vehicles were operated by 259 authorized carriers, 70 private carriers, 29 carriers of exempt commodities, and 5 persons transporting property without authority.

Although carriers of exempt commodities are subject to our accident reporting requirements, we receive relatively few reports from such carriers. Reports of 729 accidents were filed by 421 carriers in 1962. These accidents resulted in 95 deaths, injuries to 473 persons, and property damage of $2,527,440.

The following charts depict: (1) Comparisons between total inter-city miles for the 5-year period 1958 through 1962, compared with the preceding 5-year period, and a similiar comparison of fatalities reported by carriers during the same 5-year periods. These are shown separately for carriers of property and carriers of passengers; and (2) The trends in fatalities reported by motor carriers, and the trend in intercity vehicle-miles reported to the Commission by large carriers since 1946.

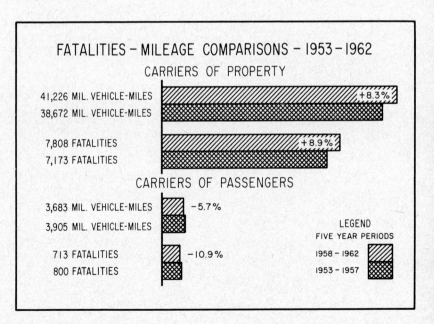

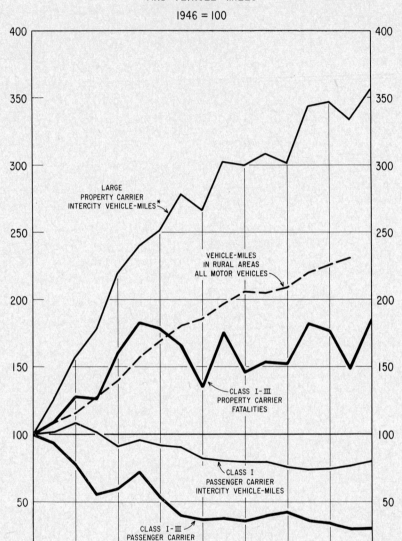

INDEXES OF MOTOR CARRIER TRAFFIC FATALITIES
AND VEHICLE-MILES

1946 = 100

LARGE
PROPERTY CARRIER
INTERCITY VEHICLE-MILES*

VEHICLE-MILES
IN RURAL AREAS
ALL MOTOR VEHICLES

CLASS I-III
PROPERTY CARRIER
FATALITIES

CLASS I
PASSENGER CARRIER
INTERCITY VEHICLE-MILES

CLASS I-III
PASSENGER CARRIER
FATALITIES

*Carriers having annual operating revenues of $200,000 and more.
Source: I.C.C., Bureau of Transport Economics and Statistics, Statistics of Class I Motor Carriers
and Statements Q-750 and Q-800, accident reports of motor carriers, and U.S. Bureau of
Public Roads, Table VM-I.

The following table contains data as to total vehicle registrations, vehicle-miles, accidents reported to the Commission, and the resultant fatalities, nonfatal injuries and property damage for 1960 through 1962:

Item	Calendar year		
	1962	1961	1960
Vehicle registrations:			
All motor vehicles	79,022,916	75,846,532	73,895,274
Trucks	12,809,150	12,291,365	11,941,071
Buses	285,219	279,668	272,167
Vehicle-miles compared with preceding year:			
All motor vehicles—rural roads _____percent		+2.2	+8.3
Trucks—intercity miles—class I and class II carriers [1] percent	+6.7	−2.2	+1.0
Buses—intercity miles—class I carriers [1] _____percent	+4.1	+2.9	+0.9
Accidents reported:			
Total [2]	29,009	25,873	28,750
Property-carrying vehicles	24,944	22,513	25,319
Passenger-carrying vehicles	4,107	3,400	3,463
Fatalities:			
Total [2]	1,811	1,494	1,767
Property-carrying vehicles	1,705	1,376	1,633
Passenger-carrying vehicles	123	122	141
Nonfatal injuries:			
Total [2]	23,213	20,054	21,265
Property-carrying vehicles	16,897	14,662	15,956
Passenger-carrying vehicles	6,697	5,565	5,558
Property damage:			
Total [2]	$52,669,080	$48,131,560	$51,080,150
Property-carrying vehicles	$50,452,690	$45,883,110	$49,101,130
Passenger-carrying vehicles	$2,512,250	$2,455,940	$2,203,160

[1] Carriers having annual operating revenues of $200,000 or more.
[2] Data relating to each accident which involved both a truck and a bus, have been included under both the property-carrying and the passenger-carrying categories. Hence a sum of the figures under these two categories for any item will exceed the "total" figure given.

The following table shows changes in deaths and injuries in accidents reported by motor carriers for 1944 through 1962:

Calendar year	Fatalities		Injuries	
	Number	Increase or decrease	Number	Increase or decrease
1962	1,811	+21	23,213	+16
1961	1,494	−15	20,054	−6
1960 [1]	1,767	−3	21,265	−4
1959 [1]	1,830	+16	22,147	+7
1958 [1][2]	1,571	----------	20,614	+10
1957 [1]	1,573	+5	18,765	+1
1956 [1]	1,498	−16	18,518	−5
1955 [1]	1,774	+27	19,415	+17
1954 [1]	1,394	−17	16,622	−14
1953 [1]	1,685	−10	19,388	−2
1952 [1]	1,877	−5	19,797	−10
1951	1,986	+14	22,070	+17
1950	1,735	+18	18,906	+6
1949	1,471	−2	17,787	−5
1948	1,501	+9	18,677	+8
1947	1,382	+3	17,367	+5
1946	1,338	+16	16,565	+15
1945	1,150	+2	14,346	+11
1944	1,133	+7	12,921	+24

[1] Data for 1952 forward relate to accidents which occurred in those years. For previous years, data are for accidents reported during the year indicated.
[2] Prior to 1958, carriers did not report accidents in intrastate operations, although they reported total miles. Beginning with 1958 such accidents were required to be reported.

Explosives and Other Dangerous Articles

On July 25, 1962, a serious explosion occurred in Berlin, N.Y., when a cargo tank motor vehicle laden with 8,000 gallons of propane overturned on a curve. The tank failed and the consequent fire and explosion resulted in the death of 10 persons and serious injuries to 17 others. A number of homes, a church, and other buildings were destroyed. A formal investigation was instituted in Ex Parte No. MC–63. Hearings were held at Albany, N.Y., before a Commissioner and a hearing examiner. We arranged for testimony and exhibits to be introduced by the National Bureau of Standards. The Commission found that the consequences of the accident were due to the failure of the tank. Its construction did not satisfy the requirements of our regulations because of improper welding procedures in the fabrication process. Subsequently, we instituted a rulemaking proceeding looking toward revising the regulations relating to design, fabrication, inspection, and operation of cargo tank vehicles transporting compressed gases.

Three other accidents were the subject of formal investigations. Hearings were held before Commissioners in cases where railroad trains collided with tank vehicles transporting flammable liquids in Alabama and Texas. Reports were issued in these cases and in a proceeding involving collision of a railroad train with a tank vehicle loaded with propane which occurred near La Porte, Ind., in April 1962.

Other accidents and incidents have occurred in the transportation by highway of dangerous materials and have been the subject of investigations. On May 6, 1963, a tank vehicle transporting a toxic fuel for the missile program overturned in Tucson, Ariz. As a precaution, residents were evacuated from their homes before the tank was righted. In January 1963, considerable effort and money were expended to decontaminate vehicles and a terminal following the leakage of liquid from a shipment of radioactive material transported from western Pennsylvania to Long Island.

A number of accidents have resulted in severe fires following the overturn of tank vehicles laden with gasoline and other flammable liquids. One of these involved explosion of vinyl acetate at Essex Junction, Vt. Others, in which gasoline shipments were involved, occurred on city streets in Detroit, Mich., Providence, R.I., Saugus, Mass., and Washington, D.C.

We have recognized the importance of furthering by every practicable means the prevention of accidents in the transportation of dangerous cargoes. We have established a close relationship with the Atomic Energy Commission to assure our being informed of every instance in which mishaps occur in highway transportation of radioactive materials. Because of a number of fires and explosions during loading of tank vehicles with flammable materials, we have consulted with the American Petroleum Institute and have received reports of their efforts to overcome this problem. The severity of collisions between railroad trains and tank vehicles transporting flammable materials at grade crossings led us to discuss this problem with the American Association of Motor Vehicle Administrators. The Association adopted a resolution urging State officials in its membership to work for adoption of regulations identical with those of this Commission concerning stop requirements at grade crossings, and to work for maximum enforcement. A similar resolution was adopted by the International Association of Chiefs of Police.

At the request of the Secretary of Commerce, we participated in conferences with that Department and others in making a review of existing legislation and regulatory requirements relating to the transportation of dangerous commodities. Recommendations by a study group established by the Secretary of Commerce have been formulated.

We have continued active participation by members of our staff in the work of the Interagency Committee on the Transportation of Radioactive materials.

In 1962 the consumption of industrial explosives in the United States amounted to 1,310,162,688 pounds, compared with 1,199,865,460 pounds in 1961. This total includes ammonium nitrate blasting agents which, under our regulations, are classified as oxidizing materials rather than as explosives. Based on estimates of the Institute of Makers of Explosives, approximately 655 million pounds of explosives and blasting agents were transported from manufacturers' plants by motor vehicles, compared with 630 million pounds in the previous year.

Insurance

As motor carriers are required to file evidence of security for the payment of bodily injury, property damage, and cargo claims, the financial and overall stability of insurance and surety companies desiring to file such security is reviewed by us. Analysis of this review indicates that substantial underwriting losses continue in the fire and casualty insurance industry. The poor income results were not compensated by investment gains as in the past. The return of the stock market to approximately its previous level by yearend did save many companies from a drastic showing. However, the experience of many of the smaller companies did not follow the general pattern of the market, and they suffered an unrealized capital loss on their stock portfolios as well as an underwriting loss. The results of operations for the first quarter of 1963 are significantly worse for the industry than in the comparable period in 1962. While the second quarter results are not generally available, there is nothing to indicate a reversal of this trend. The competition for motor carrier business by insurers remains high, and the carriers continue to enjoy a buyer's market.

In view of the worsening financial picture in the fire and casualty insurance industry, we have intensely analyzed the annual financial statements of companies qualified to file evidence of security in behalf of motor carriers. Several insurers were requested to make no further filings because of their weak financial position. Quarterly, instead of annual, financial statements are required from several other insurance companies in order that we can maintain a closer surveillance. It is interesting to note that of the several insurance companies requested to make no further filings with this Commission in the recent past, three are already in receivership; two are being rehabilitated; one has been liquidated; and one has ceased writing insurance. Our requests preceded the eventual conclusions of operations by several months to 2 years.

The bankruptcy of a large class I motor common carrier during the year provides an outstanding example of the protection afforded the public by our insurance requirements. The motor carrier's cargo insurance policy contained a $3,500 deductible provision per shipment and at the time of bankruptcy the aggregate of individual cargo claims within the deductible was approximately $185,000. Our cargo insurance requirement of a minimum of $1,000 per vehicle does not recognize private arrangements, such as deductibles, made between the insured and insurer. Thus, the insurance company is responsible for, and is paying, all outstanding claims up to $1,000 each. This will result in the prompt payment to the shippers and consignees of 99 percent of all claims as opposed to awaiting the eventual partial payment by the trustee in bankruptcy, estimated to be a maximum of ten cents on the dollar.

No applications for authority to self-insure were received during the year. Two motor carriers holding authority to self-insure their cargo liability requested and were granted authority to discontinue such authority. Self-insured carriers are required to file financial statements and claim handling data, which receive our close scrutiny to insure that such carriers are capable of discharging their obligations to the public.

Progress was made in the program requiring 100-percent compliance by carriers with the designation of process agents requirement. During the year, 4,501 designation of process agent forms were received.

The insurance compliance record of motor carriers, brokers and freight forwarders was maintained at a high level. Approximately

16,663 motor carriers and 80 freight forwarders had bodily injury and property damage security on file.   Of this number, 15,151 common carriers of property and 83 freight forwarders filed cargo security. Transportation brokers submitted 273 surety bonds insuring financial responsibility in arranging for authorized motor carrier transportation.   In maintaining the desired level of continuous compliance, 15,423 certificates of insurance and surety bonds, and 9,194 notices of cancellation were submitted during the year.

MEDALS OF HONOR

Under the Medals of Honor Act of February 23, 1905, as amended (49 U.S.C. 1201–1203), we consider applications for award of medals to persons who, by extreme daring, endanger their own lives in saving or endeavoring to save lives imperiled by any wreck, disaster or grave accident upon any railroad within the United States engaged in interstate commerce or involving any motor vehicle on a public highway, road or street of the United States.

Since enactment of the Medals of Honor Act, there have been 121 applications involving railroad incidents.   Of these, 73 have been granted, 46 denied, and 2 were pending June 30, 1963.   No applications involving motor vehicle incidents were received during the year.   No medal has yet been awarded under the street and highway provisions of the act, although six applications have been made and considered.

ACCOUNTING, COST FINDING, AND VALUATION

Accurate determination of the operating performance and financial condition of carriers is a basic requirement for meaningful regulation. With this objective in view our accounting functions include: (1) developing and prescribing uniform systems of accounts for carriers subject to the Interstate Commerce Act; (2) policing the accounts to insure compliance with prescribed accounting regulations; (3) preparing studies and analyses of transportation costs and revenues; (4) maintaining inventories of carrier property and developing relevant valuation data; and (5) prescribing specific depreciation rates for use by railroads, pipelines and water carriers.

These functions fall into the following categories:

REGULATING ACCOUNTS

We prescribe uniform systems of accounts and related regulations for carriers (except the smaller carriers) to assure uniform industry-wide classification and reporting of carriers' profits and losses, business operations, and financial condition, and to obtain adequate and reliable information essential to us for ratemaking and other regulatory work. The smaller carriers, while not required to adhere to uniform accounting rules, nevertheless file limited reports of operating income and other financial data. The number and category of carriers subject to our systems of accounts are listed in appendix I.

During the year, we processed 29 cases requesting authority to use special accounting for extraordinary transactions. These matters included principally situations involving retirements and abandonments of segments of trackage and roadway property no longer needed for transportation service, rebuilding of freight cars to extend the service life or refit the cars for special service, purchases and mergers and acquisition of control of other carriers, stock dividends and adjustment of capitalization and similar matters.

Statements and journal entries for 456 cases in finance proceedings were examined and approved after necessary adjustments had been prescribed. These proceedings involved purchases, mergers and transfers of property and certificates, acquisition of stock control of other carriers, security issues, abandonments, and construction of tracks.

A publication entitled "Accounting Series Circular No. 130, Issue of 1962," was issued by us containing interpretations of the rules in the uniform system of accounts for railroad companies. These interpretations, in the form of questions and answers, cover special or particular transactions and situations which are not suitable for definition or coverage in the general uniform system of accounts. We also issued two major orders amending (1) the uniform system of accounts and (2) the valuation regulations for railroads. These two orders are designed to require adjustments of the accounts and related valuation records to reflect accurately the cost of property used in transportation service.

The accounts and records for the cost of the various classes of property of many railroads have not been supported adequately heretofore by underlying records or reliable evidence. This is true particularly in the case of older railroads where, in their early years of existence, proper records of construction costs were not maintained. This also has developed in cases where whole railroad properties were acquired from a predecessor company in mergers or from contractors for a consideration in the form of capital stock, bonds, and sometimes in cash. Property accounts were charged often with a single lump sum in an amount necessary to balance the capitalization without suitable evidence of the true value of the property.

Under the provisions of the amended rules, primary accounts for classes of transportation property will reflect costs as of basic valuation adjusted for subsequent changes in property to date. Each account will provide a reliable statement of property costs for use in depreciation accounting, finance proceedings, cost finding and rate-making, and other regulatory work. Our order also provides procedures for handling of the unusual situation.

Federal income taxes currently payable by carriers have been materially reduced as a result of (1) new shortened tax-depreciation guideline lives authorized by the Internal Revenue Service in Revenue Procedure No. 62–21, July 1962, and (2) the investment tax credit authorized in the Revenue Act of 1962. These new tax regulations raised important questions concerning the accounting to be performed by carriers in their books of accounts and financial statements filed with us. In our report and order on this matter, docket No. 34178, issued February 1, 1963, we held that actual Federal income taxes payable for each year, based on the effective tax regulations for the year, shall be recorded in the tax accounts of carriers' books of accounts and financial statements filed with us. This confirmed conclusions set forth in a statement of policy announced on February 9, 1959, concerning accounting for Federal income taxes. No sufficient justification was presented to warrant a change in the policy enunciated in 1959 to permit some form of deferred tax or annual equalization accounting for income taxes.

During the year we completed an investigation and issued a report and order, Ex Parte No. 137, *Contracts for Protective Services*, 318 I.C.C. 111, in the matter of contracts dated August 27, 1962, between

protective service companies and railroads for protection against
heat or cold to property transported in interstate commerce. Our
report set forth a practicable procedure for handling contracts which
had proven to be burdensome and impracticable. The new procedure
will minimize the necessity for the carriers and protective service companies to enter into new contracts in situations where a fluctuation
in cost of performing services occurs and, at the same time, enable
the parties to comply with the provisions of the law.

The revision of the uniform system of accounts for pipeline companies, which we indicated in our last report had been undertaken,
is nearing completion and we expect to make the revised rules effective
for the year 1964. A complete revision of the general instructions,
the texts of the accounts and the form of financial statement is to be
made.

Revision of the uniform system of accounts for freight forwarders
is in progress. We contemplate making a general revision of the present regulations in the light of the changing business conditions and
operations of these companies. Emphasis will be placed on the important ratemaking matter of cost of service incurred in performing
operations.

The pressing economic situation in the highly competitive transportation industry has demanded increased emphasis on the adequacy
of accounting systems and costs of doing business. Accordingly, several major projects must be undertaken to prescribe new rules and to
modify existing regulations as a result of new types of facilities and
changes in operating techniques initiated by carriers. Typical of
these projects are revisions in our uniform systems of accounts for
express companies, water carriers, motor carriers, and railroads.

During the year, we continued our policy of conferring frequently
with the Committee on Relations with the Interstate Commerce Commission of the American Institute of Certified Public Accountants.
These meetings are to insure that we keep abreast of the latest con-
temporary thinking and to exchange views regarding our accounting
regulations.

FIELD EXAMINATIONS AND INVESTIGATIONS

Field auditors attached to six regional offices conduct regularly
scheduled examinations of the basic accounting and related records
which support the financial, accounting and statistical reports required
by the Commission from the carriers subject to the accounting
regulations.

Because of the extensive and important use of the data contained
in the reports, the primary purpose of the field examinations is to
ascertain that carriers conform with the prescribed uniform systems
of accounts. This will insure that the financial, statistical, opera-

tional, and other data included in reports prepared by the carrier for Commission, public and other uses correctly reflect the facts and conditions of the operation. Secondary purposes of the field audit are to detect carrier violations of laws and regulations pertaining to rebates and concession, unlawful extensions of credit, unauthorized control of other carriers, the issuance of securities without authority, various provisions of the Clayton Antitrust Act and timely remittance of c.o.d. payments received from consignees. Violations of these laws and regulations and other indications of irregular or other possible unlawful activities are reported to our Bureau of Inquiry and Compliance for appropriate action.

Annual field examinations are routinely scheduled for railroads whose revenues exceed $25 million per annum. The aggregate annual revenue of railroads in this category is approximately $9.0 billion or 96 percent of the total revenue for all line-haul railroads. Motor carriers of general commodities scheduled for annual examination are those carriers whose annual revenues exceed $1.0 million. These carriers' revenues approximate $3.8 billion or 92 percent of the total reported by general commodity carriers subject to the accounting regulations. Other carriers subject to our regulations are examined at intervals of 2 to 6 years.

During fiscal year 1963, 1,193 accounting examinations were conducted consisting of 95 railroads, 57 pipelines, 12 freight forwarders, 26 water carriers, and 1,003 motor carriers. Approximately 99 percent of the examinations required corrections in the carriers' accounts and records in order to conform to prescribed accounting rules and regulations. Due to our limited staff we were only able to accomplish approximately 67 percent of our scheduled program.

Our program included visits by our field staff to the offices of approximately 200 new carriers to advise and counsel them in the installation of their accounting systems so as to conform with the Commission's regulations.

In addition to regularly scheduled accounting examinations, our field staff was frequently called upon to conduct special investigations for the Commission and other Government agencies such as the Department of Justice and Internal Revenue Service. These involved developing facts and evidence for use in formal proceedings and cases before courts, and providing expert witness testimony. Approximately 30 such investigations were conducted in 1963.

The field activities were supplemented by an examination by the Washington staff of annual reports filed by class I and class II motor carriers of property and class I motor carriers of passengers for the purpose of detecting errors in accounting, which are directed to the carrier's attention through correspondence. There were 2,252 reports examined during the year.

COST FINDING

The general function of cost finding embraces analyses of cost evidence introduced in various rate proceedings, preparation and submission of cost data and analyses in conjunction with suspension of rates and granting of temporary authorities, preparation and introduction of cost data and testimony in investigation proceedings instituted by the Commission, cost research and formula development, and the production and publication of territorial and other cost studies.

Analyses were completed of cost evidence introduced in 143 formal cases and cost analyses were pending in 18 cases at the close of the fiscal year. These cases covered a variety of proceedings involving changes in rates on a large number of individual commodities moving by railroad, highway, barge, and coastal water carriers; divisions of rates between railroads, commutation fares by railroads and buslines; trailer-on-flatcar rates; and general increases in motor carrier rates. The 143 cases disposed of represented an increase of 8 over the indicated in the previous annual report. Paralleling this numerical increase were some 1,900 additional direct man-hours devoted to this activity over that for the prior year. This man-hour increase was attributable to the expanding complexity of cost evidence introduced in adversary rate proceedings and, particularly, intermodal rate cases.

During the year, our Bureau of Accounts received 2,843 requests to provide cost data in rate cases involving suspension of rates and granting of temporary operating authorities. These requests involved the "costing-out" of 14,420 individual point-to-point movements by railroads, motor carriers and water carriers.

There were five cases on hand covering investigations instituted by the Commission which occasioned the need to prepare and introduce cost data and testimony. Two of these investigations were completed during the fiscal year. One of the pending investigations had consumed over 50,000 man-hours by July 1, 1963. This proceeding involves the formula used in determining per diem charges for the use of freight cars.

Another important cost finding activity involves cost research and formula development. Essentially, the objective here is to search out and test in a practical fashion new and better ways of computing transportation costs.

Cost research has been spasmodic due to the limited number of personnel available for the task. Notwithstanding, a significant accomplishment was made in this area by the development and publication of a "Formula for Determining Cost of Transporting Freight by Barge Lines." This formula represents the fruits of a collaborative effort by the Commission and an industry advisory group.

Docket No. 34013, a rulemaking proceeding involving proposed rules to govern the assembling and presentation of cost evidence, is of paramount importance in our cost research and formula development activity. As of the end of fiscal 1963, this work had been limited to analyses of 41 verified statements submitted by interested parties. The investigation, aside from the legal question of prima facie evidence, raises certain controversial issues with respect to the Commission's cost formulas and principles. Considerable analysis will be necessary before a conclusion can be reached.

Through increased utilization of automatic data processing, we expect to reduce by approximately one-third the number of hours required to dispose of territorial and other cost studies. During the year we issued an "Explanation of Automatic Data Processing Procedure of Highway Form B." This statement explains a computer program for the automatic derivation of cost data for motor carriers. Further, Rail Form A, the "Formula for Use in Determining Rail Freight Service Costs," also is being adapted for automatic data processing. The program should be completed in a relatively short time. Full adaptation of automatic data processing to our cost formulas will give us the capability of developing more rail and motor costs for use of the Commission and industry.

While the foregoing represents a beginning to a continuing cost research program, much work remains. For example, the development of formulas for maritime, pipeline, motor carrier household goods, and trailers-on-flatcar operations are contemplated for the future. Also, studies directed toward the problem of comparable costs among the several modes of transportation will be amplified.

Territorial and other cost studies were published and disseminated during the year as follows:

1. Rail Carload Cost Scales by Territories for the Year 1961, Statement No. 5–63. Costs are shown on out-of-pocket and fully distributed bases by types of car, by weight of net load, and by length of haul.

2. Percent of Empty to Loaded Freight Car-Miles by Class of Equipment, Statement No. 3–62.

3. Cost of Transporting Freight by Class I and Class II Motor Common Carriers of General Commodities, East-South Territory—1961, Statement No. 1–63.

4. Cost of Transporting Freight by Class I and Class II Motor Common Carriers of General Commodities, Eastern-Central Territory—1961, Statement No. 2–63.

5. Cost of Transporting Freight by Class I and Class II Motor Common Carriers of General Commodities, Southern Region—1961, Statement No. 3–63.

6. Cost of Transporting Freight by Class I and Class II Motor Common Carriers of General Commodities, South-Central Territory—1961, Statement No. 4–63.

VALUATION OF RAILROAD AND PIPELINE CARRIER PROPERTY

Our responsibility in the area of valuation involves the maintenance of inventories of carrier property and development of relevant data. The data so developed are used in ratemaking, depreciation accounting, and other regulatory functions, and by the Department of Justice.

Annual statements show elements of value for Class I line-haul railways and switching and terminal companies. The latest compilation, as of December 31, 1961, shows the following for these carriers: original cost (not including land), $33.5 billion; cost of reproduction new, $75.6 billion; cost of reproduction new, less depreciation, $47.3 billion; and estimated present value of land, $2.0 billion.

The matter of maintaining on a current basis the original cost of railroad properties subsequent to their original inventory has been one of the more important phases of this work. The original cost of each carrier's property as perpetuated by us represents the most reliable data for use in a rate base for ratemaking purposes as well as for a depreciation base in computing proper depreciation charges.

By order dated April 17, 1963, we prescribed rules to require railroads to adjust their property accounts to conform to the valuation records. Upon final implementation of this order, our function of perpetuating original cost of railroad properties will be discontinued.

In connection with the present work of keeping valuations current, annual indices of railway construction costs are prepared. These indices are weighted averages of unit costs of physical property such as locomotives, cars, track elements, and buildings. Some indication of the pronounced fluctuations in the value of physical property of railroads in different years and periods based upon these differences in constuction costs is shown by the chart on page 155. Using the base of 100 for the period 1910–14, cost of construction reached an all-time high of 399 at the close of 1960 and declined to 396 at the close of 1962.

Pipeline valuation work principally involves preparing annual valuations of physical properties and annual indices of construction costs. The immediate prospect is that the pipeline valuation workload now at 88 reports annually will exceed 120 annual reports when basic valuations have been found by the Commission for 22 newly constructed pipeline companies and 12 pipelines which are currently planned or under construction.

Some indication of the pronounced fluctuations in the value of physical property of pipeline carriers, excluding land, in different years and periods based upon these differences in construction costs is shown by the chart on page 156.

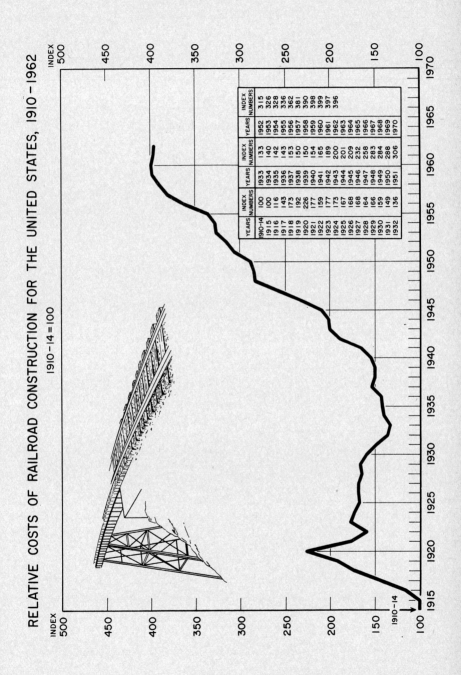

RELATIVE COSTS OF RAILROAD CONSTRUCTION FOR THE UNITED STATES, 1910-1962

1910-14=100

YEARS	INDEX NUMBERS	YEARS	INDEX NUMBERS	YEARS	INDEX NUMBERS
1910-14	100	1933	133	1952	315
1915	100	1934	140	1953	326
1916	116	1935	142	1954	328
1917	143	1936	143	1955	336
1918	173	1937	153	1956	362
1919	192	1938	150	1957	381
1920	226	1939	150	1958	390
1921	177	1940	154	1959	398
1922	159	1941	165	1960	399
1923	177	1942	189	1961	397
1924	173	1943	200	1962	396
1925	167	1944	201	1963	
1926	168	1945	209	1964	
1927	168	1946	232	1965	
1928	164	1947	258	1966	
1929	166	1948	283	1967	
1930	159	1949	284	1968	
1931	149	1950	288	1969	
1932	136	1951	306	1970	

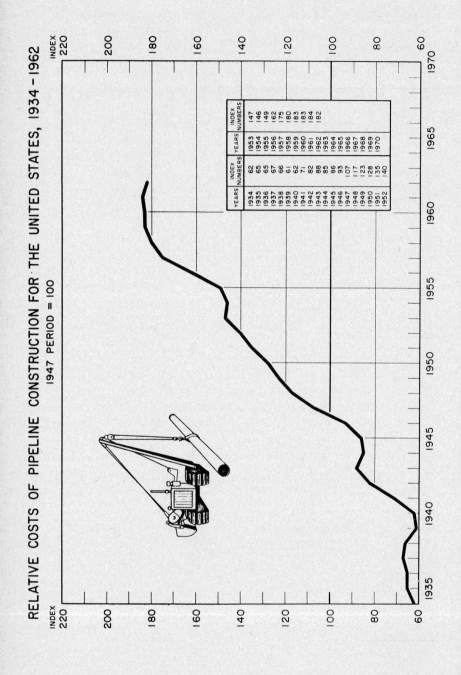

RELATIVE COSTS OF PIPELINE CONSTRUCTION FOR THE UNITED STATES, 1934-1962
1947 PERIOD = 100

YEARS	INDEX NUMBERS	YEARS	INDEX NUMBERS
1934	62	1953	147
1935	65	1954	146
1936	65	1955	149
1937	67	1956	162
1938	66	1957	175
1939	61	1958	180
1940	62	1959	183
1941	71	1960	183
1942	82	1961	184
1943	88	1962	182
1944	85	1963	
1945	86	1964	
1946	93	1965	
1947	107	1966	
1948	117	1967	
1949	123	1968	
1950	128	1969	
1951	135	1970	
1952	140		

DEPRECIATION RATES

Under the continuing responsibility of the Commission for determining the classes of property for which depreciation charges may be included by carriers in operating expenses, and the rate or rates of depreciation to be used in connection therewith, 33 formal orders and 159 informal directives were issued prescribing or approving depreciation rates. During the calendar year 1962, the application of Commission approved or prescribed depreciation rates resulted in charges in the operating expense account of railroads, pipelines, and carriers by water of an amount exceeding three-quarters of a billion dollars.

We are aware that technological changes covering introduction of new types of property such as electronic yards, jumbo and bilevel cars, centralized traffic control systems, and microwave installations have created the need for a comprehensive review of our depreciation policies. However, with our present staff, we are only able to issue orders and directives prescribing individual depreciation rates currently used by carriers in charging operating expenses.

LITIGATION INVOLVING COMMISSION ORDERS

The Office of the General Counsel during this period handled 244 cases in various stages of litigation in the Federal courts.

There were 149 cases pending on June 30, 1962, and 95 cases were instituted in the courts between that date and June 30, 1963. Of the total 120 were concluded, leaving 124 cases pending on June 30, 1963. These comprised 8 cases pending in the Supreme Court of the United States, 3 in the courts of appeals, and 113 in the district courts of the United States.

Twenty-two cases were concluded in the Supreme Court, 3 were concluded in the courts of appeals, and 95 were concluded in the district courts. The more important cases are discussed below.

INTERMODAL RATE COMPETITION

The Supreme Court in *Interstate Commerce Commission* v. *The New York, New Haven and Hartford Railroad Co., et al.*, 372 U.S. 744, vacated the judgment of a three-judge district court (199 F. Supp. 635 (1961)), which set aside so much of the Commission's order in I. and S. Docket No. 6834, *Piggy-Back Rates—Between East and Texas*, embraced in I. and S. Docket No. M–10415, *Commodities—Pan-Atlantic Steamship Corp.*, 313 I.C.C. 23 (1960), as required cancellation of certain reduced railroad trailer-on-flatcar rates. See 76th Annual Report, pp. 183–184. The Supreme Court also set aside the order of the Commission to the extent that it related to certain railroad T.O.F.C. rates and remanded the cause to the Commission for further proceedings consistent with the opinion of the court.

This was the first case in which the Supreme Court considered the interpretation and application of section 15a(3) of the Interstate Commerce Act, added by Congress in the Transportation Act of 1958, which pertains to proceedings involving rate competition between carriers of different modes. In holding that on the record before it the Commission's disallowance of the rates in question was not adequately supported, the Supreme Court stated that, in light of the legislative history of section 15a(3), it is clear Congress did not regard setting a rate at a particular level as constituting an unfair or destructive competitive practice simply because the rate would divert some or all traffic from the competing mode. The Supreme Court disagreed with the conclusions of the district court that needs of the national defense are not an operative part of the National Transportation

Policy. However, it held that the Commission's reliance on the factor of "national defense" in disallowing the rates in question was not supported by adequate findings based upon substantial evidence.

EQUALIZATION OF RATES AT PORTS

The Supreme Court, by a 4–4 vote without opinion, 373 U.S. 372 (1963), affirmed the decision of the three-judge district court in *Boston and Maine Railroad* v. *United States*, 202 F. Supp. 830 (D. Mass. 1962), which set aside our order in *Equalization of Rates at North Atlantic Ports*, 311 I.C.C. 689 (1960), 314 I.C.C. 185 (1961). The order directed cancellation of reduced rates proposed by railroads serving the ports of New York, Boston, Albany, and Portland (the northern tier ports) on export and import traffic moving between those ports and a defined interior territory. The purpose of the proposed rate reductions was to eliminate long-established differentials favoring Philadelphia, Baltimore and Hampton Roads, generally referred to as the southern tier ports, on such traffic. The district court had held that our conclusion that the proposed reduced rates by the railroads serving the northern tier ports would violate section 3(1) of the act was erroneous in that (1) we failed to give due weight to the interests of shippers, receivers, carriers, and inland communities; (2) we relied on a single subsidiary finding, namely, the distance disadvantage of the northern tier ports; and (3) while distance differences might be relevant insofar as they reflect differences in cost and value of services of competing railroads, we failed to make such cost or value findings.

In *Baltimore & Ohio, et al.* v. *U.S. and I.C.C.*, 212 F. Supp. 13 (1962), a three-judge district court for the District of Maryland held the record was deficient to support the Commission's report and order, which found just and reasonable reduced import iron ore rates through Philadelphia to 17 points in differential territory at the same level of import iron ore rates applicable through Baltimore. The matter was remanded to the Commission for further cost studies on the movement of iron ore traffic through both ports and a comparison of the total traffic through both ports.

A three-judge court for the Southern District of New York, shortly before the above opinion, had considered the Commission proceeding as related to the Port of New York and remanded the matter to the Commission. The New York court held that additional cost evidence was required to support the Commission's conclusion that equalization of rates through New York with Philadelphia and Baltimore would unduly prejudice the latter ports. *New York Central* v. *U.S. and I.C.C.*, *Erie-Lackawanna* v. *U.S. and I.C.C.*, 207 F. Supp. 483 (1962). The Commission proceeding in the New York and Baltimore cases is entitled *Iron Ore From Eastern Ports to Central Freight Association*

Points, I. and S. No. 6074.   Both proceedings are consolidated into cne report, 314 I.C.C. 149.

The Commission's decision under section 3(1) of the act, 49 U.S.C. § 3(1), *Hillsborough County Port Authority, et al.* v. *Ahnapee & Western Railway Company, et al.,* Docket No. 32456, 313 I.C.C. 691, holding rail carriers were unduly preferring Gulf and south Atlantic ports on export-import rates and unduly prejudicing the port of Tampa, Fla., on traffic moving from and to interior points which fell within a range of distances common to the competing ports, was upheld by a three-judge statutory district court.   *Alabama, Tennessee and Northern Railroad Company, et al.* v. *United States of America and Interstate Commerce Commission,* Civil Action No. 2747, U.S.D.C. S.D. Ala. (July 6, 1962).

DIVISIONS OF JOINT RATES

In *Boston and Maine Railroad, et al.* v. *United States, et al.,* 371 U.S. 26, the Supreme Court, in a *per curiam* order entered October 15, 1962 (371 U.S. 26), affirmed the judgment of a three-judge district court which dismissed the complaint of Boston and Maine Railroad and 46 other railroads who sought to set aside the Commission's order in Docket No. 32055, *Louisville and Nashville R. Co.* v. *Akron, C. & Y.R. Co.,* 309 I.C.C. 491 (1960).   *Boston and Maine Railroad, et al.* v. *United States, et al.,* 208 F. Supp. 661 (1962).   The Commission, under section 15(6) of the act, prescribed a basis for the primary division of joint rates on traffic (except coal and coke made from coal) moving between points in official territory and "border points"—i.e., points in a broader zone between the "official territory and the southern territory."   This order had the effect of completing the establishment cf a uniform basis for the division of joint rates on such interterritorial and border point traffic.

THROUGH ROUTES AND JOINT RATES

As stated in the 76th Annual Report, the court in *Atlantic Coast Line Railroad Co.* v. *United States,* 205 F. Supp. 360 (M.D. Ga. 1962), sustained the decision of the Commission in *Routing, Coal from Origins on Louisville & N.R.,* 313 I.C.C. 752.   The Commission issued its report and order following the earlier remand in *Southern Ry. Co.* v. *United States,* 167 F. Supp. 747 (M.D. Ga. 1958), and decided in the remanded proceeding that cancellation of certain circuitous routes by Southern Railway was consistent with the public interest.   Plaintiff, Atlantic Coast Line Railroad, filed a notice of appeal to the Supreme Court, which affirmed the decision below, 371 U.S. 6.

UNDUE PREFERENCE AND PREJUDICE

In *Atchison, Topeka and Santa Fe Railway Company* v. *United States*, 218 F. Supp. 359 (N.D. Ill.) (June 27, 1962), the court sustained our order in Docket No. 32551, *Cudahy Packing Company* v. *Akron, Canton & Youngstown Railroad Company*, 318 I.C.C. 229. Our order found that the rail rates on fresh meats and packinghouse products from points west of the Mississippi River to official territory were unduly prejudicial to such origins and shippers there located and unduly preferential to origins and shippers on and east of the Missississippi River, in violation of section 3(1) of the act. The effect of this order is to require railroads to give all origins west of the river the same relative level of rates as are maintained from Dubuque, Iowa, to destinations in official territory, as tested by the uniform percentages of the Docket No. 28300 first class rates, thereby eliminating not only unlawful rate differences as between origins on and east of the river, on the one hand, and origins west thereof, on the other, but also such unlawful differences that exist as between origins west of the river.

In *Class Rates, Mountain-Pacific Territory*, 296 I.C.C. 555 (1955), we approved, on an interim basis, a uniform mileage scale of class rates for rail carriers, but permitted the carriers to retain truck-competitive parity rates as to northern territory traffic. By a proceeding commenced in 1955, *Seattle Traffic Association* v. *Consolidated Freightways*, 301 I.C.C. 483 (1957), 306 I.C.C. 87 (1959), 310 I.C.C. 773 (1960), Seattle-Tacoma interests sought prescription of a similar mileage scale of class rates for motor carriers to remove an alleged undue preference and prejudice assertedly produced by Portland-Vancouver's parity position in northern territory and rate advantage in southern territory. Our decision to somewhat reduce Portland-Vancouver's rate advantage in southern territory, but not to disturb the long-standing rail-motor carrier competition on parity of rates in northern territory, was sustained in *Seattle Traffic Association* v. *United States*, Civil Action No. 5349 (W.D. Wash.) (March 27, 1963).

FOURTH SECTION APPLICATIONS

A three-judge district court in *A. L. Mechling Barge Lines, Inc., et al.* v. *United States of America and Interstate Commerce Commission, et al.*, 209 F. Supp. 744 (N.D. Ill.), upheld the Commission's order granting fourth-section relief to the rail carriers on corn and corn movements from stations on the Kankakee Belt Line in Illinois to points in official territory. *Corn and Corn Products from Illinois to Official Territory*, Fourth Section Order No. 33955, 310 I.C.C. 437. Plaintiffs, A. L. Mechling Barge Line and the Chicago Board of

Trade, contended the Commission had erred because it had considered
the entire through rate in determining whether the proposed rate was
reasonably compensatory without confining its deliberations to the
6-cent proportional rate factor which applied from origins to Kankakee on shipments destined beyond to points in official territory; and
that the Commission had erred in failing to permit submission of
evidence relating to section 3(4) violations. The court held that the
Commission had properly based its deliberations on the entire through
rate and that the Commission was not required to enlarge a section 4
proceeding into an investigation of alleged discrimination under section 3(4) of the act which relates to discriminations between connecting
carriers. Plaintiffs have taken an appeal in this case and the Supreme
Court on June 17, 1963, noted probable jurisdiction.

RATES

Upon suit of the Pennsylvania Railroad Company and 24 other
railroads operating in the eastern district of the United States, a
three-judge district court in *Pennsylvania Railroad Company, et al.*
v. *United States, et al.*, 216 F. Supp. 199, set aside that portion of the
order of the Commission entered in Ex Parte No. 223 (Sub-No. 2),
Increased Switching Charges, 315 I.C.C. 199, requiring cancellation
of tariff schedules which effected an increase of $7.50 per car in the
charges for intraterminal and interterminal switching in the eastern
district of the United States.

The report and order in Ex Parte No. 223 (Sub-No. 2), which
applied to the several rail regions in the United States, concluded that
a just and reasonable percentage increase would be 20 percent over the
prior charges, subject to varying maxima in the eastern, western and
southern regions. All the rail carriers except those operating in the
eastern district accepted the Commission's conclusion.

The court held that the increase was a general rate increase as to
which the Commission itself found use of "average figures" appropriate, and that inasmuch as the Commission found that the average
charge for such service in the eastern district was below cost, the
rates could not be characterized as unjust and unreasonable.

In *Atlantic Coast Line R. R. Co.* v. *United States*, 209 F. Supp. 157
(S.D. Fla. 1962), the court sustained our order in I. and S. Docket
No. 7443, *Phosphate Rock—Points in Florida to Points in Virginia*,
313 I.C.C. 495. Applying section 15a(2), our order rejected a reduced
rate on crude phosphate rock as unjust and unreasonable even though
the proposed rate would produce sufficient revenue to cover out-of-
pocket costs, because it would result in a reduction in net revenues.
Additionally, the court rejected the railroads' contention that we com-
mitted an abuse of discretion in denying reopening of the record to

permit introduction of evidence of increased carloadings over the published minimums which allegedly would change the net revenue figures and call for a redetermination of the lawfulness of the rate. The court concluded that since computation of revenues and loss of net revenue had been based upon projected carloadings of 71.4 tons as provided by the tariff, a showing that cars had been loaded in excess of the minimum would not create any change in the published minimum nor commit a shipper to continue to load in excess of the minimum.

In *Chicago & E. I. R. Co.* v. *United States*, 371 U.S. 69 (1962), the Supreme Court affirmed *per curiam* the lower court's dismissal of the complaint to set aside our report and order in *Bituminous Coal, Motor-Rail, Lynnville, Ind., to Chicago*, 313 I.C.C. 573 (1961), in which we held not shown to be just and reasonable a proposed motor-rail rate on bituminous coal, contemplating a 17-mile truck haul of the coal from mine to railhead, its transfer into rail hopper cars and its subsequent line-haul movement to destination, set at precisely the same level as the all-rail rate.

ABANDONMENTS

The Supreme Court in *State of Illinois, et al.* v. *United States, et al.*, 373 U.S. 378, affirmed *per curiam* the lower court decision (213 F. Supp. 83 (N.D. Ill. 1962)), sustaining the Commission. The Commission had granted a certificate of public convenience and necessity permitting abandonment of the entire line of railroad in *Chicago, North Shore & Milwaukee Railway Abandonment of Entire Operation*, Finance Docket No. 20245, 312 I.C.C. 99; 317 I.C.C. 191; 317 I.C.C. 363. Plaintiffs contended the North Shore was an interurban electric railway within the meaning of section 1(22), and thus, exempt from Commission regulation. It was further contended that even if the Commission had jurisdiction to grant a certificate to the North Shore permitting abandonment, such certificate must be limited to interstate commerce. The lower court's opinion, which was affirmed by the Supreme Court, dismissed the complaint finding that the Commission had properly determined that the North Shore was not an exempt interurban electric railway, and that the Commission's jurisdiction was not limited to the grant of a certificate to abandon operations in interstate commerce.

Appellants' appeal to the Supreme Court from the adverse judgment in *Burke County, Ga.* v. *United States*, 206 F. Supp. 586 (1962), was voluntarily dismissed by stipulation. See our 76th Annual Report, page 192. Therein the lower court had sustained our order authorizing abandonment of portions of two rail lines in *Central of Ga. Ry. Co. Abandonment*, 317 I.C.C. 184 (1961), despite the contention that officials of one of the lines had orally promised in 1950 that such line would never be abandoned.

In *State of Arizona* v. *United States*, 220 F. Supp. 337, (D. Ariz. 1963), the district court sustained the decision in *Southern Pacific Company Abandonment, Cochise County, Ariz., and Hidalgo Grant, Luna and Dona Ana Counties, N. Mex.*, 312 I.C.C. 685 (1961), authorizing the carrier to abandon a line of railroad between Douglas, Ariz., and Anapra, N. Mex., for a distance of about 233 miles. The court sustained the Commission's rules limiting the right to petition for reconsideration by the entire Commission and the basic allocation of the traffic made in the Division's report.

The decision of the district court in *Brotherhood of Locomotive Engineers* v. *United States*, 217 F. Supp. 98 (N.D. Ohio 1963), sustained the report in *Rutland Ry. Corp. Abandonment of Entire Line*, 317 I.C.C. 393 (1962), and the Commission's refusal to require financial protection for employees of a wholly abandoned line in the circumstances shown of record. The court further held Commission omission of an examiner's report did not violate the Administrative Procedure Act.

The district court in *Smith* v. *United States*, 211 F. Supp. 66 (D. Conn. 1962), sustained the retroactive imposition of conditions for the protection of rail employees adversely affected by the abandonment authorized by the Commission in *New York, N.H. & H. R. Co. Abandonment (Portion), Pomfret-Putnam, Conn.*, 312 I.C.C. 465 (1961).

DISCONTINUANCE OF PASSENGER SERVICE

The Supreme Court reversed the decision of the district court in *New York, Susquehanna and Western Railroad Company* v. *U.S. and I.C.C., et al.*, 200 F. Supp. 860, thereby upholding the Commission's order, holding it had no jurisdiction under section 13a(1) of the act to consider a notice of proposed train discontinuance where the train did not physically operate beyond the State boundaries. *New York, Susquehanna and Western Railroad Company Discontinuance of Passenger Service between New York, N.Y., and Butler, N.J.*, Finance Docket No. 21417. The mere addition of connecting-line bus transportation between Susquehanna transfer at North Bergen, N.J., and New York City did not convert the intrastate service into interstate service. *New Jersey, et al.* v. *New York, Susquehanna and Western Railroad Company*, 372 U.S. 1.

A three-judge district court reversed the order of the Commission in *The State of North Carolina, et al.* v. *U.S. and I.C.C., et al.*, 210 F. Supp. 675, which granted the application of the Southern Railroad Company to discontinue intrastate passenger train service between Greensboro and Goldsboro, N.C. The district court held the Commission erred as a matter of law in failing to take into account profits accruing to the Southern from its freight operations on the same intrastate line. The court also held that where passenger train losses are sufficiently exceeded by profits from other operations on the same intrastate line, there can be no burden on interstate commerce. *Southern Railway Company Discontinuance of Service Between Greensboro and Goldsboro, N.C.*, Finance Docket No. 21563. An appeal has been taken to the Supreme Court, which noted probable jurisdiction on May 13, 1963.

A three-judge district court held it had no jurisdiction to review the action of the Commission declining to institute an investigation into the proposed discontinuance by The Pennsylvania Railroad of the operation of passenger train service between Hagerstown, Md., and Harrisburg, Pa. The court also held that section 13a(1) is constitutional and "deprives neither the State nor any individual of any right which the Constitution of the United States guarantees." *C. J. Sludden and Cooperative Legislative Committee Railroad Brotherhoods in the State of Pennsylvania* v. *United States of America, Interstate Commerce Commission and The Pennsylvania Railroad Company*, 211 F. Supp. 150 (U.S.D.C.M.D. of Pa.). The Commission proceeding is entitled *Pennsylvania Railroad Company Discontinuance of Service Between Harrisburg, Pa. and Hagerstown, Md.*, Finance Docket No. 21936.

In *Walker* v. *United States*, 204 F. Supp. 918 (1961), 208 F. Supp. 388 (W.D. Tex. 1962), the district court sustained the acquisition of stock control by Central Freight Lines, Inc., of Alamo Express, Inc., and two affiliated companies which the Commission had approved in *Central Freight Lines, Inc.—Control—Alamo Express, Inc.*, 70 M.C.C. 610, 75 M.C.C. 731, 90 M.C.C. 96, and in *Central Freight Lines, Inc., Note*, 90 M.C.C. 246. The court initially remanded the proceedings for clarification, but then sustained the Commission, holding, *inter alia*, the existence of a contractual dispute did not cut off the Commission's jurisdiction to entertain Central's unilateral application to control the other companies. The Supreme Court affirmed, 372 U.S. 526.

In *Railway Labor Executives' Association* v. *United States*, 216 F. Supp. 101 (E.D. Va. 1963), the district court set aside the decision in *Seaboard Air Line R. Co.—Control, Etc.—Richmond Terminal Railway Co.*, 312 I.C.C. 803 (1959), 312 I.C.C. 507 (1961), insofar as the Commission had failed to require Seaboard to protect certain employees upon removal of its operation from one terminal to another in Richmond, Va. The court concluded the employees were touched sufficiently by the transaction, in that they were as much the employees of Seaboard as of the carrier remaining at the first terminal (Chesapeake & Ohio), to be treated as coming within the ambit of section 5(2)(f) of the act.

A three-judge district court upheld the Commission's power to modify a section 5 order approving the purchase of operating rights by the imposition of protective labor conditions under section 5(2)(c)(4) of the act after the consummation of the transaction and the issuance of a certificate to the vendee, where the applicants failed to comply with voluntary representations made in their application regarding employees affected by the transaction. *Baggett Transportation Company* v. *U.S. and I.C.C.*, 206 F. Supp. 835 (N.D. Ala. 1962). The Commission proceeding is entitled *Baggett Transportation Company Purchase—Hunt Freight Lines, Inc.*, Docket No. MC–F–6034.

DIVESTITURE UNDER SECTION 5(7)

In *Gilbertville Trucking Co., Inc.* v. *United States*, 371 U.S. 115 (1962), the Supreme Court unanimously sustained in part, and reversed and remanded in part, the lower court decision (196 F. Supp. 351), which had sustained our orders in 75 M.C.C. 45 (1958), and on reconsideration in 80 M.C.C. 257 (1959).

The Supreme Court held that the Commission had authority under section 5(7) to require complete divestiture; however, because the Commission did not explain why divestiture was the proper remedy, the matter was remanded for the purpose of having the Commission assign appropriate reasons for its selection of a remedial measure. See our 76th Annual Report, page 189. Following the first court test of an order requiring divestiture under section 5(7), we modified such order in 93 M.C.C. 22 (1963).

RACIAL DISCRIMINATION

As noted in the 76th Annual Report, a three-judge district court in *State of Georgia and the Public Service Commission of the State of Georgia* v. *United States*, 201 F. Supp. 813 (N.D. Ga. 1961), sustained the regulations adopted in *Discrimination in Operations of Interstate Motor Carriers of Passengers*, 86 M.C.C. 743, and codified as 49 CFR Part 180a. This decision affirms the regulations prohibiting various forms of racial segregation in motor common carrier transportation of passengers in interstate commerce. This suit also involves the first judicial interpretation of the scope of the reservation of State power over intrastate commerce under section 202(b) of the act, and of the Commission's authority to issue regulations to implement the antidiscriminatory provisions of section 216(d) of the act. The Supreme Court affirmed, 371 U.S. 9.

SEVENTY-SEVENTH ANNUAL REPORT

REPARATIONS

In *William N. Feinstein & Co., Inc.* v. *United States, et al.*, 209 F. Supp. 613 (S.D.N.Y. 1962), the district court sustained our report and order dated May 31, 1961, in *William N. Feinstein & Co., Inc.* v. *New York Central Railroad Co.* (Docket No. 32431, 313 I.C.C. 783). We had found unloading charges assessed and collected by the New York Central and other railroads at New York on past carload shipments of vegetables having origins in numerous States when "considered by themselves or as a part of the total transportation charges * * * are not shown to have been unjust, unreasonable, or otherwise unlawful." The primary contention of plaintiff was that our decision was erroneous because it was in conflict with the decision of the Supreme Court in *Secretary of Agriculture* v. *United States*, 347 U.S. 645, which set aside the Commission's decision in *Unloading Charges on Fruits and Vegetables at New York and Philadelphia*, I. and S. Docket No. 5500 (286 I.C.C. 119), and that it was contrary to our subsequent decision in the same proceeding (298 I.C.C. 637) ; and was not in accord with the decision of the Supreme Court in *Adams* v. *Mills*, 286 U.S. 397.

The district court, in sustaining our action said that the Commission "is not required to deal with a particular case as it has dealt with a prior case that seems similar since diverse factors may be present in the second determination which the Commission feels, in the exercise of its specialized experience justify a different result," and the Court is not obliged to reconcile its conclusions with decisions in earlier proceedings involving the same subject because the Court may consider only the record in the proceeding under review.

The decision of the lower court was affirmed unanimously by the United States Court of Appeals for the Second Circuit (317 F. 2d 509 (1963)).

In *Atlantic Coast Line R. Co.* v. *United States*, 213 F. Supp. 199 (M.D. Fla. 1963), a district court composed of a single judge set aside the Commission's award of reparations in *Thomson Phosphate Co.* v. *Atlantic Coast Line R. Co.*, 291 I.C.C. 1, 303 I.C.C. 25, 311 I.C.C. 315, on the grounds the court has jurisdiction to review a reparation order at the suit of the affected carrier, and the Commission unlawfully stayed the statute of limitations contained in section 16(3)(b) of the act. The jurisdictional question, whether a carrier may appeal a reparation order or must await a section 16(2) suit of the affected shipper to contest the order, is now pending appeal in the United States Court of Appeals for the Fifth Circuit, *sub. nom. Interstate Commerce Commission* v. *Atlantic Coast Line R. Co.*, No. 20485.

In *Atchison, Topeka and Santa Fe Ry.* v. *United States*, 209 F. Supp. 35 (N.D. Ill. 1962), the court reversed the Commission's decision in *Lease and Interchange of Motor Vehicles*, Second Supplemental Report, 79 M.C.C. 65 (1959). The court held, contrary to the Commission's conclusion, that carriers of fresh meat and meat products are not within the exemption from the Commission's power to regulate trip-leasing provided by section 204(f) of the act for carriers of "perishable products manufactured from perishable property of a character embraced within section 203(b)(6)." The court reasoned that the livestock from which meat and meat products are manufactured are not "perishable" property as that term is used in the Interstate Commerce Act.

MOTOR CARRIER OPERATING AUTHORITY

The Supreme Court in a majority opinion (371 U.S. 156), reversed the 2–1 decision by a three-judge district court, in *Burlington Truck Lines, Inc.* v. *United States*, 194 F. Supp. 31 (S.D. Ill. 1961), which had upheld our order in *Nebraska Short Line Carriers, Inc.—Common Carrier Application*, 79 M.C.C. 599 (1959), granting a certificate to applicant authorizing it to engage in motor carrier operations. Applicant corporation was conceived and organized by a group of nonunion motor carriers in order to combat a boycott instituted against them by several unionized motor carriers pursuant to "hot cargo" clauses in contracts with their employees. The court recognized that we are empowered to insure the provision of adequate motor carrier service through the grant of additional certificates to other motor carriers where there is a failure of existing service because of such boycotts. The Supreme Court held, however, that where "the particular deviations from an otherwise completely adequate service * * * consist solely of illegal and discriminatory refusals to accept or deliver traffic * * * the choice of the certification remedy may not be automatic," but rather must be based on a "conscious choice" that public need for adequate service "outbalances whatever public interest there is in protecting existing carriers' revenues * * *."

A three-judge district court in *Railway Express Agency, Inc.* v. *U.S.A., I.C.C., and United Parcel Service, Inc.*, 205 F. Supp. 831 (S.D.N.Y.), upheld the Commission's order in *United Parcel Service, Inc. Extension—Midwestern States*, Docket No. MC–115495 (Sub.-No. 3) and *Railway Express Agency Incorporated Extension—Several States*, Docket No. MC–66562 (Sub-No. 1671), granting a certificate of public convenience and necessity to United Parcel Service, Inc., despite the allegations by the plaintiffs, REA, that the Commission had failed to comply with the Ashbacker Doctrine (*Ashbacker Radio Co.* v. *F.C.C.*, 326 U.S. 327). The district court held that the Commission is not bound to follow any one procedure in disposing of allegedly mutually exclusive applications so long as the Commission gives comparative consideration to bona fide timely filed mutually exclusive applications.

The elimination of gateways arising from the tacking of rights acquired by purchase, which would permit direct operations between points theretofore only sparsely served because of the mileage circuity involved, was held by us to enable the applicant to render what would be tantamount to a new service for which no need had been shown. *Yale Transport Corp.* v. *United States*, 210 F. Supp. 862 (S.D.N.Y. 1962), aff'd mem., 373 U.S. 540 (1963), sustaining *Yale Transport Corp. Elimination of Gateways*, 89 M.C.C. 527.

In *Daniels* v. *United States, et al.*, 372 U.S. 704, the Supreme Court affirmed *per curiam* the judgment of the district court (210 F. Supp. 942 (D. Mont. 1962)), sustaining our order in Docket No. MC–C–2507, *W. M. Daniels—Investigation of Second Proviso Eligibility.* Our order rejected Daniels' BMC 75 statement of intent to operate in interstate commerce within the State of Montana in operations corresponding to those authorized in his Montana Interstate Permit No. MRC 284, finding that the state franchise purportedly authorized interstate and not intrastate operations and was, therefore, ineligible for registration under the partial exemption of the second proviso of section 206(a)(1) of the act, prior to the amendment in its present form.

CONTRACT CARRIERS

In *Tar Asphalt Trucking Company, Inc., Conversion Proceeding*, 88 M.C.C. 443 (1961), we ordered the conversion of a contract carrier to a common carrier against its will under section 212(c) on finding the operations of the carrier did not conform to the amended definition of a contract carrier in section 203(a)(15). Pursuant to our prior decision in *T. T. Brooks Trucking Co., Inc., Conversion Application*, 81 M.C.C. 561 (1959), we restricted the certificates to be issued in lieu of the carrier's permits against tacking. Our imposition of tacking restrictions in conversions under section 212(c), our interpretation of the criteria in section 203(a)(15) as they are to be applied in proceedings under section 212(c), and the constitutionality of our requiring involuntary conversions under that section were sustained in *Tar Asphalt Trucking Co., Inc.* v. *United States*, 372 U.S. 596 (1963), affirming, *per curiam*, the decision in *Tar Asphalt Trucking Co., Inc.* v. *United States*, 208 F. Supp. 611 (D.N.J. 1962).

In *J. B. Montgomery, Inc.* v. *United States*, 206 F. Supp. 455 (D. Colo. 1962), the district court set aside our order in *J. B. Montgomery, Inc., Conversion Proceeding*, 83 M.C.C. 457 (1960), to the extent that the Commission had imposed, in the certificate issued Montgomery upon conversion from a contract to a common carrier under section

212(c) of the act, restrictions designed to continue the effects of the Keystone restriction of the previously held permit. The court held that, under section 212(c), the Commission has no authority to impose restrictions to achieve substantial parity between prior and future operating rights. The Supreme Court noted probable jurisdiction of our appeal in No. 791, October Term, 1962.

UNAUTHORIZED MOTOR CARRIER OPERATIONS

A three-judge district court in *Jones Motor Co., Inc.* v. *The United States of America and The Interstate Commerce Commission*, 218 F. Supp. 133 (E.D. Pa.), Civil Action No. 32629, reversed the cease and desist order of the Commission in *Pennsylvania Utility Commission* v. *Jones Motor Co., Inc.*, 89 M.C.C. 605, which prohibited a motor common carrier possessing I.C.C. certificates from utilizing its certificates to conduct as a subterfuge unauthorized intrastate operations. By means of tacking, the carrier converted intrastate traffic into interstate traffic by the simple expedient of carrying shipments through an adjacent State and returning to the State of origin. The court contended that the Commission's order was not supported by substantial evidence and that the Commission cannot restrict a carrier from performing such operations without following the procedure in section 212(a) of the Interstate Commerce Act. This decision is contrary to the decisions of the lower court in *Hudson Transportation Company* v. *The United States of America, The Interstate Commerce Commission and The Pennsylvania Public Utility Commission*, 219 F. Supp. 43 (D.N.J.), Civil Action No. 362–62; and *Arrow Carrier Corporation* v. *The U.S.A., The I.C.C. and The Pennsylvania Public Utility Commission*, 219 F. Supp. 43 (D.N.J.), Civil Action No. 306–62; which upheld the Commission's precedent case in *Pennsylvania Public Utility Commission* v. *Hudson Transportation Company*, 88 M.C.C. 745. On the strength of the New Jersey decision, the district court in the *Jones* case granted a petition for rehearing. In the meantime, plaintiff Arrow Carrier Corp. has taken an appeal from the New Jersey decision to the Supreme Court.

In *John J. Casale, Inc.* v. *United States*, 208 F. Supp. 55 (S.D. N.Y. 1962), the district court sustained the determination in *John J. Casale, Inc., Contract Carrier Application*, Docket No. MC–20314 (Sub-No. 1), that the proposed operation involving the leasing of vehicles with drivers, who would be lessors' employees, would constitute for-hire carriage for which authority would be required from the Commission. The Supreme Court affirmed the decision of the district court, 371 U.S. 22.

Appeal has been noted by us from the lower court's decision in Civil Action No. 2840, *Shannon* v. *United States* (W.D. Tex. April 24, 1963), setting aside our report and orders in *Emma Shannon, et al., Investigation of Operations,* 81 M.C.C. 337 (1959), in which we found the respondent's buy-and-sell operations to constitute unauthorized for-hire carriage. We deemed it significant that the purchase and transportation of sugar by the respondent were undertaken primarily to avoid the empty return of trucks used to deliver other merchandise in private carriage and that deliveries were made directly to the ultimate consumers without warehousing of the sugar, factors which appeared to have been accorded little weight by the reviewing court.

Rejection, prior to its effective date, of a tariff naming rates on commodities which we previously had determined the motor carrier was without authority to handle was sustained in *W. J. Dillner Transfer Co.* v. *United States,* 214 F. Supp. 941 (W.D. Pa. 1963).

In *Peerless Stages, Inc.* v. *United States,* 371 U.S. 22, the Supreme Court affirmed *per curiam* the judgment of the district court sustaining our orders in Docket Nos. MC–C–2548, *Peerless Stages, Inc., Investigation and Revocation of Certificate,* and MC–66505 (Sub-No. 3), *Peerless Stages, Inc., Extension—Special and Charter Operations,* 86 M.C.C. 109. Our order found that the transportation of persons, gathered together in groups by an unlicensed broker, from points in the San Francisco Bay Area to gambling casinos in Nevada does not constitute the transportation of "special or chartered parties" as that term is used in section 208(c) of the act, and is in violation of the charter regulations and section 206(a). A certificate to conduct special or charter operations was denied because of failure to establish a public need for service additional to that existing.

In *Atwood's Transport Lines* v. *United States,* 211 F. Supp. 168 (D.D.C. 1962), affirmed, 373 U.S. 377 (1963), the Supreme Court sustained the constitutionality of rule III of the Commission's regulations governing incidental charter service by motor passenger carriers. Rule III defines the permissible origin territory of such charter parties, and provides that they may be originated at any point served by the carrier's regular routes, or at any point "within the territory served by" the carrier's regular routes. The Court rejected the plaintiff's argument that the quoted phrase is void for vagueness and uncertainty, and further sustained the Commission's application of the rule to the facts of the instant case, where it was concluded that Fort Belvoir and Alexandria, Va., are not "within the territory served by" plaintiff's regular routes, which run from downtown Washington, D.C., to Germantown and Point Lookout, Md. The Commission proceeding which was here at issue was *Alexandria, Barcroft and Washington Transit Co.* v. *Atwood's Transport Lines, Inc.,* 86 M.C.C. 399 (1961).

GRANDFATHER RIGHTS UNDER SECTION 7(c)

The disposition of grandfather applications under section 7(c) of the Transportation Act of 1958 for the transportation of frozen fruits, frozen berries and frozen vegetables were approved in Civil Action No. 62–297, *Home Transfer & Storage Co.* v. *United States* (D. Oreg. Oct. 22, 1962), sustaining *Home Transfer & Storage Co. Common Carrier "Grandfather" Application*, 88 M.C.C. 223 (1961); in Civil Action No. 5480, *Northwest Fisheries Transp., Inc.* v. *United States* (W.D. Wash. July 27, 1962), sustaining *Northwest Fisheries Transportation, Inc., Common Carrier "Grandfather" Application*, 89 M.C.C. 324; in Civil Action No. 5481, *Olmsted* v. *United States* (W.D. Wash. July 27, 1962), sustaining *Refrigerated Truck Lines Common Carrier "Grandfather" Application*, 86 M.C.C. 377, Notice of Appeal filed September 21, 1962; and in Civil Action No. 1655, *Willis Shaw Frozen Express, Inc.* v. *United States* (W.D. Ark. Feb. 11, 1963), sustaining *Willis Shaw Frozen Express, Inc., Common Carrier "Grandfather" Application*, 89 M.C.C. 377 (1961), from which an appeal has been noted in No. 1173, October Term, 1962. In Civil Action No. 13692, *J. Edward Jarman* v. *United States* (D. Md. June 19, 1963), setting aside *J. Edward Jarman Common Carrier "Grandfather" Application*, 84 M.C.C. 343 (1961), and in *Winter Garden Co.* v. *United States*, 211 F. Supp. 280 (E.D. Tenn. 1962), setting aside, *Winter Garden Co., Inc., "Grandfather" Application*, 86 M.C.C. 347 (1961), the reviewing courts remanded the proceedings for further consideration consistent with their opinions, which held, generally, that we had taken too narrow a view of the applicants' past operations.

Our determination that the past transportation of frozen french fried potatoes and other cooked vegetables failed to give rise to "grandfather" rights was sustained in *Newton Trucking Co.* v. *United States*, 209 F. Supp. 600 (D. Del. 1962), aff'd mem., 372 U.S. 702 (1963), sustaining *Frozen Cooked Vegetables—Status*, 81 M.C.C. 649 (1959).

JUDICIAL REVIEW

In *Walled Lake Door Company* v. *United States*, 31 F.R.D. 258 (E.D. Mich. 1962), the district court composed of a single judge denied plaintiff's motion to produce, and sustained objections to interrogatories, which sought to obtain certain internal memoranda and drafts of reports involved in the decision of the case. In holding that the materials were privileged and irrelevant to the review proceeding, the court broadly sustained the inviolability of the Commission's internal files. The suit arose out of *Walled Lake Door Company* v. *Atlantic Coast Line R. Co.*, 309 I.C.C. 87 (1959), and was subsequently voluntarily dismissed with prejudice by the plaintiff.

By *per curiam* memorandum denying appellant's petition for rehearing of its summary affirmance of the lower court decision, the Supreme Court announced that it had affirmed the lower court's judgment insofar as it upheld the validity of our order on the merits, but disagreed that the appellants, a motor carrier rate bureau and a motor carrier trade association, lacked standing to challenge the validity of our order. We had found that reduced freight forwarder rates on volume shipments which, at the shippers' option, would be delivered on the platform or in the boxcar at the freight forwarder's terminal, were not shown to be just and reasonable. *National Motor Freight Traffic Assn.* v. *United States*, 205 F. Supp. 592 (D.D.C. 1962), aff'd mem., 371 U.S. 223 (1962), rehearing denied, 372 U.S. 246 (1963) sustaining *Forwarder Volume Commodity Rates, Transcontinental*, 306 I.C.C. 535 (1959), 311 I.C.C. 733 (1960).

ENFORCEMENT AND COMPLIANCE

PSEUDO PRIVATE CARRIAGE

We have continued our efforts to combat unlawful activities in which for-hire motor operations are conducted without appropriate authority. Such unlawful activities usually are in the guise of private carriage, which deprives legitimate for-hire carriers of needed traffic. Several methods, of varying subtlety, to avoid the certificate and permit requirements of the act have been investigated during the past year. One arrangement involved the lease of property-carrying motor vehicles to a certificated carrier on westbound movements and to a shipper on eastbound movements, with the drivers, men otherwise regularly in the employ of the carrier, becoming the employees of the shipper on the return trip. The lease with the carrier contained a provision requiring it to relinquish possession of the equipment when needed for use by the shipper. We found, in *Zirbel Transport, Inc., Investigation and Revocation*, 91 M.C.C. 705, that the certificated carrier and the lessor of the equipment, who was also an officer of the carrier, were jointly providing for-hire motor service to the shipper. They were ordered to cease and desist from such operations. A cease and desist order entered against somewhat similar "lease-back" arrangements in 1961 was upheld by a three judge district court in *Schultz Transit, Inc.*, v. *United States*, 208 F. Supp. 537, decided August 27, 1962.

Another device to evade regulation involved an attempt to create an employer-employee or principal-agent relationship between the shippers and the actual transporter of their products. In such a case, *Kapke Investigation of Operations and Practices*, 91 M.C.C. 377, the principal respondent had entered into separate agreements with the shipper respondents under which each had agreed to employ him as its "agent" or "traffic manager." He had supplied the equipment, supervised and paid the drivers, and assumed all costs, risks and obligations connected with the operation. Shipper respondents were required to do little more than tender the traffic and pay the transportation charges. An appropriate cease and desist order was entered against all respondents.

Another attempt by a shipper to avoid having to take direct control of its motor carrier operations involved the participation of a service corporation, under common control with a certificated motor carrier which furnished the shipper with drivers and provided garage and

174

maintenance facilities for the shipper's trucks. Although the evidence indicated that the shipper performed certain functions normally assumed by a legitimate private motor carrier, we concluded that the real responsibility for direction and control of the operation was vested in the service corporation and its *alter ego*, the certificated motor carrier. *Schirmer Transp. Co., Inc.—Investigation*, 91 M.C.C. 869.

In a final decision of this type, *Car Services, Inc., Common Carrier Application*, 92 M.C.C. 595, the issue was determined on the basis of the "primary business" test codified in 1958 as section 203 (c) of the act. The proposed long-distance delivery of new automobiles to dealers by an applicant in the business of storing and checking new automobiles was here found to be beyond the scope of applicant's primary business and to be for-hire carriage requiring authority, inasmuch as the transportation of the automobiles constituted the dominant part of applicant's overall service to the dealers. Both the *Schirmer* and *Car Services* cases are pending on petition.

SHIPPER ASSOCIATION EXEMPTION

In our last report we noted certain problems arising from the shipper association exemption provisions which provide, in substance, that the provisions of the act, relating to licensing and regulation of for-hire freight forwarders, shall not be construed to apply to operations of shippers or groups or associations of shippers in consolidating and distributing freight for themselves or their members on a nonprofit basis. The continuing growth of self-styled shippers' associations and agents purportedly operating under the exemption provisions is a continuing problem. Many of these shipper associations are undoubtedly bona fide. Yet others conduct operations and provide services indistinguishable from those of authorized freight forwarders. As unauthorized freight forwarders operating under the guise of a shippers' association or agent, they are free to reduce their rates at will, in unrestrained competition with legitimate freight forwarders. Their continued existence presents a clear and constant threat to the stability of regulated transportation upon which the general public must depend. What constitutes a lawful shippers' association or agent under the statute, however, has become the subject of extensive controversy in recent years. We are now in the process of attempting to fill in the broad statutory guidelines by developing practical and meaningful standards by which to judge the operations of those asserting the right to engage in freight consolidating, forwarding and distributing operations under the exemption provisions of section 402(c).

To this end we are reconsidering and have heard oral argument in Nos. FF–C–7, *Atlanta Shippers Assn., Inc.—Investigation*, FF–C–1,

Carload Shippers Assn., Inc., Investigation, and FF–C–8, *Federal Shippers Assn., Inc.—Investigation* (prior decisions of Division 1 reported fully last year) which concern the lawfulness of the activities of three purported shippers' associations. In addition, two decisions rendered this year should prove valuable in determining the line of demarcation between the lawful operations of bona fide shippers' associations and agents and those conducted by illegal freight forwarders under the guise of the section 402(c) exemption. In the first of these, No. FF–C–3, *Southern Bonded Warehouse Co.—Investigation,* 318 I.C.C. 345, the operations performed by two purported shippers' agents, each ostensibly engaged in terminal operations at the termini of an interstate barge movement, were found to constitute a complete freight forwarding service jointly provided to the general public for compensation without appropriate authority and in violation of the act, even though no formal agency relation existed between them. The second decision, No. FF–C–4, *American Freight Forwarding Corp.* v. *Konlon and Walder,* 318 I.C.C. 507, found the combined operations of a pseudo-exempt shippers' association and certain other persons to be a single jointly conducted common carrier freight forwarder service subject to economic regulation. It was pointed out that an association of shippers of the type recognized by section 402(c) as beyond the pale of the regulatory provisions of part IV of the act must possess, as an essential attribute, the quality of subordination; i.e., the association must at all times act solely at the request, and under the direction, and for the account and benefit of its members. The effective date of the cease and desist order entered against all respondents has been postponed pending appeal to the courts.

ENFORCEMENT ACTIVITIES

During fiscal year 1963, a total of 895 court enforcement actions relating to motor carrier operations were concluded, 451 of which involved "gray area operations," as follows:

   (a) 258—undisguised unauthorized operations;
   (b) 152—alleged vehicle leasing arrangements;
   (c) 9—so-called buy and sell arrangements;
   (d) 10—alleged cooperative associations;
   (e) 22—arrangements designed to defeat the lawful rates.

In these 451 gray area cases, shippers also were included as defendants in 103 cases. In 168 of these gray area cases, the carrier defendant held operating authority of some type from the Commission and in 283 cases the carrier-defendant held no such authority. The proceedings involved criminal prosecutions in 408 instances, and a total of $359,000 in fines was assessed. The other 43 cases were civil actions in which injunctions were sought to prohibit the operations.

In addition to the 451 gray area court proceedings there was a considerable number of proceedings before the Commission itself to determine the lawfulness of operations and to order a cessation of operations found to be unlawful.

A number of proceedings have been instituted by the Commission against organizations claiming to operate as a cooperative shippers association or as a shipper's agent. In a number of such proceedings, the Commission found the organization to be engaged in unlawful freight forwarder service and issued a cease and desist order.

Although preferred attention was given to enforcement action against unauthorized transportation, the Commission also continued an active enforcement program in the area of safety of operations. Enforcement in this area relates primarily to motor and rail carriers but shippers also are included, particularly in the packaging and shipping of explosives and other dangerous articles. Approximately 425 motor carrier safety cases were concluded in the court for the year and approximately 390 rail carrier safety cases.

Enforcement activities in the field of assessment and collection of lawful rates continued. During the year over 50 cases of this type were concluded in the courts. In some instances, attempts were made to hide the practice of defeating the lawful rate. Such methods included falsely describing the property, false weights, false damage claims, and failure to abide by rules in the tariffs which governed the rate. Shippers frequently are active participants in such violations and when this can be established they are included as defendants.

As the year progressed, it was often necessary to divert enforcement personnel to special projects of major importance. Three enforcement attorneys were assigned to the hearing on the applications of the Pennsylvania Railroad and the New York Central Railroad to merge their properties. Another attorney devoted a substantial portion of his time to hearings involving piggyback service.

In addition, the enforcement staff of the Commission spent considerable time investigating complaints alleging racial discrimination. In all but a few instances, any actual racial discrimination by carrier employees was terminated when the practice was brought to the attention of the carrier management. When this type of offense was caused by persons or organizations other than the carrier and discontinuance could not be obtained by voluntary means, court actions were instituted to obtain injunctions and restrain the acts of all participants. All such actions concluded during the year resulted in judgments in favor of the Government.

Shortages of rail cars, particularly certain 40- and 50-foot boxcars, caused the Commission to issue a service order designed to return such cars as quickly as possible to the owning railroad. (See page 108.)

Initially many complaints were received alleging violations of this order, and 22 court proceedings were instituted. These actions substantially improved compliance with the order.

During the past 6 years we have more than doubled the number of enforcement cases disposed of in the courts, accomplishing this with only a modest staff increase. We believe, however, this staff has reached the maximum of its productive capacity, particularly since the schemes and devices to evade requirements of the act are becoming more subtle and sophisticated. The evasions are more difficult and time consuming to prove. As indicated, we also have had to divert some staff members to special projects. The problem of unlawful carriage and other law violations is far from solved. We recognize that continuing corrective measures must be applied and, in fact, increased. We consider that our enforcement staff is below the strength necessary to accomplish, completely, the compliance that is so necessary to effective regulation.

Summary of fiscal 1963 enforcement actions

	R-W-F	Motor	Total
Investigations:			
On hand beginning of year	225	870	1,095
Commenced during year	213	1,222	1,435
Concluded during year	248	1 1,199	1,447
Pending at end of year	190	893	1,083
Court proceedings:			
On hand beginning of year	75	528	603
Commenced during year	79	807	886
Concluded during year	77	856	933
Pending at end of year	77	479	556
Commission proceedings:			
On hand beginning of year	24	223	247
Commenced during year	2	146	148
Concluded during year	4	146	150
Pending at end of year	22	223	245
Applicant fitness:			
On hand beginning of year	0	2	2
Commenced during year	0	48	48
Concluded during year	0	50	50
Pending at end of year	0	0	0
Racial discrimination cases:	*Rail*	*Motor*	*Total*
On hand beginning of year	5	13	18
Commenced during year	0	1	1
Concluded during year	4	4	8
Pending at end of year	1	10	11

1 Includes completed final reports in the possession of the attorneys.

Railroad safety enforcement

Act	Court cases concluded	Fines imposed
Safety Appliance	311	$217,250
Hours of Service	38	19,800
Accident Reports	5	1,600
Signal Inspection	7	1,200
Locomotive Boiler Inspection	12	8,500
Total	373	248,350

Rail, water and forwarder enforcement
(not including safety)

Court cases concluded	Fines imposed
77	$152,300

Motor carrier enforcement
(including safety)

Court cases concluded	Fines imposed
856	$558,278

STANDARD TIME ZONES

No change was made during the year in our orders defining the limits of the standard time zones, although two petitions were received from groups located in the western part of South Dakota, seeking to extend the central standard time zone to the State's western border. North Dakota, except for its southwestern corner, is in the central standard time zone, but the zone boundary cuts South Dakota into two approximately equal parts. The principal contention of the western South Dakota petitioners in the mountain time zone is that they have a community of economic interests with residents of eastern South Dakota, North Dakota and the Minneapolis-St. Paul business area. To determine whether the entire States of North and South Dakota should be included within the central time zone, Division 3 reopened No. 10122, *Standard Time Zone Investigation.*

The Standard Time Act of 1918 vested authority for determining boundary lines between the different time zones in the Commission. Its requirement that railroad operations be conducted on standard time was obviously intended to protect the public against the confusion resulting from railroads conforming to local time which could vary from town to town. The railroads were the pioneers in adopting the zone system of hourly differences in standard time and, when the act was passed, exerted great influence on the standard of time observed by the areas or communities they served. But railroad time has lost most of its former significance. Contrary to the best interests of the public, the Standard Time Act now requires many railroads to observe for a good part of the year a different time from that used by most or all of their patrons and many of their own employees. For 5 or 6 months of the year, about half the population of the Nation shifts to daylight saving time, a standard of time an hour faster than railroad operating time. Under these conditions, the reasons for originally giving us the duty of determining the limits of the time zones have been lost since the important issues in time zone hearings have little bearing on the operations of common carriers.

Our experience amply demonstrates that any attempt to confine the application of the standard of time solely to federal matters or to interstate commerce, while local matters or intrastate commerce are governed by a different standard, is bound to result in chaos. Widespread variations in standard and daylight saving time, complicated by frequent time zone boundary disputes, differing standard-daylight switchover dates, and a myriad of local community options have combined to create bewildering uncertainty and confusion in the mind of the public. In the State of Iowa, for instance, only 19 cities observe daylight saving time and they begin their observance of fast time on seven different dates, ranging from April 28 to June 3. They return to standard time on six different dates during the period from August 25 to October 27. These chaotic variations in observance of daylight saving time throughout the country, together with the obsolete provisions of the Standard Time Act, emphasize more than ever the need for modern legislation based on broader public interest standards than those associated with transportation.

Since 1931 the Commission has urged enactment of measures to simplify the time problem. During this fiscal year several bills were introduced in both Houses of Congress to modernize and overhaul the 45-year old Standard Time Act and set up uniform timekeeping standards across the nation. The Senate Commerce Committee conducted hearings on a number of proposals seeking elimination of costly confusion in our timekeeping system. The salient features of the bills would carry out substantially the Commission's past recommendations to establish a uniform system of time standards and time measurement, and require observance of such time standards. Under the terms of the bills, an area within a zone observing daylight saving time would be transferred temporarily to the standard time zone immediately to the east. Thus, an area which has observed "central daylight saving time" in the summer months would now observe "eastern standard time," since each refers to the same time standard of the 75th degree of longitude. Uniform standard-daylight changeover dates would also be provided, and the standard time zone system would be extended to Alaska and Hawaii.

The time of the zones would be the exclusive time for the transaction of public business by all Federal departments and agencies and by all common carriers. Competitors of the railroads are subject to the present law, but largely ignore it since there is no power to compel compliance. Administrative and procedural safeguards (public hearings and judicial review) would be provided as well as enforcement provisions (injunctions, fines, and civil forfeitures) necessary to fully implement the proposals. So far as the dispute between daylight saving time and standard time is concerned, the bills provide sufficient flexibility to authorize advanced time in areas where it is desired and has been observed, while still retaining standard time in those areas, such as the South and parts of the Midwest where daylight saving time is considered a detriment. Its popularity in other areas, however, is attested by the fact that it is now being observed by more than 45 percent of the Nation's population.

ECONOMIC RESEARCH AND STATISTICS

Statistical and economic information, research, and advisory services required to carry out our regulatory responsibilities are obtained through our Bureau of Transport Economics and Statistics. This Bureau also administers the Commission's major statistical reporting systems and the RCA 301 computer installation, and publishes summaries of financial and operating statistics collected from carriers.

ECONOMIC RESEARCH

The expanding scope, volume, and complexity of the Commission's responsibilities have increased the need for carefully defined statistical information and economic research. With growing frequency, the basic issues in regulatory problems are found to be economic in nature.

During the year, there was a marked increase in the use of our research staff for preparation of analytical material, exhibits, and testimony to supplement the record in proceedings involving issues of general transportation importance and significant cases such as *Finance Docket Nos. 21989 and 21990*, the applications of the Pennsylvania Railroad and the New York Central Railroad for approval of merger.

Special studies and analyses included, for example, an estimate of the proportion of 1961 carload or truckload traffic that would be exempt from minimum-rate regulation under provisions of the Presidential recommendation embodied in H.R. 4700 and S. 1061, and of the proportion of regulated carrier revenue represented by the potentially exempt traffic; an analysis of the movement of ore through the St. Lawrence Seaway and North Atlantic ports; and development of a proposed revision of the Commission's commodity classification code compatible with (*a*) the Standard Industrial Classification, (*b*) the commodity code developed by the Bureau of the Budget, and (*c*) a classification plan formulated by the railroad industry.

Our recent annual reports to the Congress have noted the rapid development of trailer-on-flatcar (TOFC) or piggyback service. To meet the Commission's growing need for information concerning these operations as a basis for the solution of various regulatory problems, we instituted, in June 1962, an investigation in this area designated as *Docket Ex Parte No. 230, Substituted Service Charges and Practices of For-Hire Carriers and Freight Forwarders (Piggyback Service)*.

The services and experience of our economic research staff were used to collect and analyze information concerning the practices of the various modes of transportation participating in piggyback service. An additional project in this area is the development of adequate forms for the reporting of piggyback traffic data by carriers of the different modes.

Three economic and statistical studies of transportation problems completed during the fiscal year were considered of sufficient general interest to justify release for publication:

Statement No. 6301, *Fluctuations in Railroad Freight Traffic Compared with Production, Class I Railroads, 1958, 1959, and 1960.* This analysis (thirteenth of a series) compares changes in traffic volume and revenue with changes in commodity output. Comparisons are made between tons actually carried in a given year and "potential" tons, i.e., tons the railroads would have carried in that year if they had handled the same proportion as they did in 1947, the base year. The study also shows the absolute percentages of production which the railroads transported in several years, as well as the effects of tonnage changes on gross freight revenue.

Statement No. 6207, *Rail-Highway-Grade-Crossing Accidents for the Year Ended December 31, 1961.* This annual study indicates conditions existing in each accident, the number of deaths and injuries, and the trends for the past 10 years.

Accident Bulletin No. 130, *Summary and Analysis of Accidents of Railroads in the United States Subject to the Interstate Commerce Act, Calendar Year 1961.* Class I line-haul railroads, class I switching and terminal companies, and class II railroads are required to report to the Commission all collisions, derailments, or other accidents resulting in casualties to persons or in damage to equipment, track, or roadbed in excess of specified amounts. This publication contains the statistical summaries and analysis of these reports.

A monthly publication, *Transport Economics*, serves as a vehicle for the early release of statistical information and analytical comment concerning current operating and financial developments.

CARRIERS' REPORTS AND STATISTICS

The tabulation below classifies the 18,287 carriers and organizations subject to Commission statistical reporting requirements at the end of fiscal year 1963. During the year, these carriers and organizations filed a total of approximately 95,800 financial and operating reports, a reduction of about 3,900 under fiscal year 1962. There were 17,950 annual, 36,517 quarterly and monthly reports, and 41,297 railroad accident and supplemental reports of individual train and train-service accidents.

Number of carriers subject to Uniform System of Accounts and required
to file annual and periodic reports as of June 30, 1963 [1]_____ 4, 934

Number of carriers and organizations required to file annual reports but
not subject to Uniform System of Accounts :
    Car lines (companies which furnish cars for use on lines of rail-
roads) _____ 166
    Class II and class III motor carriers of passengers_____ 874
    Class III motor carriers of property_____ 12, 078
    Water carriers (less than $100,000 gross revenue)_____ 104
    Freight forwarders (less than $100,000 gross revenue)_____ 21
    Holding companies (motor)_____ 23
    Street electric lines_____ 5
    Rate bureaus and organizations_____ 82

    Total _____ 13, 353

    Grand total_____ 18, 287

[1] A listing by class of carrier is shown in appendix I.

The above table reflects a net decrease of about 350 in the total number of carriers subject to our reporting requirements.

During the year, we continued our review of reporting requirements, keeping in mind the desirability of reducing the paperwork burden on carriers where possible. A comprehensive investigation and analysis of the frequency requirement for rail wage and employment data reported by class I railroads resulted in the issuance of an order, April 26, 1963, continuing monthly reporting. The dispute and threatened work stoppage over railroad operating rules emphasized the importance of currency in these statistics. Water carriers, other than class C, subject to regulation under the act, are now required to report quarterly the number of revenue ton-miles of service. Revision of seven reports of operating statistics filed quarely by class I railroads was initiated with the view toward reducing the reporting burden on these carriers.

Other reporting activities under investigation at the end of the fiscal year included revision of the Freight Commodity Classifications (Docket No. 34206), the development of procedures for reporting of TOFC traffic, and the occupational classifications used for railroad wage statistics.

We continued our program of publishing statistics derived from the reports filed by carriers, including *Transport Statistics in the United States*, quarterly releases showing results of carrier operations, monthly reports of railroad employment and wages and of railroad accidents, with a quarterly cumulative supplement of the latter, and motor carrier and railroad freight commodity statistics on an annual basis. Carrier reports are made available to the public in the public reference room of the Bureau of Transport Economics and Statistics.

The necessity for adequate statistics prompted a new quarterly series for class II motor carriers of property. A quarterly publication under consideration at the end of the fiscal year is designed to present useful statistics exclusively related to class I motor common carriers of general freight, similar to existing Statement No. Q–800, which contains data related to all class I motor carriers of property. The projected publication became practicable with the installation in January 1963, of the RCA 301 electronic data processing equipment. Addition of these publications will extend quarterly statistical coverage to all segments of the regulated motor carrier transportation industry, except those in class III which file only annual reports.

Some improvement in timely filing of reports occurred during fiscal year 1963, compared to fiscal year 1962, and it was necessary to refer the records of only 225 carriers, predominantly motor, for enforcement action, compared with 412 delinquent carriers in 1962.

STATISTICAL ADVISORY SERVICES

The increasing frequency of the use of modern statistical methods by parties to proceedings and the continuing need for reliable statistical data and estimates have given added significance to statistical advisory services rendered by the staff. This group advises, applies, plans, designs, and interprets sampling and other statistical techniques to meet special needs, in addition to administering the continuous rail carload waybill sample and other statistical programs.

Typical of such special services was a professional appraisal of conflicting testimony on statistical techniques and inferences from data presented in a rate proceeding. Advice and guidance in regard to regression analyses and probability sampling have been of value in connection with a number of administrative and regulatory matters.

TRAFFIC ANALYSIS

The rail carload waybill sample provides on a continuing basis significant information on the characteristics of rail carload traffic. We published a number of studies derived from the waybill sample:

Statement MS–1, *Distribution of Freight Traffic and Revenue Averages by Commodity Classes*, shows by commodity groups and classes, for the entire United States, the number of carloads, tons, revenues, average tons per car, average miles per ton, average miles per car, average revenue per 100 pounds, average revenue per car, average revenue per car-mile, and average revenue per ton-mile.

Statement TD–1, *Territorial Distribution, Traffic and Revenue by Commodity Classes*, contains data similar to those in Statement MS–1 on the movement of traffic within and between major territories. In addition, Statement TD–1 shows short-line ton-miles and short-line car-miles.

Statements MB–1, 2, 3, 4, and 5, *Mileage Block Distributions*. This series of publications is designed to analyze rail carload traffic in terms of length of haul. Carloads, tons, revenue, short-line ton-miles, short-line car-miles, average tons per car, average short-line haul, and average revenues per hundredweight, per car, per short-line car-mile and per short-line ton-mile data are distributed by commodity, territorial movement, and type of rate for selected mileage or short-line length of haul blocks. Statement MB–1 covers data for products of agriculture, MB–2 for animals and products, MB–3 for products of mines, MB–4 for products of forests, and MB–5 for manufactures and miscellaneous and forwarder traffic. MB–6, *Mileage Block Progressions*, shows similar data for each commodity class for a lesser number of mileage blocks than those presented in the other MB publications.

Statements SS–1, 2, 3, 4, 5, and 6, *State-to-State Distribution*, show data for the same characteristics as shown in TD–1. Each publication covers commodity classes in a major commodity group or groups, similarly to the MB publications. SS–7 shows tons of freight originated and terminated by State and by commodity class.

Statements TC–1, 2, and 3, *Distributions by Type of Car*. Publications in this series develop rail carload traffic charactertistics in terms of the type of car equipment used. Statement TC–1 shows the number of carloads by commodity class, type of car, and mileage block. Statement TC–2 contains data for the number of carloads by commodity class, type of car, and weight category. Statement TC–3 shows the number of carloads by commodity class, type of car, and territorial movement.

Statement MS–2A, *Petroleum Products*, publishes the number of carloads and tons for selected petroleum products by movement between Petroleum Administration Districts.

Statement RI–1, *Indexes of Average Freight Rates*, is designed to estimate the annual changes in average freight rates for selected commodity classes and groups due to changes in tariffs. Index numbers are also developed for territorial and for interstate and intrastate movements. This series covers the years from 1947, using 1950 as the base period.

Statement MS–2, *Distribution of Petroleum Products by Petroleum Administration Districts*. This publication contains 3-month totals for characteristics similar to those in Statement MS–2A.

A number of special traffic studies and analyses were made from the waybill sample for various rail merger proceedings. For example, a study based on a probability sample drawn from the waybill file was undertaken to develop information on the practices of shippers and carriers in routing carload traffic. Some of the data were presented by staff members in the Pennsylvania-New York Central merger case mentioned previously.

At year end, a special study of piggyback (TOFC) traffic contained in the carload waybill sample was being designed and tested as a basis for analyses of TOFC operations.

A new publication, *Deep-Sea Domestic Waterborne Traffic, 1956–1960*, shows ton-miles and average haul per ton for dry cargo and tanker ships, by origin and destination trade areas and by movements between trade areas.

Important developments in data processing operations are reported at page 22 in the section relating to management activities.

LAURENCE K. WALRATH, *Chairman*
ABE McGREGOR GOFF, *Vice Chairman*
HOWARD G. FREAS
KENNETH H. TUGGLE
EVERETT HUTCHINSON
RUPERT L. MURPHY
CHARLES A. WEBB
CLYDE E. HERRING
JOHN W. BUSH
WILLIAM H. TUCKER
PAUL J. TIERNEY

APPENDIX A

OFFICE AND BUREAU ORGANIZATION

There are 3 staff offices and 10 bureaus, the heads of which report to the Chairman. However, the Managing Director and the seven regulatory bureaus report through the Vice Chairman; while each of the three proceedings bureaus reports through the Chairman of the Division responsible for its work; and the Secretary and General Counsel report directly to the Chairman.

Officials

(Updated to November 1, 1963)

Office of the Chairman :
    Legislative Counsel_____ Robert T. Wallace
    Congressional Liaison Officer_____ Hiram H. Spicer
Office of the Managing Director :
    Managing Director_____ Bernard F. Schmid
    Assistant Managing Director_____ Ernest Weiss
    Budget Officer_____ J. Neil Ryan
    Director of Personnel_____ Curtis F. Adams
    Chief of Section of Administrative Services_____ John A. Nolin
    Chief of Section of Systems Development_____ Robert J. Hartel
Office of the Secretary :
    Secretary _____ Harold D. McCoy
    Assistant Secretary_____ Bertha F. Armes
    Public Information Officer_____ Warner L. Baylor
    Chief, Reference Service_____ Walter W. Dwyer
    Librarian _____ Glennie M. Norman
Office of the General Counsel :
    General Counsel_____ Robert W. Ginnane
    Deputy General Counsel_____ I. K. Hay
Bureau of Accounts :
    Director _____ Matthew Paolo
    Assistant Director_____ Bernard V. Moffett
    Assistant Director_____ Howard L. Domingus
Bureau of Finance :
    Director _____ Irving J. Raley
    Assistant Director_____ Thaddeus W. Forbes
Bureau of Inquiry and Compliance :
    Director _____ Asa J. Merrill
    Assistant Director_____ Bernard A. Gould
    Assistant Director_____ Marcus L. Meyer
Bureau of Motor Carriers :
    Director _____ Herbert Qualls
    Assistant Director_____ George A. Meyer

Officials—Continued

Bureau of Operating Rights:
    Director _____ Bertram E. Stillwell
    Assistant Director_____ Sheldon Silverman
Bureau of Rates and Practices:
    Director _____ Alvin L. Corbin
    Assistant Director_____ Charlie H. Johns
    Assistant Director_____ Harold A. Downs
Bureau of Safety and Service:
    Director _____ Charles W. Taylor
    Assistant Director_____ Robert D. Pfahler
    Assistant Director and Chief of Section of Car   Paul J. Reider
        Service.
    Assistant Director and Chief of Section of Loco-   John A. Hall
        motive Inspection (Director of Locomotive In-
        spection).
    Assistant Director and Chief of Section of Rail-   H. R. Longhurst
        road Safety.
Bureau of Traffic:
    Director _____ Edward H. Cox
    Assistant Director_____ Robert Newel
    Assistant Director and Chief of Section of   Grayson B. Robinson
        Tariffs.
    Assistant Director and Chief of Section of Rates   Radway R. Gibbs
        and Informal Cases.
Bureau of Transport Economics and Statistics:
    Director _____ Edward Margolin
    Assistant Director_____ Robert G. Rhodes
Bureau of Water Carriers and Freight Forwarders:
    Director _____ Lee R. Nowell
    Assistant Director_____ Raymond Krebill

Office of the Managing Director

The Managing Director is responsible for the day-to-day administration of the Commission and management of its operations.

Office of the Secretary

The Secretary is the official through whom the Commission, its Divisions, individual Commissioners, boards of employees, joint boards, and examiners issue their orders and decisions. He is custodian of the seal and records of the Commission and is responsible for the proper documentation of Commission decisions, procedures, and other transactions. Pursuant to the Rules of Practice, he is responsible for processing the official documents pending before the Commission and for service on parties to formal proceedings. The Secretary's Office is the medium through which decisions, orders, statements, releases, and other information, including individual votes contained in the Commission's minutes, are made available to the press and public.

Office of the General Counsel

The Office of the General Counsel furnishes general legal advisory service to the Commission in all matters involving its functions and activities under the act and other statutes administered by it and concerning other laws or statutes

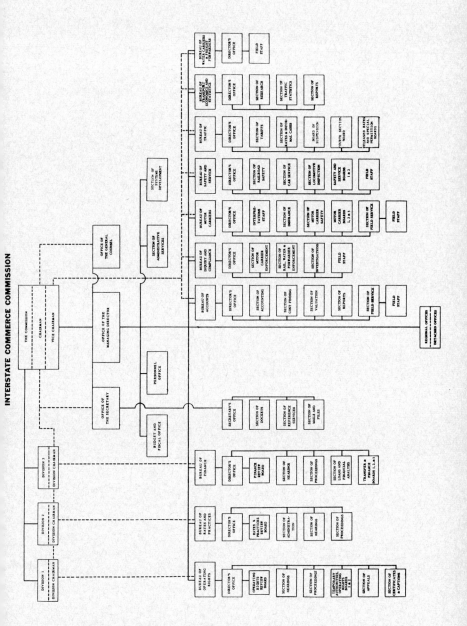

applicable to or affecting the Commission; and defends, on behalf of the Commission, in all court proceedings to set aside, enjoin, cancel, or annul orders of the Commission.

Bureau of Accounts

The Bureau of Accounts performs the accounting, cost finding and valuation functions necessary in the regulatory work of the Commission to bring about accurate, uniform and comprehensive disclosure of financial data by carriers in the public interest. This includes the development of uniform systems of accounts, valuation regulations, regulations governing the destruction of carrier records, and other related regulations for all transportation companies subject to the act; examining the accounts, records and financial statements filed by such companies to ascertain compliance with Commission accounting and related regulations; development of equitable and reasonable depreciation rates for carrier property; preparing studies and analyses of the costs and revenues of transportation services of carriers subject to the act; maintaining inventories of railroad and pipeline properties, and developing property valuation data; preparing accounting, cost and valuation data for use in proceedings before the Commission; rendering assistance in accounting matters in finance proceedings; and analyzing cost evidence presented by other parties in rate proceedings.

Bureau of Finance

The Bureau of Finance handles proceedings involving rail carriers, motor carriers, water carriers, and freight forwarders, under the various sections of the act, relative to: authority to construct, acquire or abandon lines of a railroad or the operation thereof; proposed discontinuance or changes in the operation by railroads of trains or ferries; approval for motor carriers, water carriers, and railroads to enter into contracts and agreements for the pooling or division of traffic and earnings; authority to consolidate, merge, transfer ownership, or acquire control of carriers, and when directly related to such authority the granting of certificates or permits to motor carriers in connection therewith; authority for a railroad to acquire trackage rights over, or joint ownership or use of railroad lines and terminals; ordering the use by one railroad of terminal facilities of another; authority to issue securities or to assume obligation and liability with respect to securities of others; authority to sell securities without competitive bidding; authority to alter or modify outstanding securities and obligations; transfers of brokers' licenses and of certificates and permits of motor carriers, water carriers, and permits of freight forwarders; authority to hold position of officer or director of more than one railroad; the guaranty of loans to railroads in financing additions or betterments or other capital expenditures, or for the financing of expenditures for maintenance of property; and formal investigations concerning possible violations of the act relating to the foregoing subjects; and, under provisions of the Uniform Bankruptcy Act, the approval of plans of reorganization, the submission thereof to creditors and stockholders for acceptance or rejection, the recommendation of formulas for the segregation of earnings, the ratification of trustees, the fixing of maximum limits of allowances to trustees and other parties in interest, and the authorization of persons, including protective committees, to solicit and act under proxies, authorizations or deposit agreements in connection with railroad reorganization or receivership proceedings.

Bureau of Inquiry and Compliance

The Bureau of Inquiry and Compliance investigates violations, prosecutes in court and assists the Department of Justice in prosecuting civil and criminal proceedings arising under all parts of the act (except violations of the Safety Acts which are handled by the Section of Railroad Safety, Bureau of Safety and Service), and related acts such as the Elkins Act, the Clayton Anti-Trust Act and the Transportation of Explosives Act. When specifically authorized by the Commission, a division thereof or the Vice Chairman, in any particular case or class of cases, participates in Commission proceedings for the purpose of developing the facts and issues.

Bureau of Motor Carriers

The Bureau of Motor Carriers performs duties in connection with the Commission's programs involving the regulation of motor carriers and brokers under part II of the act insofar as they involve: initiating and administering the rules and regulations governing the filing and approval of security or insurance for the protection of the public and designation of agents for service of process; initiating and administering safety regulations concerning qualifications and maximum hours of service of employees and safety of operation and equipment of all for-hire and private carriers in interstate or foreign commerce; initiating and administering the rules and regulations governing the lease and interchange of vehicles by motor carriers; investigating and reporting on serious accidents and the transportation of explosives and other dangerous articles; initiating and administering regulations relating to the safe transportation of migratory workers; inspecting the operations and records of the carriers and others in the field to inform them of the requirements of the act and regulations and to discover unauthorized operations or violations with regard to tariffs, rebates, accounts, insurance, annual reports, extensions of credit, or unsafe operating practices; and issuing informal interpretations of Commission's certificates, permits and regulations affecting motor carrier operations.

Bureau of Operating Rights

The Bureau of Operating Rights performs duties in connection with the Commission's proceedings involving motor common and contract carriers, brokers of motor carrier transportation, water carriers, and freight forwarders, under the various sections of the act, relative to operating authority matters, provisions and exemptions, including investigations looking to the prescription of rules and regulations governing operations of such carriers; formal complaints and investigations concerning failure of carriers to comply with the act or any requirement established thereunder, with respect to operating practices under the jurisdiction of Division 1; the suspension, change or revocation of certificates, permits and licenses; and the granting of temporary authorities for motor carrier service. Operations are conducted on functional bases by and through the Director's Office, the Sections, the Review Board, the Temporary Authorities Board, and Operating Rights Boards Nos. 1 and 2. The Director's Office is responsible for, among other things, maintenance of the case processing and other statistical records; handling of correspondence; official travel authorizations; Joint Board appointments; case status information; special studies and projects; clerical support for the scheduling and postponement of hearings and modified procedure; extensions of dates for filing pleadings: and the handling of uncontested requests for authority under the Deviation Rules.

Bureau of Rates and Practices

The Bureau of Rates and Practices performs duties in connection with Commission proceedings involving rail carriers, motor carriers, water carriers, and freight forwarders, under the various sections of the act, relative to rates, fares, charges, and practices and relief from antitrust laws relative to collective ratemaking agreements; and conducts proceedings arising under a number of miscellaneous provisions of the act and other acts such as the Railway Mail Service Pay Act, Railroad Retirement Act, etc., which require Commission findings and determinations.

Bureau of Safety and Service

The Bureau of Safety and Service performs duties in connection with the Commission's programs respecting: (1) car service provisions of the Act which include preparing proposed regulations and emergency orders regarding the use, control, supply, movement, distribution, interchange, and return of locomotives, cars and other vehicles used in the transportation of property; (2) the Locomotive Inspection Act, to promote safety of employees and travelers on railroads, making the inspections to determine that locomotives are in proper condition, safe to operate and comply with the rules and regulations, and to determine that the required inspections of locomotives are made by the carriers and the defects are repaired before the locomotive is returned to service; (3) the Safety Appliance Act, the Ash Pan Act, the Hours of Service Act, Accident Reports, Block Signal Resolution, Power Brake Law of 1958, etc., relating to investigation of safety appliances or systems intended to promote safety of railway operation; and (4) the transportation of explosives and other dangerous articles by rail, highway and water.

Bureau of Traffic

The Bureau of Traffic performs duties relative to filing of schedules or tariffs of rates, fares and charges, and of transportation and protective service contracts, of carriers subject to the act; the suspension of tariff provisions pending investigation of their lawfulness; and the administration of the long-and-short-haul and aggregates-of-intermediate-rate provisions of the act; confers and corresponds with carriers, shippers and other interested parties, expressing its views, concerning the application of rates and other tariff provisions, as a possible means of settling controversies; processes applications of carriers requesting authority to make reparation on past shipments; and advises with, and acts as consultant to, the Commission and its staff with respect to tariff policies, rate adjustments, general rate investigations, tariff interpretations, and ratemaking principles.

Bureau of Transport Economics and Statistics

The Bureau of Transport Economics and Statistics performs economic, statistical and related analytical work concerning transportation, necessary to the Commission in the performance of its functions to foster sound economic conditions consistent with the National Transportation Policy. In performing this work, the bureau advises the Commission on economic matters and develops and prepares for publication data concerning such matters as finances, physical characteristics, operations, and traffic consist of the various carriers, as well as statistical and economic evaluations of the effects of the Commission's regulatory policies on carriers, shippers, consumers, and the national economy, and the effects of development pertaining to the latter on the Commission's responsibilities.

Bureau of Water Carriers and Freight Forwarders

The Bureau of Water Carriers and Freight Forwarders performs duties in connection with the Commission's programs involving the regulation of water carriers, freight forwarders and rate bureaus under parts III and IV, and section 5a of the act. It processes the applications (1) of water carriers for temporary authorities and exemptions, and (2) of common carriers for approval of collective ratemaking agreements. The bureau inspects the operations of water carriers, freight forwarders and rate bureaus to inform them of the requirements of the act and Commission regulations and to discover unauthorized operations or violations with regard to tariffs, rebates, accounts, annual reports, extensions of credit, or procedures for collective ratemaking under approved agreements.

Field Organization

Programs conducted by the field staff, which is approximately 33 percent of the total staff of the Commission, are largely in the area of enforcement and compliance. They include inspection of carrier accounts and other records for compliance with regulations, inspection of equipment and facilities, investigation of accidents, and investigation of complaints from shippers, other carriers and the general public. The work of the field staff is discussed in the chapters on "Accounting, Cost Finding, and Valuation"; Enforcement and Compliance"; "Promotion of Safety"; and "Service and Facilities." Directory of ICC field offices follows.

DIRECTORY OF INTERSTATE COMMERCE COMMISSION FIELD OFFICES (REVISED TO REFLECT REORGANIZATION OF FIELD APPROVED BY THE COMMISSION ON SEPTEMBER 20, 1963)

Region	Territory	Regional Managers and addresses
1	Massachusetts	Martin E. Foley, Regional Manager, 15 Court Square, Boston, Mass., 02108.
	Maine	
	New Hampshire	6 Campbell Street, Lebanon, N.H., 03766.
	Vermont	305 Post Office and Courthouse, 76 Pearl Street, Portland, Maine, 04112. Mail address: P. O. Box 167, P.S.S.
	Rhode Island	
	New York	
	New Jersey	187 Westminster Street, Providence, R.I., 02903.
	Connecticut	
		338 Federal Building, 436 Dwight Street, Springfield, Mass., 01103.
		Room 1111, 346 Broadway, New York, N.Y., 10013.
		518 Federal Building, Maiden Lane and Broadway, Albany, N.Y., 12207.
		215 Post Office and Courthouse, Binghamton, N.Y., 13902.
		324 Post Office Building, 121 Ellicott Street, Buffalo, N.Y., 14203.

DIRECTORY OF FIELD OFFICES—Continued

Region	Territory	Regional Managers and addresses
		223 Federal Building, 135 High Street, Hartford, Conn., 06101.
		363 Industrial Office Building, 1060 Broad Street, Newark, N.J., 07102.
		1025 Chimes Building, 109 West Onondaga Street, Syracuse, N.Y., 13202.
		410 Post Office Building, 402 East State Street, Trenton, N.J., 08608.
2	Pennsylvania	Fred E. Cochran, Regional Manager, 900
	Maryland	Customhouse, Second and Chestnut Streets
	Delaware	Philadelphia, Pa., 19106.
	District of Columbia	312 Appraisers Stores Building, 103 South
	Ohio	Gay Street, Baltimore, Md., 21202.
	Virginia	218 Central Industrial Building, 100 North
	West Virginia	Cameron Street, Harrisburg, Pa., 17101.

250 Post Office Building, 600 Granby Street Norfolk, Va., 23501.

10–502 Federal Building, 400 North Eighth Street, Richmond, Va., 23240.

215 Campbell Avenue SW., Roanoke, Va., 24011.

206–B Post Office Building, East Main and Baptist Streets, Salisbury, Md., 21801.

309 Post Office Building, North Washington Avenue and Linden Street, Scranton, Pa., 18503.

12th and Constitution Avenue NW., Washington, D.C., 20423.

236 New Post Office Building, 85 Marconi Boulevard, Columbus, Ohio, 43215.

3202 Federal Office Building, 500 Quarrier Street, Charleston, W. Va., 25301.

753 Post Office and Courthouse, Cincinnati, Ohio, 45202.

435 Federal Building, 215 Superior Avenue NE., Cleveland, Ohio, 44114.

303 Victory Building, 212 Ninth Street, Pittsburgh, Pa., 15222.

5234 Federal Building, 234 Summit Street, Toledo, Ohio, 43604.

531 Hawley Building, 1025 Main Street, Wheeling, W. Va., 26003.

610 Schween Wagner Building, 125 West Commerce Street, Youngstown, Ohio, 44503.

DIRECTORY OF FIELD OFFICES—Continued

Region	Territory	Regional Managers and addresses
3	Georgia Florida Alabama North Carolina South Carolina Kentucky Tennessee Mississippi	James B. Weber, Regional Manager, 680 West Peachtree Street NW., Atlanta, Ga., 30308. 1325 City Federal Building, 2026 Second Avenue, North, Birmingham, Ala., 35203. Room 206, 327 North Tryon Street, Charlotte, N.C., 28202. 509 Federal Office Building, 901 Sumter St., Columbia, S.C., 29201. Room 3, 4112 Aurora Street, Coral Gables, Fla., 33146. 428 Post Office Building, 311 West Monroe, Jacksonville, Fla., 32201. Mail address: Post Office Box 4969. 317 U.S. Court and Customhouse, Mobile, Ala., 36602. 401 Oberlin Road, Raleigh, N.C. Mail address: Post Office Box 10885, Cameron Village Station, Raleigh, N.C., 27605. Room 154, 300 Tampa Street, Tampa, Fla., 33602. 706 U.S. Courthouse, 801 Broadway, Nashville, Tenn., 37203. 320 Post Office and Courthouse, Jackson, Miss., 39201. 207 Exchange Building, 147 North Upper Street, Lexington, Ky., 40507. 426 Post Office Building, 601 West Broadway, Louisville, Ky., 40202. 390 Federal Office Building, 167 North Main Street, Memphis, Tenn., 38103.
4	Indiana Illinois Michigan Wisconsin Minnesota North Dakota South Dakota	George L. Wilmot, Regional Manager, 852 Customhouse, 610 South Canal Street, Chicago, Ill., 60607. 1439 Book Building, 1249 Washington Boulevard, Detroit, Mich., 48226. 308 Federal Building, Fort Wayne, Ind., 46802. Eighth Floor, Century Building, 36 South Pennsylvania Street, Indianapolis, Ind., 46204. 221 Federal Building, 325 West Allegan Street, Lansing, Mich., 48923. 719 Meyers Building, Fifth and Washington Streets, Springfield, Ill., 62701

DIRECTORY OF FIELD OFFICES—Continued

Region	Territory	Regional Managers and addresses
		448 Federal Building and U.S. Courthouse, 110 South Fourth Street, Minneapolis, Minn., 55401.
		425 Post Office Building, Duluth, Minn., 55801.
		116 South Plaza Building, 1621 South University Drive, Fargo, N. Dak., 58101. Mail address: Post Office Box 26.
		214 North Hamilton Street, Room 100, Madison, Wis., 53703.
		511 Cawker Building, 108 West Wells Street, Milwaukee, Wis., 53203.
		Karcher Building, 366½ South Pierre Street, Pierre, S. Dak., 57501. Mail address: Post Office Box 94.
5	Texas Oklahoma Arkansas Louisiana Iowa Missouri Nebraska Kansas	Bernard H. English, Regional Manager, 816 Texas and Pacific Building, Throckmorton and Lancaster Streets, Fort Worth, Tex., 76102.
		918 Tyler Street, Amarillo, Tex., 79101.
		3–101 Mart Building, 500 South Ervay Street, Dallas, Tex., 75201.
		203 U.S. Courthouse, El Paso, Tex., 79901.
		8610 Federal Building and U.S. Courthouse, 515 Rusk Avenue, Houston, Tex., 77061. Mail address: Post Office Box 61212.
		705 Federal Building, 106 South 15th Street, Omaha, Nebr., 68102.
		304 Post Office Building, Sioux City, Iowa, 51101.
		3248 Federal Building, 1520 Market Street, St. Louis, Mo., 63103.
		309 Federal Building, Topeka, Kans., 66603.
		906 Schweiter Building, 106 North Main Street, Wichita, Kans., 67202.
		1100 Federal Office Building, 911 Walnut Street, Kansas City, Mo., 64106.
		235 Post Office Building, Fourth and Perry Streets, Davenport, Iowa, 52801.
		227 Federal Office Building, Fifth Street and Court Avenue, Des Moines, Iowa, 50309.
		315 U.S. Courthouse and Post Office Building, Lincoln, Nebr., 68508.
		2519 Federal Office Building, Little Rock, Ark., 72201.

DIRECTORY OF FIELD OFFICES—Continued

Region	Territory	Regional Managers and addresses
		709 Masonic Temple, 333 St. Charles Avenue, New Orleans, La., 70130.
		4019 Federal Office Building, 200 Northwest Fourth, Oklahoma City, Okla., 73102.
		583 Post Office and Courthouse, 615 East Houston Street, San Antonio, Tex., 78206. Mail address: Post Office Box 628.
		625 Ricou-Brewster Building, 425 Milam Street, Shreveport, La., 71102. Mail address: Post Office Box 1784.
6	Oregon Washington Idaho Montana Wyoming Alaska	N. Thomas Harris, Regional Manager, 538 Pittock Block, 921 Southwest Washington Street, Portland, Oreg., 97205.
		203 Eastman Building, 105 North Eighth Street, Boise, Idaho, 83702.
		6130 Arcade Building, 1319 Second Avenue, Seattle, Wash., 98101.
		401 Post Office Building, West 914 Riverside Avenue, Spokane, Wash., 99201.
		318 Post Office and Courthouse, Billings, Mont., 59101.
		Civic Center Building, Great Falls, Mont., 59401.
		Room 51-52 Federal Building, Anchorage, Alaska, 99501. Mail address: Post Office Box 1532.
7	Arizona California Nevada Colorado Utah New Mexico	Phillip J. Brannigan, Regional Manager, 602 Sheldon Building, 9 First Street, San Francisco, Calif., 94105.
		212 Telegraph Building, 11 West Telegraph Street, Carson City, Nev., 89701.
		1819 West Sixth Street, Los Angeles, Calif., 90057.
		5045 Federal Building, 230 North First Avenue, Phoenix, Ariz., 85025.
		502 Denham Building, 635 18th Street, Denver, Colo., 80202.
		109 U. S. Courthouse, Fourth and Gold Streets, Albuquerque, N. Mex., 87101.
		114 Atlas Building, 36½ West Second South Street, Salt Lake City, Utah, 84101.

APPENDIX B

ANNUAL RECEIPTS AND DISPOSITIONS OF FORMAL PROCEEDINGS CASES, FISCAL YEARS 1960, 1961, 1962, 1963, 1964*

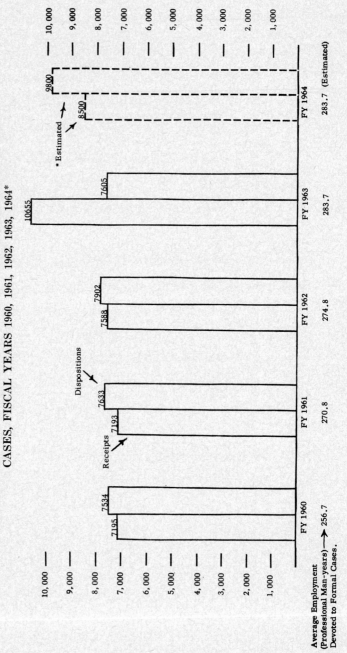

200

AVERAGE ELAPSED TIME REQUIRED TO DISPOSE OF FORMAL
PROCEEDINGS CASES, FISCAL YEARS 1960, 1961, 1962, 1963

	8 Months	7 Months	6 Months	5 Months	4 Months	3 Months	2 Months	1 Month
FY 1960	8.6							
FY1961	8.8							
FY1962	7.8							
FY 1963		6.9						

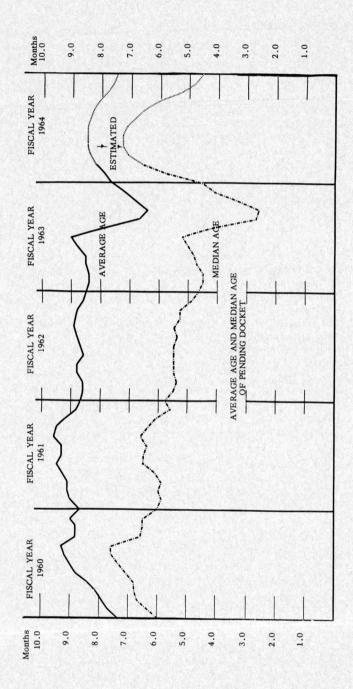

APPENDIX C

ADVISORY COMMITTEES REORGANIZED PURSUANT TO EXECUTIVE ORDER NO. 11007 DATED FEBRUARY 26, 1962, A DESCRIPTION OF THE FUNCTIONS OF EACH COMMITTEE, THE DATES OF MEETINGS HELD DURING PERIOD JULY 1, 1962–JUNE 30, 1963, AND THE NAMES AND AFFILIATIONS OF COMMITTEE MEMBERS AS OF JUNE 30, 1963, AND EXPIRATION DATES OF THE COMMITTEE

I. THE OIL PIPELINE ADVISORY COMMITTEE ON VALUATION

A. *Purpose.*—The committee was established to cooperate with the Bureau of Accounts in valuation matters generally, in the interest of assisting the Commission in more effectively performing its valuation work with respect to oil pipeline companies, and more specifically, in the area of collecting, summarizing and considering data used in the development of annual price indices. The committee serves in an advisory capacity, only, and completely independent and final evaluation of committee deliberations is made by the Bureau of Accounts.

B. *Dates of meetings.*—The committee held meetings on April 24, 1962, November 6, 1962, and May 7, 1963.

C. *Membership.*—The committee consists of oil pipeline company representatives selected for membership by the Bureau of Accounts, with representatives of the Bureau serving as chairman and secretary. Committee members serve at the pleasure of the Bureau for an indefinite period; however, continued existence of the committee is currently limited to July 1, 1964. There follows a list of the present committee members and their addresses as shown according to the Commission's records:

Officers

Chairman: Howard L. Domingus, Assistant Director, Bureau of Accounts, Interstate Commerce Commission, Washington, D.C., 20423.
Secretary: William E. Sturges, Valuation Engineer, Bureau of Accounts, Interstate Commerce Commission, Washington, D.C., 20423.

Members

F. W. Abbott, Portland Pipe Line Corp., 335 Forest Avenue, Portland, Maine

Charles E. Alexander, Atlantic Pipe Line Co., 260 South Broad Street, Philadelphia, Pa.

Vern E. Archer, Wolverine Pipe Line Co., 8500 North Michigan Road, Indianapolis, Ind.

E. P. Baker, Pure Transportation Co., 200 East Golf Road, Palatine, Ill.

C. V. Baxter, Salt Lake Pipe Line Co., Post Office Box 117, Salt Lake City, Utah

G. D. Beard, The Texas Pipe Line Co., Houston, Tex.

H. C. Bloomfield, Humble Pipe Line Co., Houston, Tex.

Members—Continued

W. K. Borland, Plantation Pipe Line Co., Post Office Box 1743, Atlanta, Ga.

Donald R. Casisky, Cooperative Refinery Association, Post Office Box 7305, Kansas City, Mo.

C. S. Cone, Jr., Magnolia Pipe Line Co., Post Office Box 900, Dallas, Tex.

George W. Conrad, Gulf Refining Co., Post Office Drawer 2100, Houston, Tex.

C. M. Cotten, Sinclair Pipe Line Co., Sinclair Building, Independence, Kans.

W. S. Deppen, Marathon Pipe Line Co., Findlay, Ohio

W. D. Farr, Pure Transportation Co., 200 East Golf Road, Palatine, Ill.

J. R. Fredenberger, Service Pipe Line Co., Tulsa, Okla.

L. E. Frensley, Magnolia Pipe Line Co., Post Office Box 900, Dallas, Tex.

G. D. Griffee, Okan Pipeline Co., 1350 South Boulder Avenue, Tulsa, Okla.

P. H. Gutknecht, Jayhawk Pipeline Corp., Denver Club Building, Denver, Colo.

J. P. Harshfield, Phillips Petroleum Co., Pipe Line Department, Bartlesville, Okla.

R. E. Higginbotham, Oklahoma Mississippi River Products Line, Inc., Post Office Box 2139, Tulsa, Okla.

C. R. Hodges, Texas Eastern Transmission Corp., Post Office Box 1612, Shreveport, La.

F. S. Howard, Humble Pipe Line Co., Post Office Box 2220, Houston, Tex.

C. Wilkes Keith, Service Pipe Line Co., Tulsa, Okla.

J. G. Kline, Atlantic Pipe Line Co., 260 South Broad Street, Philadelphia, Pa.

K. M. Leask, Trans Mountain Oil Pipe Line Corp., 400 East Broadway, Vancouver, British Columbia, Canada

Fred Lee, The Shell Pipe Line Corp., Houston, Tex.

J. J. Lowe, Ashland Pipe Line Co., Ashland, Ky.

E. F. Males, Mid-Valley Pipe Line Co., Post Office Box 2388, Longview, Tex.

J. D. Marshall, Continental Pipe Line Co., Ponca City, Okla.

Morgan Martin, Gulf Refining Co., Post Office Drawer 2100, Houston, Tex.

Alfred W. Martinelli, The Buckeye Pipe Line Co., 100 Buckeye Road, Macungie, Pa.

Earl A. Matheney, Mid-American Pipeline Co., Post Office Box 2401, Tulsa, Okla.

R. R. McDaniel, Chief Engineer, Southern Pacific Pipe Line, Inc., 610 South Main Street, Los Angeles, Calif.

G. S. McDonald, Phillips Petroleum Co., Bartlesville, Okla.

W. E. McKee, Sohio Pipe Line Co., Post Office Box 5774, Cleveland, Ohio

Stell Meador, Cities Service Pipe Line Co., Bartlesville, Okla.

J. G. Miranda, Michigan-Ohio Pipeline Corp., East Superior Street, Post Office Box 231, Alma, Mich.

C. K. Monroe, Shell Pipe Line Corp., Post Office Box 2648, Houston, Tex.

W. R. Nelson, Wyco Pipe Line Co., 910 South Michigan Avenue, Chicago, Ill.

R. J. Northway, Manager, Tax Department, Shell Pipe Line Corp., Post Office Box 2648, Houston, Tex.

John T. Osborn, Platte Pipe Line Co., 106 West 14th Street, Kansas City, Mo.

C. R. Perkins, Mid-Valley Pipe Line Co., Post Office Box 2388, Longview, Tex.

P. D. Phillips, Jr., Humble Pipe Line Co., Post Office Drawer 2220, Houston, Tex.

G. E. Pierce, The Buckeye Pipe Line Co., 30 Broad Street, New York, N.Y.

J. Arnold Pittman, Texas Eastern Transmission Corp., Post Office Box 1189, Memorial Professional Building, Houston, Tex.

Members—Continued

C. L. Place, Lakehead Pipe Line Co., 2206 East Fifth Street, Superior, Wis.

J. T. Robb, Great Lakes Pipe Line Co., Post Office Drawer 2239, Kansas City, Mo.

J. R. Sanders, Shamrock Pipe Line Corp., Post Office Box 631, Amarillo, Tex.

E. C. Schoenfeldt, Sinclair Pipe Line Co., Sinclair Building, Independence, Kan.

M. G. Shoup, Kaneb Pipe Line Co., 3431 West Alabama, Post Office Box 22146, Houston, Tex.

W. N. Stivers, Service Pipe Line Co., Tulsa, Okla.

John D. Sturtevant, Humble Pipe Line Co., Post Office Drawer 2220, Houston, Tex.

J. M. vonAlmen, Dixie Pipeline Co., Post Office Box 4673, Atlanta, Ga.

W. F. Yorty, Sun Pipe Line Co., 1608 Walnut Street, Philadelphia, Pa.

II. THE OIL PIPELINE ADVISORY COMMITTEE ON ACCOUNTING

A. *Purpose.*—The committee was established to cooperate with the Bureau of Accounts in matters pertaining to the maintenance of the Commission's Uniform System of Accounts for Pipeline Companies in conformance with generally accepted accounting principles, and in recognition of considerations peculiar to the oil pipeline industry.

The committee serves in an advisory capacity, only, and completely independent and final evaluation of committee deliberations is made by the Bureau of Accounts.

B. *Dates of meetings.*—The committee held meetings on July 9 and 10, 1962, and on May 8 and June 27 and 28, 1963.

C. *Membership.*—The committee consists of oil pipeline company representatives selected for membership by the Bureau of Accounts, with a representative of the Bureau serving as chairman. Committee members serve at the pleasure of the Bureau for an indefinite period; however, continued existence of the committee is currently limited to February 13, 1965. There follows a list of the present committee members and their addresses as shown according to the Commission's records:

Officer

Chairman: Matthew Paolo, Director, Bureau of Accounts, Interstate Commerce Commission, Washington, D.C.

Members

G. D. Beard, The Texas Pipe Line Co., 1111 Rusk Avenue, Houston, Tex.

H. G. Bloomfield, Humble Pipe Line Co., Post Office Box 2220, Houston, Tex.

Mr. C. S. Cone, Jr., Magnolia Pipe Line Co., Post Office Box 900, Dallas, Tex.

C. M. Cotton, Sinclair Pipe Line Co., Sinclair Building, Independence, Kans.

W. D. Farr, Pure Transportation Co., 200 East Golf Road, Palatine, Ill.

R. E. Higgenbotham, Oklahoma Mississippi River Products Line, Inc., Sunray Building, Tulsa, Okla.

C. W. Keith, Service Pipe Line Co., Service Pipe Line Building, Tulsa, Okla.

Fred Lee, Shell Pipe Line Corp., 607 Fannin Street, Houston, Tex.

J. D. Marshall, Continental Pipe Line Co., Drawer 1267, Ponca City, Okla.

Morgan Martin, Gulf Refining Co., Post Office Drawer 2100, Houston, Tex.

Members—Continued

A. W. Martinelli, The Buckeye Pipe Line Co., Post Office Box 68, Emmaus, Pa.

W. E. McKee, Sohio Pipe Line Co., Midland Building, Cleveland, Ohio.

Stell Meador, Cities Service Pipe Line Co., Masonic-Empire Building, Bar-

tlesville, Okla.

J. T. Robb, Great Lakes Pipe Line Co., Post Office Drawer 2239, Kansas City, Mo.

W. F. Yorty, Sun Pipe Line Co., 1608 Walnut Street, Philadelphia, Pa.

III. THE INDUSTRY ADVISORY COMMITTEE ON PER DIEM COSTS

A. *Purpose.*—The committee was established to cooperate with the Bureau of Accounts in matters pertaining to the development of cost formula for computation of per diem charges for the use of freight-train cars in conformance with generally accepted railroad cost accounting principles, and in recognition of considerations peculiar to the use of freight-train cars in interchange service. The committee serves in an advisory capacity, only, and completely independent and final evaluation of committee deliberations is made by the Bureau of Accounts.

B. *Dates of meetings.*—No meetings have been held by the committee during the period July 1, 1962–June 30, 1963.

C. *Membership.*—The committee consists of railroad company representatives selected for membership by the Bureau of Accounts, with representatives of the Bureau serving as chairman and secretary. Committee members serve at the pleasure of the Bureau for an indefinite period; however, continued existence of the committee is at present limited to May 23, 1965. There follows a list of the present committee members and their addresses as shown according to the Commission's records:

Officers

Chairman: Samuel A. Towne, Chief, Section of Cost Finding, Bureau of Accounts, Interstate Commerce Commission, Washington, D.C.

Secretary: Ralph W. Fondersmith, Transportation Cost Analyst, Bureau of Accounts, Interstate Commerce Commission, Washington, D.C.

Members

H. H. Coyle, Comptroller, New York, New Haven & Hartford Railroad Co., New Haven, Conn.

J. T. Cunningham, Auditor of Disbursements, Long Island Railroad Co., Jamaica Station, Jamaica, N.Y.

G. F. Glacy, Vice President, Accounting and Finance, Boston & Maine Railroad, Boston, Mass.

H. Lyrla, Assistant Comptroller, Illinois Central Railroad Co., Chicago, Ill.

E. M. Talboth, Assistant Comptroller, Baltimore & Ohio Railroad Co., Baltimore, Md.

E. A. White, General Auditor, Chicago, Burlington & Quincy Railroad Co., Chicago, Ill.

IV. ADVISORY COMMITTEE TO THE INTERSTATE COMMERCE COMMISSION ON MOTOR VEHICLE PARTS AND ACCESSORIES

A. *Purpose.*—The committee was established to cooperate with the Bureau of Motor Carriers in motor vehicle technical matters generally, in the interest of assisting the Commission to perform its regulatory work with respect to motor vehicle safety requirements, and more specifically, in the area of furnishing technical advice on motor vehicles and their component parts as to design, performance and maintenance.

B. *Dates of meetings.*—No meetings have been held since reorganization of the committee, pursuant to the provisions of Executive Order No. 11007, was approved on November 15, 1962.

C. *Membership.*—The Committee consists of representatives of Government agencies, and organizations of vehicle manufacturers, component parts manufacturers, vehicle service equipment manufacturers, technical societies, motor carriers, and industry members-at-large, selected for membership by the Bureau of Motor Carriers with a representative of the Bureau serving as chairman. Committee members serve at the pleasure of the Bureau for an indefinite period; however, continued existence of the committee is currently limited to July 1, 1964. There follows a list of the present committee members and their addresses as shown according to the Commission's records:

Regular members

J. R. Almond, Vice President, Owosso Division, Midland Ross Corp., Owosso, Mich.

Earl T. Andrews, Bendix Westinghouse Automotive Air Brake Co., 901 Cleveland Street, Elyria, Ohio

Harry B. Barrett, President, Barrett Equipment Co., 21st and Cass, St. Louis, Mo.

J. V. Bassett, 5196 Greenview Drive, Route 1, Clarkston, Mich.

J. Douglas Bennett, Fawick Brake Division, Fawick Corp., 9921 Clinton Road, Cleveland, Ohio

Arthur A. Berg, Berg Manufacturing & Sales Co., 1712 South Michigan Avenue, Chicago, Ill.

Frank A. Carter, Director, Motor Equipment Management Division, GSA, Washington, D.C.

Ernest G. Cox (Chairman), Bureau of Motor Carriers, Interstate Commerce Commission, Washington, D.C.

Wilbur L. Cross, Jr., Director, Division of Engineering, Connecticut Department of Motor Vehicles, 165 Capitol Avenue, Hartford, Conn.

C. B. Fites, Wagner Electric Corp., 6400 Plymouth Avenue, St. Louis, Mo.

M. T. Hayes, GMC Truck & Coach Division, General Motors Corp., Pontiac, Mich.

Alternates

S. A. Tilden, Permafuss Corp., 675 Main Street, Westbury, N.Y.

Carl W. Cowan, Marshal-Eclipse Division, Bendix Corp., General Motors Building, Detroit, Mich.

I. W. Rhodes, Deputy Director, Motor Equipment Management Division, GSA, Washington, D.C.

B. G. Milster, Bureau of Motor Carriers, Interstate Commerce Commission, Washington, D.C.

Charles W. Reed, Chief, Vehicle Inspection Section, District of Columbia Department of Vehicles and Traffic, Washington, D.C.

R. A. Goopfrich, Chief Engineer, Bendix Products Division, Bendix Corp., South Bend, Ind.

J. H. Letsinger, International Harvester Co., Motor Truck Engineering Department, Post Office Box 1109, Meyer Road, Fort Wayne, Ind.

Regular Members—Continued

C. Roy Herring, Sealco Air Brakes, Inc., 13530 Nelson Avenue, City of Industry, Calif.

William R. Hummel, Chief Engineer, Trailmobile, Inc., 31st and Robertson Avenue, Cincinnati, Ohio

Stephen Johnson, Jr., Bendix Westinghouse Automotive Air Brake Co., 901 Cleveland Street, Elyria, Ohio

T. A. Kreuser, Manager, Automotive Service Sales, Bendix Products Division, Bendix Corp., South Bend, Ind.

J. W. Riesing, P.I.E. Building, Post Office Box 958, Oakland, Calif.

Carl G. Saal, Bureau of Public Roads, Room 1009, 1717 H Street NW., Washington, D.C.

Arthur C. Schmidt, Manager, Automotive Department, Armour & Co., Chicago, Ill.

Herman P. Simon, Deputy Chief, Motor Transport Division, U.S. Army Transportation Research and Engineering Command, Fort Eustis, Va.

Alternates—Continued

Henry C. Stricker, Jr., Chief Engineer, Highway Trailer Co., Edgerton, Wis.

Lewis C. Kibbee, Director, Engineering Department, American Trucking Associations, Inc., 1616 P Street NW., Washington, D.C.

F. W. Petring, Bureau of Public Roads, Room 1015, 1717 H Street NW., Washington, D.C.

John W. Limpert, Fleet Manager, Standard Brands, Inc., 625 Madison Avenue, New York, N.Y.

J. R. Bracewell, Jr., Technical Director, Surface Transport Research and Development Program, Office of Chief of Transportation, Washington, D.C.

V. SPECIAL ADVISORY COMMITTEE ON INTERSTATE COMMERCE COMMISSION PRACTICES AND PROCEDURES

A. *Purpose.*—The committee was established to obtain the benefit of the recommendations of a representative group of transportation lawyers for the improvement of the Commission's organization and procedures.

B. *Dates of meetings.*—No meetings have been held since reorganization of the committee pursuant to Executive Order No. 11007, was approved on December 3, 1962.

C. *Membership.*—The committee is composed of lawyers representing the different modes of surface transportation, shippers and State Commissions. They are appointed by the Commission for an indefinite tenure. Existence of the committee is limited to December 3, 1964. There follows a list of the committee members and their addresses as shown according to the Commission's records:

Officer

Chairman: Sam H. Flint, General Traffic Manager, Quaker Oats Co., 345 Merchandise Mart Plaza, Chicago, Ill.

Members

J. Haden Alldredge,[1] Attorney, law firm of Knabe & Nachman, Hill Building, Montgomery, Ala.

Harry C. Ames, Member of law firm of Ames, Hill & Ames, Transportation Building, Suite 529, Washington, D.C.

Robert N. Burchmore, Attorney, law firm of Burchmore, Good & Bobinette, 2106 Field Building, Chicago, Ill.

John F. Donelan, Attorney, law firm of Pope, Ballard & Loos, Munsey Building, Washington, D.C.

Richard J. Hardy, Member of law firm of Belnap, Spencer, Hardy & Freeman, One North LaSalle Street, Chicago, Ill.

Richard H. Heilman, Director of Transportation, A. O. Smith Corp., Post Office Box 384, Milwaukee, Wis.

Marion F. Jones, Attorney, law firm of Jones, Micklejohn & Kilroy, Denham Building, Denver, Colo.

Gordon C. Locke, General Counsel, Association of Oil Pipe Line, 1725 K Street NW., Washington, D.C.

David G. Macdonald, Member of law firm of Macdonald & McInerny, 602 Solar Building, Washington, D.C.

Walter R. McDonald, Commissioner, Georgia Public Service Commission, 244 Washington Street SW., Atlanta, Ga.

James F. Pinkney, Counsel for Public Affairs, American Trucking Association, 1616 P Street NW., Washington, D.C.

Robert E. Powell, Attorney, 1005–6 Trust Building, Lincoln, Nebr.

John B. Prizer, Vice President and General Counsel, The Pennsylvania Railroad Co., Six Penn Center Plaza, Philadelphia, Pa.

Lee Reeder, Attorney, law firm of Reeder, Griffin & Dysart, 1012 Baltimore Avenue, Kansas City, Mo.

Roland Rice, Attorney, law firm of Rice, Carpenter & Carraway, 1111 E Street NW., Washington, D.C.

Reagan Sayers, Attorney at Law, 304 Century Life Building, Fort Worth, Tex.

Douglas F. Smith, Member of law firm of Sidley, Austin, Burgess & Smith, 11 South LaSalle Street, Chicago, Ill.

James L. Tapley, Commerce Counsel, Southern Railway Co., Southern Railway Building, Washington, D.C.

Starr Thomas, General Solicitor, Atchison, Topeka & Santa Fe Railway System, 80 East Jackson Boulevard, Chicago, Ill.

Clarence D. Todd, Attorney, law firm of Todd, Dillon & Sullivan, 1825 Jefferson Place NW., Washington, D.C.

John R. Turney, Member of law firm of Turney, Major, Markham & Sherfy, 2001 Massachusetts Avenue NW., Washington, D.C.

[1] Deceased—December 5, 1962.

VI. JOINT EQUIPMENT COMMITTEE

A. *Purpose for which used by ICC.*—To cooperate with the Bureau of Accounts in an advisory capacity only in assisting the Commission in performing its railroad valuation work and more specifically in the area of collecting, summarizing and considering data used in the development of annual railroad construction indices.

B. *Dates of meetings.*—The committee met on June 4, 1963.

C. *Membership.*—The Joint Equipment Committee is a subcommitee of the Association of American Railroads. Committee members consist of railroad company representatives with its chairman appointed by and selected from the committee members. An ICC employee is present at all meetings and acts as the committee's secretary during those periods when the committee is utilized by the Commission. Existence of the committee is scheduled to be terminated on July 31, 1963. There follows a list of the present committee members and their affiliations as shown according to the Commission's records:

Officer

Chairman: E. W. Preble, Valuation and Research Engineer, Southern Railway System, 15th and K Streets NW., Washington, D.C.

Members

D. R. Alexander, Mechanical Engineer, Pennsylvania Railroad Co., 15 North 32d Street, Philadelphia, Pa.

F. E. Bryant, Mechanical Valuation Engineer, Union Pacific Railroad Co., 1416 Dodge Street, Omaha, Nebr.

P. L. Conway, Jr., Assistant to Vice President, Association of American Railroads, Transportation Building, Washington, D.C.

A. L. DeMontfredy, Mechanical Accountant, Southern Railway System, 15th and K Streets NW., Washington, D.C.

F. H. DeMoyer, Valuation Engineer, Pennsylvania Railroad Co., 15 North 32d Street, Philadelphia, Pa.

Leo Gunderson, Valuation Electrical and Mechanical Engineer, Southern Pacific Railroad Co., 65 Market Street, San Francisco, Calif.

F. W. Jacobsen, Accountant, New York Central Railroad Co., 466 Lexington Avenue, New York, N.Y.

G. J. Lehnerer, Assistant Mechanical and Research Engineer, Illinois Central Railroad Co., 135 East Eleventh Place, Chicago, Ill.

L. M. Rothberger, Mechanical Valuation Engineer, Atchison, Topeka & Santa Fe Railroad Co., Topeka, Kans.

VII. JOINT VALUATION SIGNAL COMMITTEE

A. *Purpose for which used by ICC.*—To cooperate with the Bureau of Accounts in an advisory capacity only in assisting the Commission in performing its railroad valuation work and more specifically in the area of collecting, summarizing and considering data used in the development of annual railroad construction indices.

B. *Dates of meetings.*—The committee met on June 3, 1963.

C. *Membership.*—The Joint Valuation Signal Committee is a subcommittee of the Association of American Railroads. Committee members consist of railroad company representatives with its chairman appointed by and selected from the committee members. An ICC employee is present at all meetings and acts as the committee's secretary during periods when the committee is utilized by the Commission. Existence of the committee is scheduled to be terminated on July 31, 1963. There follows a list of the present committee members and their affiliations as shown according to the Commission's records:

Officer

Chairman: H. A. Hudson, Assistant to Vice President, Southern Railway System, 15th and K Streets NW., Washington, D.C.

Members

L. E. Bottinelli, Chief Signal Engineer, New York Central System, 1324 West Third Street, Cleveland, Ohio

F. H. DeMoyer, Valuation Engineer, Pennsylvania Railroad Co., 15 North 32d Street, Philadelphia, Pa.

E. D. Feak, Assistant Engineer Signal and Electrical Department, Southern Railway System, 15th and K Streets NW., Washington, D.C.

Leo Gunderson, Valuation Electrical and Mechanical Engineer, Southern Pacific Railroad Co., 65 Market Street, San Francisco, Calif.

A. L. Jordon, Signal Engineer, Baltimore and Ohio Railroad Co., Baltimore, Md.

George Pipas, Signal Engineer, Illinois Central Railroad Co., 135 East 11th Place, Chicago, Ill.

VIII. WESTERN RAILROAD GROUP PRICE COMMITTEE

A. *Purpose for which used by ICC.*—To cooperate with the Bureau of Accounts in an advisory capacity only in assisting the Commission in performing its railroad valuation work and more specifically in the area of collecting, summarizing and considering data used in the development of annual railroad construction indices.

B. *Dates of meetings.*—The committee met on June 6, 1963.

C. *Membership.*—Committee members consist of railroad company representatives with its chairman appointed by and selected from the committee members. An ICC employee is present at all meetings and serves as the committee's secretary during periods when the committee is utilized by the Commission. Existence of the committee is scheduled to be terminated on July 31, 1963. There follows a list of the present committee members and their affiliations as shown according to the Commission's records.

Officer

Chairman: C. F. Olson, Great Northern Railway Co., 175 East 4th Street, St. Paul, Minn.

Members

R. B. Aldridge, Missouri-Kansas-Texas Railroad Co. of Texas, Denison, Tex.

B. H. Benson, Chicago & Northwestern Railway Co., 400 W. Madison Street, Chicago, Ill.

J. R. Clayton, Atchison, Topeka & Santa Fe Railway System, 80 East Jackson Boulevard, Chicago, Ill.

P. L. Conway, Jr., Assistant to Vice President, Association of American Railroads Transportation Building, Washington, D.C.

C. R. Dolan, Missouri Pacific Railroad Co., Missouri Pacific Building, St. Louis, Mo.

E. W. Gibson, Chicago, Burlington & Quincy Railroad Co., 547 West Jackson Boulevard, Chicago, Ill.

J. E. Hebbron, Southern Pacific Railroad Co., 65 Market Street, San Francisco, Calif.

R. D. Igou, Chicago, Rock Island & Pacific Railroad Co., LaSalle Street Station, Chicago, Ill.

A. R. Johnson, Chicago, Milwaukee, St. Paul & Pacific Railroad Co., Union Station, Chicago, Ill.

J. E. Manthey, Elgin, Joliet & Eastern Railway Co., 208 South LaSalle Street, Chicago, Ill.

W. J. Pease, Illinois Central Railroad Co., 135 East 11th Place, Chicago, Ill.

H. R. Williams, Union Pacific Railroad Co., 1416 Dodge Street, Omaha, Nebr.

M. C. Wolf-J. G. Maher, Northern Pacific Railroad Co., 176 East Fifth Street, St. Paul, Minn.

APPENDIX D

STATEMENT OF APPROPRIATION AND OBLIGATION FOR THE FISCAL YEAR ENDED JUNE 30, 1963

An Act making appropriations for sundry independent, executive bureaus, boards, commissions, corporations, agencies, and offices, for the fiscal year ending June 30, 1963, and for other purposes. (Public Law 87–741, 87th Cong., approved October 3, 1962.)

Salaries and expenses: For necessary expenses of the Interstate Commerce Commission, including not to exceed $5,000 for the employment of special counsel; services as authorized by section 15 of the Act of August 2, 1946 (5 U.S.C. 55a), at rates for individuals not to exceed $100 per diem; and purchase of not to exceed fifty-seven passenger motor vehicles of which fifty-five shall be for replacement only; $22,606,000, of which not less than $1,753,700 shall be available for expenses necessary to carry out railroad safety activities and not less than $1,170,800 shall be available for expenses necessary to carry out locomotive inspection activities; *Provided,* That Joint Board members and cooperating State commissioners may use Government transportation requests when traveling in connection with their duties as such__ $22,606,000

Supplemental Appropriation Act, 1963, Public Law 88–25, 88th Congress, approved May 17, 1963—Providing for increased pay costs for the fiscal year 1963_____ 896,800

    Amount available_____ 23,502,800

Obligations and unobligated balance of appropriation as of June 30, 1963. The obligations shown represent net obligation after deducting reimbursements from non-Federal sources and all credits for services and salaries charged to other Government activities.

    Net obligations under appropriation for the fiscal year ended June 30, 1963: Salaries and expenses_____ 23,496,960

Unobligated balance of appropriation:

    Salaries and expenses_____ 5,840

Statement of receipts from fees and charges during the fiscal year ended June 30, 1963:

    Fees and other charges for other administrative services_____ 4,888

    Miscellaneous fees for permits and licenses, not otherwise classified _____ 6,940

    Sale of publications and reproductions_____ 35,584

    Fees and other charges for miscellaneous services_____ 18,540

    Fees and other charges for special benefits, not otherwise classified _____ 88,706

    Total receipts from fees and charges_____ 154,658

212

APPENDIX E

AUTHORIZATIONS UNDER VARIOUS SECTIONS OF THE INTERSTATE COMMERCE ACT AS AMENDED

Certificates of convenience and necessity for construction and/or operation of lines of railroad under section 1 (18) of the Interstate Commerce Act, as amended

Name of applicant	Location of line	Miles
Baltimore & Ohio R. Co_____	Sangamon County, Ill_____	.6566
Chicago & North Western Ry. Co_____	Polk County, Iowa_____	1.6
Chicago, Milwaukee, St. Paul & Pacific R. Co.	Fond du Lac County, Wis_____	.32
Erie-Lackawanna R. Co_____	Passaic County, N.J_____	.204
Georgia Railroad_____	Baldin and Putnam Counties, Ga_____	10.2
Marquette & Huron Mountain R. Co., Inc____	Marquette County, Mich_____	1.25
Pacific Electric Ry. Co. and Union Pacific R. Co.	Orange and Los Angeles Counties, Calif_____	.10
Southern Pacific Co_____	Orange and Los Angeles Counties, Calif_____	.0866
Do_____	Washoe County, Nev_____	.172
Southern Pacific Co. and Harris County Houston Ship Channel Navigation District.	Harris County, Tex_____	.9
Total number of miles_____		15.4892

	Miles
20 applications filed involving_____	164.1286
10 certificates issued authorizing_____	15.4892
2 applications dismissed involving_____	28.7400
1 application denied involving_____	.9510
Authorized since effective date of act_____	11,610.793
Portion thereof actually constructed_____	8,423.809
Portion thereof deferred or abandoned_____	3,054.060
Portion in which time for construction has not expired_____	113.851

Certificates of convenience and necessity for abandonment of lines of railroad or the operation thereof, issued under section 1(18) of the Interstate Commerce Act, as amended

Name of applicant	Location of line	Miles
Angelina & Neches River R. Co___	Angelina and Nacogdoches Counties, Tex____	22. 92
Atchison, Topeka & Santa Fe Ry. Co_____	Greenwood County, Kans_____	10. 42
Do____	Pottawatomie and McClain Counties, Okla___	34. 42
Atlantic & Danville Ry. Co_____	Portsmouth County, Va_____	7. 3
Atlantic Coast Line R. Co_____	Lake County, Fla_____	2. 53
Do____	Marion County, Fla_____	20
Do____	Citrus County, Fla_____	2. 48
Do____	Orange County, Fla_____	4. 2
Do____	Marion County, Fla_____	6. 21
Do____	Seminole County, Fla_____	1. 03
Baltimore & Ohio R. Co_____	Cuyahoga County, Ohio_____	2. 18
Do____	Lucas County, Ohio, and Monroe and Wayne Counties, Mich.	57. 6
Do____	Jackson County, W. Va_____	12. 46
Berlin Mills Ry. Co_____	Coos County, N.H_____	1. 325
Boston & Maine R_____	Rensselaer and Albany Counties, N.Y_____	. 40
Campbell Hall Connecting Ry_____	Orange County, N.Y_____	4. 08
Central Vermont Ry., Inc_____	Franklin County, Vt., and Clinton County, N.Y.	7. 4
Chesapeake & Ohio Ry. Co_____	Albemarle County, Va_____	7. 24
Do____	Jefferson County, Ky_____	1. 07
Chicago & North Western Ry. Co_____	Pipestone and Murray Counties, Minn_____	18. 5
Do____	Polk County, Iowa_____	3. 25
Do____	Nicollet County, Minn_____	4. 77
Chicago Great Western Ry. Co_____	Webster County, Iowa_____	. 394
Do____	____do_____	. 581
Chicago, Milwaukee, St. Paul & Pacific R. Co__	Carroll County, Ill_____	6. 80
Do____	Gallatin County, Mont_____	5. 2
Do____	Fond du Lac County, Wis_____	1. 47
Chicago, Rock Island & Pacific R. Co_____	Fayette and Winneshiek Counties, Iowa_____	23. 37
Do____	Peoria and Stark Counties, Ill_____	25. 44
Cincinnati, Indianapolis & Western R. Co. and Baltimore & Ohio R. Co.	Sangamon County, Ill_____	3. 199
Cleveland, Cincinnati, Chicago & St. Louis Ry. Co. and New York Central R. Co.	Hardin and Logan Counties, Ohio_____	8. 7
Connellsville & Monongahela Ry. Co., Pennsylvania R. Co., and Monongahela Ry. Co.	Fayette County, Pa_____	2. 27
Delaware & Hudson R. Corp_____	Albany and Rensselaer Counties, N.Y_____	. 36
Denver & Rio Grande Western R. Co_____	Arapahoe County, Colo_____	2. 22
Des Moines & Central Iowa Ry. Co_____	Polk County, Iowa_____	1. 79
Erie-Lackawanna R. Co_____	Orange County, N.J_____	11. 68
Do____	Tioga County, N.Y., and Bradford County, Pa.	11. 80
Do____	Bergen and Passaic Counties, N.J_____	4. 93
Do____	Passaic County, N.J_____	3. 9
Do____	Steuben County, N.Y_____	3. 30
Do____	Morris County, N.J_____	. 62
Fort Dodge, Des Moines & Southern Ry. Co__	Webster and Calhoun Counties, Iowa_____	20. 05
Fort Worth & Denver Ry. Co_____	Gray County, Tex_____	3. 47
Grasse River R. Corp_____	St. Lawrence County, N.Y_____	2. 375
Great Northern Ry. Co_____	Skagit County, Wash_____	9. 24
Illinois Central R. Co_____	Franklin County, Ill_____	6. 32
Kansas, Oklahoma & Gulf Ry. Co_____	Wagoner, Mayes, Craig & Ottawa Counties, Okla.	103. 44
Do____	Ottawa County, Okla., and Cherokee County, Kans.	8. 91
Lehigh Valley R. Co_____	Tompkins County, N.Y_____	11
Do____	Carbon County, Pa_____	5. 302
Los Angeles & Salt Lake R. Co. and Union Pacific R. Co.	Orange and Los Angeles Counties, Calif_____	4. 68
Michigan Central R. Co. and New York Central R. Co.	Bay and Gladwin Counties, Mich_____	27. 9
Milwaukee Electric Ry. & Transport Co. and Wisconsin Electric Power Co.	Milwaukee County, Wis_____	2. 25
Missouri-Kansas-Texas R. Co_____	Allen County, Kans_____	12. 32
Missouri Pacific R. Co_____	Moniteau and Miller Counties, Mo_____	31. 97
Do____	Orange, Jasper, and Newton Counties, Tex___	48. 18
Do____	Brazoria County, Tex_____	14. 38
Do____	Grant and Jefferson Counties, Ark_____	19. 24
Do____	Morehouse Parish, La., and Union County, Ark.	29. 72
Monongahela Ry. Co_____	Fayette County, Pa_____	. 73
Do____	Monongalia County, W. Va_____	1. 59
Nelson & Albemarle Ry. Co_____	Nelson and Albemarle Counties, Va_____	8. 84

Certificates of convenience and necessity for abandonment of lines of railroad or the operation thereof, issued under section 1 (18) of the Interstate Commerce Act, as amended—Continued

Name of applicant	Location of line	Miles
New York Central R. Co	Westchester and Putnam Counties, N.Y	21. 8
Do	Jefferson and St.Lawrence Counties, N.Y	41. 9
Do	Hillsdale and Lenawee Counties, Mich	10. 1
Do	Genesee County, N.Y	5. 2
Do	Erie County, N.Y	6. 1
Do	Genesee County, N.Y	10. 24
Do	Rensselaer and Albany Counties, N.Y	.3
Do	Muskingum County, Ohio	9. 8
New York, New Haven & Hartford R. Co	Providence County, R.I	19. 34
Do	Litchfield County, Conn	7. 9
Do	Windham County, Conn	17. 82
Do	Plymouth County, Mass	.454
Do	do	1. 87
Do	Plymouth and Norfolk Counties, Mass	9. 67
Do	Fairfield County, Conn	4. 67
Do	Washington County, R.I	2. 52
New York, Susquehanna & Western R. Co	Sussex and Warren Counties, N.J	26. 45
Oahu Ry. & Terminal Warehousing Co., Ltd	Honolulu County, Hawaii	8. 765
Pacific Electric Ry. Co	San Bernardino County, Calif	.966
Do	Orange and Los Angeles Counties, Calif	3. 818
Penndel Co. and Pennsylvania R. Co	Cattaraugus, Allegany, Wyoming, and Livingston Counties, N.Y.	86
Pennsylvania R. Co	Clarion County, Pa	1. 17
Do	Lancaster and York Counties, Pa	1. 16
Do	Columbia County, Pa	.57
Do	Chester County, Pa	1. 89
Do	Fayette County, Pa	2. 49
Pittsburgh, McKeesport & Youghiogheny R. Co. and Pittsburgh & Lake Erie R. Co.	do	3. 69
Reading Co	Berks and Lehigh Counties, Pa	11. 37
Do	Northumberland County, Pa	.09
Rutland Ry. Corp	St. Lawrence, Franklin, Clinton, and Rensselaer Counties, N.Y., and Grand Isle, Chittenden, Addison, Rutland, Bennington, Windsor, and Windham Counties, Vt.	391. 47
Saint Paul Union Stockyards Co	Yellowstone County, Mont	
San Diego & Arizona Eastern Ry. Co	San Diego County, Calif	1. 261
Shamokin Valley & Pottsville R. Co. and Pennsylvania R. Co.	Northumberland County, Pa	1. 05
Soo Line R. Co	Barron and Dunn Counties, Wis	18. 52
Do	Douglas County, Wis., and St. Louis County, Minn.	1. 15
Southern Pacific Co	Quay, San Miguel, Harding and Colfax Counties, N. Mex.	114. 070
Do	Lavaca, De Witt, and Karnes Counties, Tex	63. 92
Do	Butte and Yuba Counties, Calif	19. 28
Do	Polk County, Oreg	3. 6
Do	Imperial County, Calif	13. 116
Do	Marion County, Oreg	2. 278
Staten Island Rapid Transit Ry. Co	Richmond County, N.Y	2. 05
Stockyards Ry. Co	Yellowstone County, Mont	
Troy Union R. Co	Rensselaer and Albany Counties, N.Y	2. 45
Tuskegee R. Co	Macon County, Ala	9. 38
United New Jersey R. & Canal Co. and Pennsylvania R. Co.	Hudson and Essex Counties, N.J	.51
Washington & Old Dominion R	Arlington County, Va	2. 94
Wisconsin Central R. Co	Cook County, Ill	1. 03
Zanesville Terminal R. Co	Muskingum County, Ohio	.5
Total		1,688. 404

	Miles
127 applications filed involving	1, 937. 400
110 certificates issued permitting abandonment	1, 688. 404
6 applications dismissed involving	76. 820
3 applications denied involving	72. 652
Abandonments permitted since effective date of act	49, 373. 666

Certificates of convenience and necessity for acquisition and/or operation of lines of railroad issued under section 1(18) of the Interstate Commerce Act, as amended

Name of applicant	Location of line	Miles
Chattahoochee Industrial R	Early County, Ga	15.072
Kansas City Southern Ry. Co	Cherokee County, Kans	8.3472
Louisville & Nashville R. Co	Monroe County, Ala	4.5
Marquette & Huron Mountain R. Co., Inc	Marquette County, Mich	23.74
New York Central R. Co	Rensselaer County, N.Y	.5
Port Authority Trans-Hudson Corp	Hudson County, N.J., and New York County, N.Y.	8.5
Western Maryland Ry. Co	Grant County, W. Va	15.75
Total number of miles		71.9092

Miles
12 applications filed involving _____ 93. 5972
7 certificates issued involving _____ 76. 4092

Authorizations under section 5(2) of the Interstate Commerce Act, as amended, involving railroad properties

Acquiring carrier	Owning carrier	Miles	How acquired
Atchison, Topeka & Santa Fe Ry. Co	Gulf, Mobile & Ohio R. Co	15.5	Trackage rights.
Do	Southern Pacific Co	66	Operating agreement.
Do	California, Arizona & Santa Fe Ry. Co.	702.35	Merger.
Do	Union Pacific R. Co	.21	Trackage rights.
Belt Railway Co. of Chicago	Chicago & Western Indiana R	376.30	Purchase.
Belt Ry. Co. of Chicago	Indiana Harbor Belt R. Co	10	Trackage agreement.
Berlin Mills Ry	Boston & Maine R	1.356	Trackage rights.
Boston & Maine R	Stony Brook R. Corp	10.99	Control.
Carolina & Northwestern Ry. Co., Live Oak, Perry & Gulf R. Co., and South Georgia Ry. Co.	Georgia & Florida Ry. Co	314	Do.
Central of Georgia Ry. Co	Georgia R	3.53	Trackage rights.
Central Vermont Ry., Inc	Canadian National Ry. Co	15	Do.
Central R. Co. of New Jersey	Wilkes-Barre & Scranton Ry. Co	11.56	Purchase.
Chesapeake & Ohio Ry. Co	Baltimore & Ohio R. Co	5,911.21	Control.
Do	Louisville & Nashville R. Co	5.03	Trackage rights.
Chicago & North Western Ry. Co	Chicago, Rock Island & Pacific R. Co.	3.9	Do.
Do	Wisconsin Electric Power Co	1.95	Lease.
Chicago, Milwaukee, St. Paul & Pacific R. Co.	Chicago & North Western R. Co	1.34	Trackage rights.
Cincinnati, Indianapolis & Western R. Co. and Baltimore & Ohio R. Co.	Illinois Central R. Co	3.630	Do.
Colorado & Southern Ry. Co	Denver & Rio Grande R. Co	1.28	Joint operation.
Delaware & Hudson R. Corp	New York Central R. Co	6.5	Trackage rights.
Detroit, Toledo & Ironton R. Co	Ann Arbor R. Co	331.96	Control.
Erie-Lackawanna R. Co	Delaware & Hudson R. Corp	.68	Trackage rights.
Fort Dodge, Des Moines & Southern Ry. Co.	Des Moines Western Ry. Co	———	Lease agreement.
Georgia & Florida Ry. Co	Georgia & Florida R	314	Purchase.
Georgia-Pacific Corp	Oregon Pacific & Eastern Ry. Co. and Brimstone R. Co.	44.90	Control.
Illinois Central R. Co	Chicago, Memphis & Gulf R. Co	48.53	Merger.
Lehigh Coal & Navigation Co	Nesquehoning Valley R. Co. and Tresckow R. Co.	24.60	Do.
Los Angeles & Salt Lake R. Co. and Union Pacific R. Co.	Pacific Electric Ry. Co	6.62	Joint use.
Louisville & Nashville R. Co	Louisville & Nashville Terminal Co.	15.85	Purchase.
Louisiana Midland Ry. Co	Missouri Pacific R. Co	26.05	Lease and trackage rights.
Mahoning & Shenango Valley R. Co	Shenango Valley R. Co. and Stewart Ry. Co.	7.84	Merger.
Maine Central R. Co	Bangor & Aroostook R. Co	.82	Trackage rights.
Missouri-Kansas-Texas R. Co	Atchison, Topeka & Santa Fe Ry. Co.	3.69	Do.
New York Central R. Co	Delaware & Hudson R. Corp	6.5	Do.

Authorizations under section 5(2) of the Interstate Commerce Act, as amended, involving railroad properties—Continued

Acquiring carrier	Owning carrier	Miles	How acquired
Norfolk & Western Ry. Co. and Norfolk, Franklin & Danville Ry. Co.	Norfolk, Franklin & Danville Ry. Co. and Atlantic & Danville Ry. Co.	203 29.31	Control. Trackage rights.
Pacific Electric Ry. Co	Southern Pacific Co	2.105	Do.
Do	Los Angeles & Salt Lake R. Co. and Union Pacific R. Co.	8.69	Joint use.
Pennsylvania R. Co	Lehigh Valley R. Co	61.53	Trackage rights.
Pennsylvania R. Co. and New York Central R. Co.	Cherry Tree & Dixonville R. Co	58.201	Trackage agreement.
W. L. Pippin, Edward H. Lewis, and Lucile Pidcock Mullins.	Albany & Northern Ry. Co	36	Control.
Pittsburgh, Fort Wayne & Chicago Ry. Co. and Pennsylvania R. Co.	Pittsburgh Joint Stock Yards Co	4.18	Purchase and lease.
Reading Co	Lehigh Coal & Navigation Co	130.89	Purchase.
Soo Line R. Co	Chicago & North Western R. Co	2.809	Trackage rights.
Do	Lake Superior Terminal & Ry. Co.	.492	Do.
Southern Pacific Co	Central Pacific Ry	—	Control.
Do	Western Pacific R. Co	27	Trackage rights.
Do	Southern Pacific Terminal Co	8.49	Merger.
Do	Western Pacific R. Co	151.597	Trackage rights.
Harris County Houston Ship Channel Navigation District.	Southern Pacific Co., Chicago, Rock Island & Pacific R. Co., Fort Worth & Denver Ry. Co., Gulf, Colorado & Santa Fe Ry. Co., Houston Belt & Terminal Ry.Co., Missouri-Kansas-Texas, R. Co., Missouri Pacific R. Co., and Port Terminal R. Assn. and Galveston, Houston & Henderson R. Co.		Operating agreement.
Southern Ry. Co	Central of Georgia Ry. Co	2,395	Control.
Do	Atlanta & Charlotte Air Line Ry. Co.	255	Lease agreement.
Texas South-Eastern R. Co	Texas State R	33.03	Lease.

62 applications filed.
52 applications granted.
1 application denied.
1 application dismissed.

Authorizations under section 5 (2) of the Interstate Commerce Act, as amended, for unifications involving the 100 largest motor carriers of property

Acquiring carrier	1962 revenues (000)	Rank	Acquired carrier	Revenues Year	Revenues (000)	Rank	How acquired
Arkansas-Best Freight System, Inc.	16,855	64	Orville M. Fine, d/b/a Fine Truck Line	1962	74		Purchase (portion).
			Delta Motor Line, Inc.	1962	8,207		Control.
			Eastern Arkansas Truck Lines, Inc.	1962	53		Control and merger.
			Healzer Cartage Co.	1962	3,088		Merger.
B & P Motor Express, Inc.	13,211	92	Hicks Express, Inc.	1961	355		Purchase.
Consolidated Copperstate Lines	13,531	91	Paul W. Nielsen (Dale M. Belts, receiver)	1960	147		Purchase (portion).
Consolidated Freightways Corp. of Delaware.	85,330	2	Belmap Freight Lines, Inc.	1961	830		Purchase.
Greyhound Van Lines, Inc.	8,152		Consolidated Freightways Corp. of Delaware.	1962	85,330	2	Purchase (portion).
Helm's Express, Inc.	17,152	61	Keystone Transfer Co., Inc.	1961	127		Purchase.
			The Royal Transportation Co	1962	1,032		Control and merger.
			Zeno Freightways	1961	3,355		Merger.
Huber & Huber Motor Express, Inc.	18,512	54	The C & D Motor Delivery Co	1961	4,174		Control and merger.
Interstate Motor Lines, Inc.	26,270	36	Husmann & Roper Freight Lines, Inc.	1962	5,325		Do.
Johnson Motor Lines, Inc.	16,349	67	Emmott-Valley Transportation Co., Inc.	1962	1,538		Merger.
Jones Motor Co., Inc.	18,568	53	Atlanta-New Orleans Motor Freight Co.	1962	5,347		Control and merger.
Kramer-Consolidated Freight Lines, Inc. (formerly Kramer Bros. Freight Lines, Inc.).	17,304	60	Mundy Motor Lines	1962	3,466		Do.
			Consolidated Freight Co	1962	8,191		Do.
Lee Way Motor Freight, Inc.	15,780	72	Pioneer Freight, Inc.	1962	635		Do.
Mason & Dixon Lines, Inc.	24,561	38	Silver Fleet Motor Express, Inc.	1962	7,579		Control.[1]
Merchants Fast Motor Lines, Inc.	14,010	90	R. A. Wright, d/b/a Wright Motor Freight Lines	1962	320		Purchase.
			Union Truck Lines, Inc.	1962	984		Control and merger.
Midwest Emery Freight System, Inc.	26,641	34	Pampa Motor Freight Lines, Inc.	1962	225		Do.
Navajo Freight Lines, Inc.	30,244	25	James F. Lee, d/b/a Lee Transport.	1961	296		Purchase (portion).
North American Van Lines, Inc.	44,708	9	Brooks Truck Lines, Inc.	1962	1,077		Merger.
			Fort Smith Furniture Transportation Co.	1962	1		Purchase.
Overnight Transportation Co	19,469	49	Kleitner Van Lines, Inc.	1961	323		Do.
Pilot Freight Carriers, Inc.	18,827	52	Hill City Transfer, Inc.	1962	348		Do.
Ringsby Truck Lines, Inc.	20,776	44	Bison Fast Freight, Inc.	1962	70		Do.
			Colonial & Pacific Frigidways, Inc.	1962	2,337		Purchase (portion).
			Fortier Transportation Co.	1962	3,940		Do.
			Converse Trucking Service.	1962	1,281		Control.
Ruan Transport Corp	17,930	57	Hillside Transit Co., Inc.	1962	2,973		Purchase (portion).
Smith's Transfer Corp. of Staunton, Va.	14,450	84	Pitzer Transfer, Storage & Fuel Corp.	1961	116		Purchase.
Transcon Lines	26,519	35	Charles Meek, d/b/a C & M Trucking Co.	1962	63		Do.
			Houston & North Texas Motor Freight Lines, Inc.	1962	659		Do.
Valley Motor Lines, Inc. (including Valley Express Co.).	15,062	78	Oakridge-Westfir Truck Lines, Inc., d/b/a Klamath Falls Fast Freight.	1961	187		Merger.
Viking Freight Co.	17,801	58	Mid-Continent Freight Lines, Inc.	1962	3,651		Control.
Whitehouse Trucking, Inc.	917		Commercial Carriers, Inc.	1962	14,688	81	Purchase (portion).
							Do.

[1] Petition for reconsideration pending.

Authorizations under the Interstate Commerce Act for unifications and transfers involving water carriers and freight forwarders

Acquiring carrier	From	How acquired
Day Line, Inc	Hudson River Day Line Inc	Water carrier certificate transfer.
Hawaiian Express Service, Inc	Milton J. Daly Hawaiian Express & Dillon Drayage Co.	Freight forwarder permit transfer.
Isbrandtsen Company, Inc	Isbrandtsen Steamship Company, Inc	Water carrier certificate transfer.
McAllister Brothers, Inc	McAllister Lighterage Line, Inc	Control.
Do	Russell Bros. Towing Co., Inc	Merger.
McGrath & Kuskokwin Freight Service Inc.	Eugene Tibbs, McGrath & Kuskokwin Freight Service.	Water carrier certificate transfer.
A. S. Mechling Barge Lines, Inc	John I. Hay Co	Control.
Star Forwarders, Inc	Merchants Carloading Co., Inc., Globe Freight Service, and Flynn Forwarding Company Inc.	Freight forwarder permit transfer.
Weyerhaeuser Co	Weyerhaeuser Steamship Co	Merger.

9 applications filed.
8 applications granted.
1 application dismissed.

APPENDIX F

RAILROAD COMPANIES IN REORGANIZATION (OR RECEIVERSHIP) PROCEEDINGS

Proceedings under section 77 of the Bankruptcy Act: *Miles of line operated [1]*

Boston & Providence R. Corp.[2] _____ 64

New Jersey & New York R. Co _____ 38

New York, New Haven & Hartford R. Co _____ 1, 697

Receivership proceedings:

Georgia & Florida R. _____ 321

Waco, Beaumont, Trinity & Sabine Ry. Co.[3] _____ 18

Tennessee R. Co _____ 57

[1] As of June 30, 1963.

[2] Owned mileage 64. Leased to Old Colony R. Co.; operated by New York, New Haven & Hartford R. Co.

[3] Not in operation. Owned mileage 18.

Mileage of line-haul railroads operated by receivers or trustees at various dates

Year [1]	Miles of road operated by receivers at close of year	Miles of road operated by trustees at close of year	Miles of road operated by both receivers and trustees at close of year	Total miles of road operated at close of year, All line-haul companies	Percent of total mileage operated by receivers or trustees
1895	37, 855. 80		37, 855. 80	177, 746	21. 30
1900	4, 177. 91		4, 177. 91	192, 556	2. 17
1905	795. 82		795. 82	216, 974	. 37
1910	5, 257. 03		5, 257. 03	240, 831	2. 18
1915	30, 223. 05		30, 223. 05	257, 569	11. 73
1920	16, 290. 17		16, 290. 17	259, 941	6. 27
1925	18, 686. 99		18, 686. 99	258, 631	7. 23
1930	9, 486. 28		9, 486. 28	260, 440	3. 64
1935	15, 920. 00	52, 425. 00	68, 345. 00	252, 930	27. 02
1940	11, 658. 00	63, 612. 00	75, 270. 00	245, 740	30. 63
1945	5, 088. 00	34, 626. 00	39, 714. 00	239, 438	16. 59
1950	638. 00	11, 585. 00	12, 223. 00	236, 857	5. 16
1955	441. 00	1, 497. 00	1, 938. 00	233, 955	. 83
1956	982. 00	612. 00	1, 594. 00	233, 509	. 68
1957	441. 00	612. 00	1, 053. 00	232, 177	. 45
1958	427. 00	613. 00	1, 040. 00	231, 494	. 45
1959	484. 00	613. 00	1, 097. 00	230, 933	. 48
1960	435. 00	824. 00	1, 259. 00	230, 169	. 55
1961	378. 00	1, 987. 00	2, 365. 00	229, 369	1. 03
1962	378. 00	1, 735. 00	2, 113. 00	227, 851	. 93

[1] As of June 30, 1895 to 1915, inclusive. As of Dec. 31, 1920 to 1962, inclusive.

APPENDIX G

STATISTICS OF RAILROAD DEVELOPMENT FROM ANNUAL REPORTS OF CARRIERS

Data for years preceding 1952 for most of the tables appear in prior reports

TABLE I.—*Mileage operated and mileage owned by railroads in the United States, 1952–62*

Year ended Dec. 31—	Road owned in the United States [1] (first main track)	Total miles of all tracks operated, excluding trackage rights [2]	Mileage operated by classes I and II line-haul railroads (including trackage rights)			
			First main track	Second or additional main tracks	Yard track and sidings	All tracks
1952	222,508	373,571	235,545	39,977	119,109	394,631
1953	221,758	372,584	234,959	39,794	118,983	393,736
1954	221,098	371,339	234,342	39,520	118,718	392,580
1955	220,670	369,401	233,955	38,825	118,185	390,965
1956	220,221	368,020	233,509	37,908	118,251	389,668
1957	219,067	365,915	232,177	37,123	117,678	386,978
1958	218,399	364,353	231,494	36,448	117,322	385,264
1959	217,565	362,506	230,930	35,746	117,236	383,912
1960	217,552	360,566	230,169	34,800	116,776	381,745
1961	216,445	357,917	229,369	33,853	116,193	379,415
1962	215,090	354,460	227,851	32,719	115,720	376,290

[1] Includes mileage of some small companies that do not make annual reports to the Commission.
[2] Includes mileage of classes I and II line-haul railroads and switching and terminal companies.

TABLE II.—*Equipment of railroads, including switching and terminal companies, in service at the close of each year, 1952–62* [1]

Year ended Dec. 31—	Locomotives							
	Steam		Electric		Diesel		Other	
	Number	Average tractive effort [2]	Number	Average tractive effort [2]	Number	Average tractive effort [2]	Number	Average tractive effort [2]
		Pounds		*Pounds*		*Pounds*		*Pounds*
1952	16,738	59,966	791	60,415	22,118	58,918	52	[3] 59,176
1953	12,274	61,339	713	62,060	24,209	59,393	55	[3] 77,150
1954	9,041	63,152	669	62,605	25,256	59,692	67	[3] 108,114
1955	6,266	65,005	639	64,577	26,563	63,644	34	[3] 111,353
1956	3,918	68,745	616	64,198	28,001	60,489	58	[3] 117,031
1957	2,608	72,030	597	65,696	29,137	60,479	49	[3] 117,567
1958	1,488	73,692	562	66,914	29,515	60,593	51	[3] 135,875
1959	871	73,298	517	71,221	30,097	60,911	54	[3] 156,297
1960	374	76,920	498	64,102	30,240	61,122	66	[3] 169,592
1961	210	77,651	484	66,539	30,123	61,829	72	[3] 174,732
1962	136	45,020	441	69,274	30,057	61,323	67	[3] 180,140

See footnotes at end of table.

TABLE II.—*Equipment of railroads, including switching and terminal companies, in service at the close of each year, 1952–62* [1]—Continued

Year ended Dec. 31—	Cars					
	Freight cars (excluding caboose)		Passenger train	Coaches		
	Number	Average capacity [2]	Number	Number	Average seating capacity [2]	Number air-conditioned [2]
		Tons				
1952	1,783,352	53.2	34,942	14,957	74	7,356
1953	1,801,874	53.5	34,106	14,460	74	7,427
1954	1,761,386	53.7	33,035	14,210	74	7,689
1955	1,723,747	53.7	32,182	13,543	75	7,378
1956	1,738,631	54.0	30,817	12,867	75	7,414
1957	1,777,557	54.5	29,564	12,328	75	7,295
1958	1,755,775	54.8	28,999	11,934	76	7,118
1959	1,708,116	55.0	27,419	11,121	76	6,751
1960	1,690,396	55.4	25,746	10,287	76	6,316
1961	1,635,342	55.7	24,433	9,840	76	6,053
1962	1,581,213	56.3	23,430	9,432	77	5,934

[1] Privately owned cars and cars owned or leased by the Pullman Co., are not included. In 1962 privately owned freight carrying cars, other than those leased to railroads, numbered 269,475 and cars owned or leased by the Pullman Co., 2,220.

[2] Class I railroads.

[3] Includes gas turbine electric locomotives having average tractive effort as follows: 1952, 6 locomotives of 138,000 pounds; 1953, 10 locomotives of 137,900 pounds; 1954 through 1957, 25 locomotives of 137,920 pounds; 1958, 29 locomotives of 147,931 pounds; 1959, 36 locomotives of 160,111 pounds; 1960, 48 locomotives of 172,729 pounds; 1961, 55 locomotives of 177,564 pounds; 1962, 49 locomotives of 183,429 pounds.

TABLE III.—*Shareholders' equity and long-term debt, 1952–62: Class I line-haul railroads and their lessor subsidiaries*

Year ended Dec. 31—	Shareholders' equity					Total long-term debt [1]	Total equity and debt	Ratio of debt to total equity and debt
	Total	Common stock	Preferred stock	Capital surplus	Retained income			
	Thousands	*Thousands*	*Thousands*	*Thousands*	*Thousands*	*Thousands*	*Thousands*	*Percent*
1952	$17,091,459	$7,105,639	$1,942,964	$283,107	$7,759,749	$10,082,143	$27,173,602	37.10
1953	17,469,719	6,890,010	1,857,735	318,194	8,403,780	10,016,006	27,485,725	36.44
1954	17,584,070	7,187,290	1,521,179	319,445	8,556,156	9,893,291	27,477,361	36.01
1955	17,879,591	7,213,028	1,300,596	433,058	8,932,909	9,910,592	27,790,183	35.66
1956	18,080,027	6,744,889	1,382,058	721,113	9,231,967	9,989,378	28,069,405	35.59
1957	18,306,144	6,138,281	1,356,468	1,250,820	9,560,575	10,139,252	28,445,396	35.64
1958	18,369,390	6,086,580	1,253,146	1,300,608	9,729,056	10,080,345	28,449,735	35.43
1959	18,504,534	6,076,283	1,234,569	1,294,674	9,899,008	9,865,743	28,370,277	34.77
1960	18,527,246	6,028,793	1,206,710	1,327,193	9,964,550	9,700,783	28,228,029	34.37
1961	18,462,947	5,370,943	1,200,985	1,909,967	9,981,052	9,542,193	28,005,140	34.07
1962	18,751,740	5,384,374	1,190,201	1,947,310	10,229,855	9,433,447	28,185,187	33.47

[1] Excludes amounts payable to affiliated companies.

TABLE IV.—*Dividends, 1952–62: Line-haul railroads and their lessor subsidiaries*

Year ended Dec. 31—	Proportion of stock-paying dividends [1]	Amounts of dividends [1]	Average rate on—		Dividends declared [2]	
			Dividend-paying stock [1]	All stock	On preferred stock	On common stock
	Percent	*Thousands*	*Percent*	*Percent*		
1952	73.23	$394,042	5.85	4.28	$75,376,804	$262,688,453
1953	81.57	445,145	6.14	5.01	77,974,384	334,089,068
1954	74.82	405,410	6.13	4.58	72,738,779	306,605,209
1955	84.39	476,748	6.53	5.51	70,768,164	377,450,539
1956	81.69	487,905	7.19	5.87	46,239,794	415,468,274
1957	84.41	466,415	7.21	6.09	46,500,614	391,889,328
1958	70.45	444,982	8.41	5.93	42,258,920	376,506,263
1959	76.89	431,860	7.51	5.77	40,996,898	364,643,640
1960	75.88	411,650	7.33	5.56	36,454,767	349,040,714
1961	64.74	385,017	8.83	5.71	31,259,322	328,192,149
1962	63.60	394,116	9.20	5.85	30,338,958	339,735,118

[1] Includes figures for lessors and operating railroads without excluding duplications on account of intercorporate payments. Stock dividends for the last 11 years have been as follows: $767,537 in 1952, $26,035,890 in 1953, $5,000,000 in 1954, $2,130,100 in 1955, $22,038,223 in 1956, $635,174 in 1957, $46,282,730 in 1958, $2,402,789 in 1959, of which $65,364 was credited to "Capital Surplus" for amount in excess of par value of stock dividends declared; $2,329 in 1960, $1,890,200 in 1961, and $1,910,451 in 1962.
[2] By class I line-haul railroads.

TABLE V.—*Reported property investment and selected income items, 1952–62: Line-haul railroads and their lessor subsidiaries*

Year ended Dec. 31—	Investment [1]	Investment per mile of road	Depreciation reserve [2]	Net railway operating income [3]	Other income [4]	Fixed charges and other deductions [5]	Net income
	Thousands		*Thousands*	*Thousands*	*Thousands*	*Thousands*	*Thousands*
1952	[6] $31,822,114	$143,238	$6,926,771	$1,091,657	$269,614	[5]$25,746	$900,472
1953	[6] 32,416,389	146,414	7,009,758	1,122,512	290,116	498,995	939,887
1954	[6] 32,709,615	148,183	7,175,101	887,816	257,364	452,958	712,252
1955	[6] 33,034,952	149,950	7,313,951	1,144,347	250,503	453,918	958,849
1956	[6] 33,714,159	153,303	7,542,856	1,083,708	259,677	451,169	908,416
1957	[6] 34,614,517	158,255	7,800,925	934,645	277,634	460,730	765,227
1958	[6] 34,934,471	160,179	8,043,497	772,898	323,153	482,439	630,033
1959	[6] 35,157,554	161,834	8,295,563	760,140	306,732	475,575	607,924
1960	[6] 35,513,351	163,885	8,532,411	594,618	338,466	475,520	473,175
1961	[6] 35,541,973	164,842	8,792,724	547,045	312,524	464,552	410,140
1962	[6] 34,361,477	160,440	8,982,196	735,266	313,199	464,228	600,393

[1] Includes investment of operating, lessor, and proprietary companies. Proprietary companies do not render annual reports to the Commission but information concerning them is given in reports of the operating companies.
[2] Includes amortization of defense projects.
[3] Classes I and II line-haul railroads.
[4] Includes amounts received as interest or dividends on railroad securities owned by reporting carriers. See Transport Statistics in the United States, table 109. Figures represent classes I and II line-haul railroads.
[5] The interest included represents accruals, not payments. In 1962, the interest payments on unmatured funded debt and long-term debt in default in excess of accruals was $740,356 for class I railroads. Figures represent classes I and II line-haul railroads.
[6] Includes investment of lessor and proprietary companies, as follows, but excludes investment of proprietary companies in systems which file consolidated annual reports combining the mileage, investment and other items on a net system basis:

Year	Lessor companies	Proprietary companies	Year	Lessor companies	Proprietary companies
	Thousands	*Thousands*		*Thousands*	*Thousands*
1952	$3,173,506	$594,910	1958	$2,238,968	$501,004
1953	2,289,043	551,485	1959	2,194,123	512,011
1954	2,273,924	522,611	1960	2,171,069	510,363
1955	2,243,939	521,665	1961	2,102,273	502,164
1956	2,234,533	506,107	1962	2,039,217	494,198
1957	2,335,220	500,539			

TABLE VI.—*Selected balance sheet items, 1952–62: Class I line-haul railroads and their lessor subsidiaries*

Year ended Dec. 31—	Current assets	Net investment in transportation property	All other assets	Current liabilities [1]	Long-term debt	All other liabilities	Shareholders' equity
	Thousands	Thousands	Thousands	Thousands	Thousands	Thousands	Thousands
1952	$3,844,904	$23,996,214	$3,858,193	$2,300,046	$11,107,148	$1,200,657	$17,091,460
1953	3,673,098	24,545,352	3,433,061	2,191,795	10,870,601	1,119,395	17,469,720
1954	3,346,911	24,702,048	3,278,552	1,805,377	10,744,715	1,193,348	17,584,071
1955	3,790,710	24,883,508	3,289,814	2,151,157	10,741,077	1,192,206	17,879,592
1956	3,575,204	25,285,612	3,262,526	2,130,785	10,801,320	1,111,210	18,080,027
1957	3,221,842	25,928,467	3,182,141	1,928,844	10,977,187	1,120,275	18,306,144
1958	3,147,256	26,012,615	3,015,483	2,129,840	10,614,720	1,061,404	18,369,390
1959	3,154,043	25,967,635	3,110,464	2,260,406	10,386,430	1,080,772	18,504,534
1960	2,939,773	26,098,028	3,089,336	2,259,987	10,244,727	1,095,178	18,527,245
1961	3,004,927	25,878,373	2,965,344	2,396,721	10,072,311	916,665	18,462,947
1962	3,055,840	24,595,106	4,376,231	2,371,290	9,927,493	956,654	18,751,740

[1] Includes long-term debt due within 1 year in 1958–62. This item included in long-term debt in prior years.

TABLE VII.—*Operating revenues, operating expenses, and taxes: Class I line-haul railroads, 1952–62*

Year ended Dec. 31—	Operating revenues	Freight revenues	Passenger revenues	Operating expenses	Railway tax accruals [1]			Ratio of total operating expenses to total operating revenues
					U.S. Government taxes	Other than U.S. Government taxes	Total	
	Thousands	Thousands	Thousands	Thousands	Thousands	Thousands	Thousands	Percent
1952	$10,580,762	$8,788,635	$906,185	$8,052,518	$908,729	$355,535	$1,264,264	76.11
1953	10,664,169	8,950,522	841,962	8,135,229	824,704	362,722	1,187,426	76.29
1954	9,370,826	7,797,885	767,283	7,384,499	500,788	361,801	862,589	78.80
1955	10,106,330	8,538,286	742,945	7,646,418	702,765	379,602	1,082,367	75.66
1956	10,550,943	8,931,423	756,582	8,108,353	730,619	392,910	1,123,529	76.85
1957	10,491,390	8,928,511	735,339	8,227,522	666,171	404,246	1,070,417	78.42
1958	9,564,568	8,070,826	675,296	7,543,842	560,564	398,269	958,833	78.87
1959	9,825,060	8,312,181	651,168	7,704,815	644,889	404,322	1,049,211	78.42
1960	9,514,294	8,025,423	640,268	7,565,336	600,610	400,231	1,000,841	79.52
1961	9,189,138	7,739,044	624,688	7,274,260	609,723	382,943	992,666	79.16
1962	9,439,895	7,991,146	619,056	7,418,562	541,303	365,080	906,383	78.59

[1] Includes lessor companies.

TABLE VIII.—*Net railway operating income, net income, and rates of return, class I line-haul railroads, 1952–62*

Year ended Dec. 31—	Elements of value after depreciation and amortization, end of preceding year	Net railway operating income, current year	Ratio of net railway operating income to elements of value	Shareholders' equity	Net income	Ratio of net income to shareholders' equity
	Thousands	Thousands	Percent	Thousands	Thousands	Percent
1952	$23,735,874	$1,078,455	4.54	$15,376,024	$825,396	5.37
1953	24,360,748	1,109,434	4.55	16,236,952	903,227	5.56
1954	24,893,120	874,092	3.51	16,359,168	681,690	4.17
1955	24,849,863	1,128,082	4.54	16,657,939	927,122	5.57
1956	25,020,645	1,068,344	4.27	16,861,286	876,333	5.20
1957	25,517,763	923,285	3.62	17,102,896	737,431	4.31
1958	26,193,911	761,773	2.91	17,142,266	601,737	3.51
1959	26,190,059	749,476	2.86	17,291,787	577,719	3.34
1960	26,247,426	584,016	2.23	17,312,733	444,640	2.57
1961	26,396,665	537,771	2.04	17,283,908	382,444	2.21
1962	26,372,540	725,679	2.75	17,559,195	571,017	3.25

NOTE.—Ratios of net railway operating income to elements of value are from *Transport Economics* and predecessor publications. Elements of value are from Bureau of Accounts annual publication "Elements of Value of Property Used in Common Carrier Service."

TABLE IX.—*Number and compensation of employees: Class I line-haul railroads, 1952–62*

Year ended Dec. 31—	Average number of employees during year [1]	Total hours paid for	Compensation of railroad employees [2]			
			Total	Average per hour	Ratio to revenues	Ratio to expenses
		Thousands	*Thousands*		*Percent*	*Percent*
1952	1, 226, 421	2, 845, 217	$5, 326, 804	$1. 872	50. 34	66. 15
1953	1, 205, 966	2, 777, 235	5, 324, 951	1. 917	49. 93	65. 46
1954	1, 064, 337	2, 467, 515	4, 853, 660	1. 967	51. 80	65. 73
1955	1, 057, 866	2, 502, 608	4, 992, 235	1. 995	49. 40	65. 29
1956	1, 043, 447	2, 466, 176	5, 324, 672	2. 159	50. 47	65. 67
1957	984, 974	2, 314, 973	5, 358, 049	2. 315	51. 07	65. 12
1958	840, 580	1, 980, 557	4, 929, 906	2. 489	51. 54	65. 35
1959	815, 509	1, 924, 500	4, 986, 251	2. 591	50. 75	64. 72
1960	780, 971	1, 840, 615	4, 893, 622	2. 659	51. 43	64. 68
1961	715, 985	1, 698, 704	4, 623, 981	2. 722	50, 32	63. 57
1962	700, 146	1, 672, 389	4, 662, 113	2. 788	49. 39	62. 84

[1] This is the average of 12 counts made at middle of month and differs from the number of persons receiving pay during the month of year regardless of whether for a long or short period.
[2] In 1962, $4,452,443,605, or 95.50 percent of the reported compensation was chargeable to operating expenses.

TABLE X.—*Freight transportation service performed by line-haul railroads, 1952–62*

Year ended Dec. 31—	Revenue tons originated	Revenue tons carried 1 mile	Loaded car miles	Average haul		Average amount received for each ton originated	Revenue per ton-mile
				United States as a system	For the individual road		
	Thousands	*Millions*	*Millions*	*Miles*	*Miles*		*Cents*
1952	1, 447, 410	617, 941	19, 919	426. 93	223. 11	$6. 159	1. 443
1953	1, 447, 655	608, 964	19, 863	420. 66	221. 36	6. 271	1. 491
1954	1, 279, 267	552, 197	18, 239	431. 65	227. 81	6. 187	1. 433
1955	1, 455, 625	626, 892	20, 226	430. 67	227. 88	5. 953	1. 382
1956	1, 521, 163	651, 188	20, 364	428. 09	228. 02	5. 975	1. 396
1957	1, 449, 007	621, 907	19, 183	⸣29. 20	230. 77	6. 255	1. 457
1958	1, 247, 407	554, 534	17, 273	444. 55	239. 30	6. 568	1. 477
1959	1, 292, 581	578, 637	17, 905	447. 66	239. 36	6. 531	1. 459
1960	1, 301, 303	575, 360	17, 379	442. 14	238. 83	6. 264	1. 417
1961	1, 252, 868	566, 295	16, 753	452. 00	244. 56	6. 273	1. 388
1962	1, 293, 572	597, 774	17, 086	460. 57	248. 22	6. 273	1. 362

TABLE XI.—*Carload, trainload, and density of traffic: Class I line-haul railroads, 1952–62*

Year ended Dec. 31—	Ton-mile revenue and nonrevenue freight per loaded freight-car-mile	Revenue ton-miles per train-mile	Passenger-miles per car-mile	Passenger-miles per train-mile	Revenue ton-miles per mile of road	Passenger-miles per mile of road
1952	32. 42	1, 236	18	99	2, 722, 052	154, 299
1953	31. 97	1, 243	18	95	2, 687, 176	143, 889
1954	31. 26	1, 240	17	92	2, 440, 924	133, 993
1955	31. 97	1, 322	18	95	2, 773, 638	131, 272
1956	32. 83	1, 375	18	97	2, 893, 286	130, 454
1957	33. 29	1, 396	18	94	2, 776, 983	120, 456
1958	32. 89	1, 388	19	94	2, 486, 153	109, 152
1959	33. 08	1, 401	19	98	2, 602. 794	103. 658
1960	33. 86	1. 426	19	102	2, 592, 653	100, 761
1961	34. 53	1, 469	20	102	2, 552, 143	96, 139
1962	35. 62	1, 519	20	103	2, 707, 807	96, 111

TABLE XII.—*Passenger transportation service performed by line-haul railroads, 1952–62*

Year ended Dec. 31—	Passengers carried	Passenger-miles	Average journey per passenger [1]	Average receipts per passenger	Revenue per passenger-mile
	Millions	*Millions*	*Miles*		*Cents*
1952	471	34,033	72.26	$1.925	2.665
1953	458	31,679	69,13	1.839	2.660
1954	441	29,310	66.50	1.742	2.620
1955	433	28,548	65.88	1.716	2.605
1956	430	28,216	65.62	1.762	2.685
1957	413	25,914	62.80	1.785	2.842
1958	382	23,295	61.04	1.772	2.903
1959	354	22,075	62.42	1.845	2.955
1960	327	21,284	65.05	1.961	3.014
1961	318	20,308	63.79	1.966	3.082
1962	313	19,926	63.65	1.981	3.113

[1] This average is affected by the changing ratio of commutation traffic to the total traffic.

TABLE XIII.—*Fuel consumed by motive-power units, and rails and ties laid: Class I line-haul railroads, 1952–62*

Year ended Dec. 31—	Coal (net tons)	Fuel oil (thousands of gallons)	Diesel oil (thousands of gallons)	Electricity (thousands of kilowatt-hours)	Rails applied in replacement and betterment (all tracks) (tons) [1]	Ties laid in previously constructed tracks	
						Crossties (numbers)	Switch and bridge ties (feet (b.m.))
1952	32,885,246	1,505,068	2,653,579	2,237,481	1,835,090	30,331,899	96,917,440
1953	23,402,162	995,199	2,980,008	2,135,968	2,057,492	29,808,949	99,791,974
1954	12,701,795	466,780	3,121,244	2,044,607	1,710,740	23,173,611	85,346,254
1955	11,427,313	375,580	3,393,103	2,082,350	1,890,002	24,149,169	79,098,327
1956	8,581,869	191,426	3,565,919	2,091,478	1,731,234	23,646,332	74,099,682
1957	4,866,198	89,300	3,535,849	2,024,608	1,592,124	22,082,225	71,582,096
1958	1,150,102	67,172	3,381,838	1,805,676	920,780	16,029,558	54,985,488
1959	300,216	81,776	3,483,959	1,748,480	1,011,745	16,423,307	54,378,386
1960	39,307	89,270	3,471,781	1,641,243	914,733	14,318,721	49,902,467
1961	9,394	93,570	3,382,015	1,625,397	758,269	12,019,255	50,187,247
1962	8,256	100,871	3,462,725	1,686,923	822,931	13,428,392	48,717,261

[1] Tons of 2,240 pounds prior to 1955; tons of 2,000 pounds subsequent years.

APPENDIX H

STATISTICS FROM MONTHLY AND OTHER PERIODICAL REPORTS OF CARRIERS

TABLE A.—*Selected data and analysis of operating revenues, expenses, and income class I line-haul railroads, 1961–62 and first 6 months of 1962 and 1963*

Item	Calendar year		First 6 months	
	1961 [1]	1962	1962 [1]	1963
Operating revenues:	*Thousands*	*Thousands*	*Thousands*	*Thousands*
Freight	$7,736,599	$7,990,791	$4,000,180	$4,026,955
Passenger	624,688	619,057	301,779	292,319
Mail	341,697	343,587	164,139	161,618
Express	83,019	81,957	39,443	37,901
All other	401,120	404,503	198,368	196,095
Total	9,187,123	9,439,895	4,703,909	4,714,888
Percent of total:				
Freight	84.21	84.65	85.04	85.40
Passenger	6.80	6.56	6.42	6.20
Mail	3.72	3.64	3.49	3.43
Express	.90	.87	.84	.81
All other	4.37	4.28	4.21	4.16
Operating expenses:	*Thousands*	*Thousands*	*Thousands*	*Thousands*
Maintenance of way and structures	$1,118,187	$1,154,802	$580,187	$577,213
Maintenance of equipment	1,683,596	1,743,639	883,815	858,488
Traffic	247,586	251,754	126,022	125,499
Transportation	3,711,410	3,755,092	1,867,994	1,868,697
General	432,985	436,458	217,433	218,642
All other	77,396	76,810	37,508	35,454
Total	7,271,160	7,418,555	3,712,959	3,683,993
Percent of total:				
Maintenance of way and structures	15.38	15.57	15.63	15.67
Maintenance of equipment	23.16	23.50	23.80	23.31
Traffic	3.41	3.39	3.39	3.41
Transportation	51.04	50.62	50.31	50.72
General	5.95	5.88	5.86	5.93
All other	1.06	1.04	1.01	.96
Operating ratio, percent	79.1	78.6	78.9	78.1
	Thousands	*Thousands*	*Thousands*	*Thousands*
Railway tax accruals	$991,556	$905,044	$523,653	$464,644
Equipment rents—debit	345,047	348,632	170,987	185,960
Joint facility rents—debit	41,665	41,978	21,039	20,537
Net railway operating income	537,695	725,686	275,271	359,754
Other income	324,010	325,574	140,173	147,711
Interest, rents, and other deductions	477,111	480,236	234,125	237,158
Net income	384,594	571,024	181,319	270,307
Federal income and excess-profits taxes [2]	243,191	156,785	140,012	97,167
Net railway operating income before provisions for Federal income and excess-profits taxes	780,886	882,471	415,283	456,921
Net income before provisions for Federal income and excess-profits taxes	627,785	727,809	321,331	367,474

[1] Revised.
[2] Included in railway tax accruals shown above.

227

TABLE B.—*Selected operating statistics in freight and passenger service, class I line-haul railroads, 1961–62 and first 6 months of 1962 and 1963*

Item	Calendar year		First 6 months	
	1961 [1]	1962	1962 [1]	1963
Freight service:				
Average miles of road operated	218, 586	217, 344	217, 000	215, 937
Total revenue ton-miles (million)	561, 837	591, 718	294, 757	306, 057
Tons of revenue freight carried (thousands)	2, 190, 700	2, 277, 645	1, 124, 534	1, 141, 823
Revenue tons originated (thousands)	1, 193, 740	1, 233, 597		
Revenue per ton-mile (cents)	1. 37	1. 35	1. 35	1. 31
Miles per revenue ton per road (average haul)	256. 5	259. 8	262. 1	268. 0
Freight-train miles (thousands)	386, 332	393, 344	196, 518	198, 149
Net ton-miles per train-mile (including nonrevenue tons)	1, 507	1, 557	1, 550	1, 598
Train-miles per mile of road per day	4. 8	4. 9	5. 0	5. 0
Net ton-miles per mile of road per day	7, 237	7, 657	7, 692	8, 032
Loaded car-miles (thousands)	16, 647, 801	16, 994, 155	8, 471, 267	8, 557, 425
Empty car-miles (thousands)	10, 541, 250	10, 755, 127	5, 343, 075	5, 424, 430
Percent loaded of total freight car-miles	61. 2	61. 2	61. 3	61. 2
Percent eastbound or northbound of loaded car-miles	54. 9	54. 0	53. 7	53. 6
Net ton-miles per loaded car-mile	34. 7	35. 7	35. 7	36. 7
Freight car-miles per train-mile—Total	70. 9	71. 1	70. 9	71. 1
—Loaded	43. 4	43. 5	43. 5	43. 5
—Empty	27. 5	27. 6	27. 4	27. 6
Gross ton-miles per train-mile (excluding locomotives and tenders)	3, 332	3, 402	3, 383	3, 453
Gross ton-miles of locomotives and tenders per locomotive-mile	387	395	393	397
Train-miles per train-hour (average)	19. 9	20. 0	20. 0	20. 1
Gross ton-miles per train-hour	65, 598	67, 529	67, 091	68, 863
Car-miles per car-day	40. 6	42. 8	42. 7	44. 8
Net ton-miles per freight car-day	862	937	933	1, 005
Percent of freight locomotives unserviceable	7. 0	7. 3	6. 8	7. 1
Percent of freight cars unserviceable	8. 2	7. 5	7. 5	7. 3
Pounds of coal per 1,000 gross ton-miles (including locomotives and tenders)	284	268	290	338
Gallons of diesel oil per 1,000 gross ton-miles (including locomotives)	1. 78	1. 77	1. 79	1. 78
Passenger service:				
Average miles of road operated	89, 044	86, 101	86, 070	85, 042
Passengers carried (thousands)	315, 954	311, 220	157, 108	155, 669
Total passenger-miles (millions)	20, 131	19, 760	9, 415	8, 947
Revenue passenger-miles per train-mile	101. 5	102. 4	98. 3	94. 8
Revenue passenger-miles per car-mile	19. 8	20. 0	19. 5	19. 2
Revenue per passenger per mile:				
Including commutation passengers (cents)	3. 08	3. 11	3. 18	3. 26
Excluding commutation passengers (cents)	3. 08	3. 10	3. 19	3. 29
Average journey per passenger per road (miles)	63. 7	63. 5	59. 9	57. 5
Passenger-train miles (thousands)	198, 497	193, 211	95, 408	94, 019
Passenger-train car-miles (thousands)	2, 026, 549	1, 988, 358	963, 580	938, 801
Passenger-train cars per train	10. 21	10. 29	10. 10	9. 99
Train-miles per mile of road per day	6. 1	6. 1	6. 1	6. 1
Train-miles per train-hour	40. 9	40. 9	40. 9	40. 9
Percent of passenger locomotives unserviceable	8. 4	9. 0	8. 9	9. 4
Percent of passenger cars unserviceable	9. 6	10. 5	10. 4	11. 5
Cost of fuel, all services (including freight charges):				
Average cost of coal per ton	$6. 03	$5. 94	$5. 90	$6. 08
Average cost of diesel oil per gallon (cents)	9. 53	9. 41	9. 66	9. 66

[1] Revised.

TABLE C.—*Average number of employees and total compensation, by groups of employees class I railroads, excluding switching and terminal companies, 1962-63*

Group of employees	Calendar year 1962		6 months, January to June, inclusive	
	Average number of employees middle of month	Total compensation	Average number of employees middle of month	
			1962	1963 [1]
I. Executives, officials, and staff assistants	14,454	$184,024,483	14,478	14,421
II. Professional, clerical, and general	145,903	891,706,492	147,214	140,425
III. Maintenance of way and structures	102,274	562,337,935	102,694	96,659
IV. Maintenance of equipment and stores	161,080	943,711,588	165,074	156,007
V. Transportation (other than train, engine, and yard)	77,743	460,521,885	78,048	72,448
VI. (a) Transportation (yardmasters, switchtenders, and hostlers)	10,713	87,865,115	10,816	10,307
(b) Transportation (train and engine service)	187,979	1,531,897,140	187,953	184,353
All employees	700,146	4,662,064,638	706,277	674,620

[1] Preliminary.

TABLE D.—*Carloads and tons of revenue freight originated and freight revenue, by commodities, calendar year 1962, class I railroads*

Commodity groups	Number of carloads	Number of tons (2,000 pounds)	Freight revenue
Products of agriculture:			
Wheat	637, 582	36, 171, 152	$219, 999, 533
Corn	524, 006	29, 263, 627	159, 356, 217
Other grains	377, 983	19, 529, 310	123, 433, 106
Flour, wheat	295, 597	10, 365, 042	78, 444, 160
Other mill products	335, 578	9, 490, 494	66, 792, 363
Cotton in bales	190, 256	3, 713, 765	49, 823, 471
Citrus fruits	44, 979	953, 590	30, 463, 359
Other fresh fruits	119, 905	1, 899, 786	72, 426, 236
Potatoes, other than sweet	145, 409	3, 375, 115	68, 472, 105
Other fresh vegetables	144, 384	2, 452, 700	99, 226, 491
Sugar beets	229, 101	10, 895, 338	16, 188, 531
All other	686, 985	27, 186, 603	179, 139, 932
Total	3, 731, 765	155, 296, 522	1, 163, 765, 504
Animals and products:			
Live animals	192, 862	2, 193, 900	50, 170, 751
Meats and other edible packinghouse products	218, 854	3, 746, 117	100, 025, 156
Poultry, live and dressed	7, 082	184, 676	4, 898, 019
Dairy products	42, 008	959, 958	17, 335, 879
Wool and mohair	8, 833	177, 986	4, 729, 002
Hides and leather	26, 162	730, 410	16, 794, 337
All other	46, 866	1, 459, 026	16, 357, 239
Total	542, 667	9, 452, 073	210, 310, 383
Products of mines:			
Anthracite coal [1]	161, 301	9, 093, 271	33, 399, 210
Bituminous coal	4, 930, 847	312, 178, 807	1, 035, 122, 493
Coke	345, 458	15, 466, 767	63, 072, 124
Iron ore	1, 116, 409	79, 036, 271	180, 751, 059
Other ores and concentrates	275, 448	20, 561, 011	75, 435, 855
Gravel and sand	957, 434	61, 956, 395	107, 692, 371
Stone and rock: Broken, ground, and crushed	908, 898	56, 060, 771	94, 070, 057
Fluxing stone and raw dolomite	205, 745	14, 284, 773	29, 806, 865
Petroleum, crude	46, 299	1, 755, 547	6, 793, 918
Phosphate rock	324, 311	22, 620, 837	47, 297, 822
All other	769, 168	41, 732, 549	242, 045, 740
Total	10, 041, 318	634, 746, 999	1, 915, 487, 514
Products of forests:			
Logs, butts, and bolts	136, 114	4, 975, 540	10, 262, 640
Posts, poles, and piling, wooden	74, 709	2, 367, 231	23, 488, 079
Pulpwood	924, 456	44, 251, 130	83, 755, 521
Lumber, shingles, and lath	441, 586	15, 563, 263	365, 065, 371
All other	320, 920	10, 947, 315	164, 661, 427
Total	1, 897, 785	78, 104, 479	647, 233, 038
Manufactures and miscellaneous:			
Refined petroleum products	803, 810	24, 246, 555	191, 219, 747
Vegetable oils	119, 635	3, 801, 424	44, 237, 939
Chemicals	547, 486	25, 286, 292	289, 631, 559
Fertilizers, n.o.s.	408, 288	21, 318, 546	165, 057, 436
Metals and alloys, other than iron and steel	139, 157	6, 231, 712	116, 314, 896
Pig iron	51, 083	3, 290, 351	16, 591, 250
Semifinished iron and steel	206, 677	12, 519, 887	59, 550, 706
Manufactured iron and steel	877, 012	35, 352, 710	407, 313, 924
Vehicles and parts, motor and other	847, 349	15, 630, 317	461, 973, 783
Cement, natural and portland	361, 300	22, 513, 197	78, 563, 112
Paper and paper products	1, 161, 862	35, 193, 227	499, 988, 005
Alcoholic beverages	144, 701	4, 692, 995	78, 509, 436
Sugar	139, 697	6, 629, 514	56, 743, 106
Food products, n.o.s., in cans and packages, not frozen	483, 602	14, 241, 096	238, 893, 223
Feed, animal and poultry, n.o.s.	576, 025	16, 458, 686	85, 934, 393
Containers, metal, wooden and paper	333, 835	4, 141, 250	75, 455, 702
Scrap iron and steel	351, 605	17, 901, 422	72, 901, 161
All other	2, 950, 895	79, 610, 646	1, 232, 459, 285
Total	10, 504, 019	349, 059, 827	4, 171, 338, 663
Forwarder traffic	392, 825	4, 754, 615	177, 145, 167
Grand total carload traffic	27, 110, 379	1, 231, 414, 515	8, 285, 280, 269
All l.c.l. freight		2, 182, 805	99, 663, 026
Grand total, carload and l.c.l		1, 233, 597, 320	8, 384, 943, 295

[1] Excludes coal to breakers and washeries.

TABLE E.—*Revenues, expenses, and income of class I motor carriers* [1] *of property for the calendar year 1962 compared with the same carriers for 1961* [2]

Item	1961	1962
INTERCITY CARRIERS		
Number of carriers represented	954	954
Revenues:		
Freight revenue—Intercity—Common carrier	$4,574,801,778	$5,017,433,486
Freight revenue—Intercity—Contract carrier	194,353,625	207,725,909
Freight revenue—Local cartage	56,466,204	65,767,328
Revenue—Transportation for other class I and class II motor carriers	33,063,817	37,158,143
Other operating revenue	43,911,946	45,664,631
Total operating revenues	4,902,597,370	5,373,749,497
Expenses:		
Equipment maintenance expense	467,695,646	516,889,592
Transportation expense	2,405,354,154	2,641,381.462
Terminal expense	679,560,260	755,844,907
Traffic expense	154,956,339	164,359,506
Insurance and safety expense	203,353,721	216,995,047
Administrative and general expense	282,219,551	295,803,646
Total operation and maintenance expenses	4,193,139,671	4,591,274,160
Depreciation expense	225,064,463	237,504,269
Depreciation adjustment	d *13,135,221*	d *18,973,665*
Amortization chargeable to operations	28,918	26,493
Operating taxes and licenses	298,554,397	333,948,045
Total expenses	4,703,652,228	5,143,779,302
Operating ratio (percent)	95.9	95.7
Net operating revenue	$198,945,142	$229,970,195
Other income	19,356,165	15,257,613
Other deductions	53,733,810	53,764,417
Net income before income taxes	164,567,497	191,463,391
Net income after income taxes [3]	90,093,057	109,424,845
LOCAL CARRIERS		
Number of carriers represented	85	85
Total operating revenues	$309,368,660	$334,190,263
Total expenses	300,661,716	325,963,229
Operating ratio (percent)	97.2	97.5
Net operating revenue	$8,706,944	$8,227,034
Other income	2,753,197	2,582,684
Other deductions	1,876,698	1,843,580
Net income before income taxes	9,583,443	8,966,138
Net income after income taxes [3]	4,929,050	4,889,978

Deficit and contra items shown in italics.
[1] Class I motor carriers are those having average gross operating revenues of $1,000,000 or over annually.
[2] This table does not include data for 35 carriers that failed to furnish complete records. The total figures for these 35 carriers amounted to the following for 1962: Operating revenues, $69,007,875; operation and maintenance expenses, $58,524,039; other expenses, $7,541,297; total expenses, $66,065,336; net operating revenue, $2,942,539; net income before income taxes, $2,582,715; net income after income taxes, $1,582,401.
[3] Net income is overstated to the extent that income taxes are reported by corporations only. Income taxes of sole proprietorships and partnerships involve factors that do not arise from motor-carrier operations and, therefore, are not reported to the Commission.

TABLE F.—*Revenues, expenses, and income of class I motor carriers* [1] *of passengers for the calendar year 1962, compared with the same carriers for 1961* [2]

Item	1961	1962
INTERCITY CARRIERS		
Number of carriers represented	140	140
Operating revenues:		
Passenger revenue—Intercity schedules	$369,749,201	$401,506,064
Passenger revenue—Local and suburban schedules	22,912,086	23,691,889
Passenger revenue—Charter or special service	38,237,825	41,448,362
Other operating revenue	51,569,215	57,992,342
Total operating revenues	482,468,327	524,638,657
Operating expenses:		
Equipment maintenance and garage expenses	71,104,121	73,161,764
Transportation expense	152,853,394	162,019,299
Station expenses	59,229,082	64,935,646
Traffic, solicitation, and advertising expense	14,509,949	15,731,966
Insurance and safety expense	15,447,798	17,701,935
Administrative and general expense	34,841,143	37,718,362
Total operation and maintenance expenses	347,985,487	371,268,972
Depreciation expense	27,643,579	29,682,990
Amortization chargeable to operations	41,043	32,805
Operating taxes and licenses	37,527,287	39,426,783
Operating rents—net	6,260,847	6,700,340
Total expenses	419,458,243	447,111,890
Operating ratio (percent)	86.9	85.2
Net operating revenue	$63,010,084	$77,526,767
Other income	1,408,988	1,631,504
Other deductions	4,386,229	3,387,089
Net income before income taxes	60,032,843	75,771,182
Net income after income taxes [3]	32,520,605	42,639,559
LOCAL CARRIERS		
Number of carriers represented	68	68
Total operating revenues	$130,514,943	$133,222,567
Total expenses	126,993,558	130,076,101
Operating ratio (percent)	97.3	97.6
Net operating revenue	$3,521,385	$3,146,466
Other income	1,776,978	1,887,276
Other deductions	1,413,606	1,592,656
Net income before income taxes	3,884,757	3,441,086
Net income after income taxes [3]	2,462,761	2,588,833

Deficit and contra items in italics.

[1] Class I motor carriers are those having average gross operating revenues of $200,000 or over annually.

[2] This table does not include data for 8 carriers that failed to furnish complete reports. The total figures for these 8 carriers amounted to the following for 1962: Operating revenues, $2,763,525: operation and maintenance expenses, $2,179,267: other expenses, $398,573; total expenses, $2,577,840; net operating revenue, $185,685: net income before taxes, $161,460: net income after taxes, $132.138.

[3] Net income is overstated to the extent that income taxes are reported by corporations only. Income taxes of sole proprietorships involve factors that do not arise from motor carrier operations and, therefore, are not reported to the Commission.

TABLE G.—*Revenues, expenses, and statistics of freight forwarders for the years 1961 and 1962* [1]

Item	1961 [2]	1962
Number of forwarders represented	64	64
Operating revenues:		
Transportation revenue	$442,767,684	$464,582,799
Transportation purchased—Dr.:		
Railroad transportation	179,144,943	179,654,289
Motor transportation	60,927,786	68,722,351
Water transportation	1,642,555	1,446,230
Pickup, delivery, and transfer service	60,898,444	66,559,585
Other transportation purchased	1,813,998	2,066,120
Total transportation purchased	304,427,726	318,448,575
Forwarder revenue from transportation	138,339,958	146,134,224
Incidental revenues	4,711,903	4,249,558
Total operating revenues	143,051,861	150,383,782
Operating expenses:		
Salaries, wages, and expenses of employees	61,527,831	63,930,635
Paid to others for services rendered	36,915,118	37,222,440
Operating rents	9,092,646	9,737,195
Communications and postage	4,346,221	4,467,230
Payroll taxes	2,495,066	2,691,804
All other operating expenses	17,549,247	18,790,128
Total operating expenses	131,926,129	136,839,432
Income items:		
Revenue from forwarder operations	11,125,732	13,544,350
Transportation tax accruals	292,950	309,151
Revenue, less taxes, from forwarder operations	10,832,782	13,235,199
Other income	4,480,135	5,782,702
Total income	15,312,917	19,017,901
Miscellaneous deductions from income	4,657,073	6,170,892
Net income before fixed charges and income taxes	10,655,844	12,847,009
Fixed charges	187,751	190,101
Net income before provisions for income taxes	10,468,093	12,656,908
Provisions for income taxes	4,388,080	5,886,134
Net income	6,080,013	6,770,774
Statistics:		
Tons of freight received from shippers	4,009,740	4,310,706
Number of shipments received from shippers	26,002,025	21,705,625

[1] Confined to forwarders having gross revenues of $100,000 or more per annum.
[2] Revised.

TABLE H.—*Selected statistics of nonrailroad controlled private car owners,*[1] *year 1962*

Item	Refrigerator cars	Tank cars		Other cars[2]	Total
		Petroleum	Other		
Cars owned at close of year	17,453	128,368	27,783	87,076	260,680
Serviceable cars	15,682	123,501	27,155	86,414	252,752
Unserviceable cars	1,771	4,867	628	662	7,928
Miles made by owned cars (thousands):					
Loaded	241,666	783,014	131,424	589,884	1,745,988
Empty	227,797	798,339	134,931	284,369	1,445,436
Not separable	29,313	32,643	60,998	35,983	158,937
Total	498,776	1,613,996	327,353	910,236	3,350,361
Revenue receivable, on (thousands):					
Car mileage basis	$24,361	$60,241	$7,155	$13,451	$105,208
Car rental basis	729	103,207	21,265	70,318	195,519
Other car service basis	15	136	85	37	273
Total	25,105	163,584	28,505	83,806	301,000

[1] Confined to owners of 10 or more cars. Does not include railroad owned or controlled refrigerator carlines. Compiled from annual reports of 169 owners.
[2] Includes such cars as stock, gondola, hopper, airdump, box, cradle, flat, vat, et cetera.

TABLE I.—*Selected statistics of refrigerator carlines owned or controlled by railroads, for the years 1961 and 1962*

Item	1961	1962
Number of companies represented	8	8
Operating revenues:		
Car service	$98,748,767	$98,864,965
Icing protective service	26,491,132	25,719,696
Mechanical protective service	8,112,041	8,925,964
Heater service	1,632,331	1,725,376
Other services	3,037,667	5,088,417
Total	138,021,938	140,324,418
Operating expenses:		
Car service	58,479,845	55,372,121
Icing protective service	18,907,264	18,342,177
Other icing service	6,163,504	5,930,804
Mechanical protective service	8,634,269	10,010,141
Heater service	1,919,271	1,934,207
Miscellaneous	4,618,427	6,434,024
General	3,603,416	3,631,327
Total	102,325,996	101,654,801
Net income after fixed charges and tax accruals	$8,878,573	$13,830,014
Carline tax accruals	$11,909,097	$9,404,044
Investment in cars or protective service property less recorded depreciation and amortization	[1]$310,738,146	$320,875,655
Rolling stock owned at close of year:		
Refrigerator cars	61,916	63,172
Other cars	796	1,337
Mileage made by owned refrigerator cars:		
Loaded	1,264,775,131	1,266,330,187
Empty	903,598,086	866,398,115
Not separable	12,228,383	3,547,409
Total	2,180,601,600	2,136,275,711
Total employees at close of year	6,608	6,583
Total compensation for the year	$39,169,375	$37,666,715

[1] Revised.

TABLE J.—*Selected financial and operating data of oil pipeline companies, 1960, 1961, and 1962*

Item	1960	1961	1962
Miles of line operated:			
Gathering lines	49,401	49,656	48,063
Trunk lines	102,567	104,081	106,990
Investment in carrier property	$3,299,501,127	$3,406,830,415	$3,518,419,962
Capital stock [1]	383,826,501	338,028,237	340,373,346
Funded debt unmatured [1]	1,055,501,963	1,058,721,769	1,043,106,588
Accrued depreciation—Carrier property [2]	1,332,190,497	1,429,116,884	1,523,221,548
Operating revenues	770,417,060	786,717,567	810,605,133
Operating expenses	417,640,213	419,853,655	426,362,651
Pipeline taxes:			
U.S. Government taxes	115,234,824	111,358,769	115,284,481
Other than U.S. Government taxes	38,631,096	40,888,996	41,928,173
Pipeline operating income	198,910,927	214,616,147	227,029,828
Net income	169,398,118	180,697,972	203,799,801
Dividend appropriations [1]	143,459,767	153,062,714	174,185,295
Number of barrels of oil received into system	4,783,055,042	4,940,907,441	5,122,942,814
Number of barrel-miles (trunk lines):			
Crude oil (thousands)	976,357,818	995,642,315	998,096,023
Refined oils (thousands)	304,448,973	317,141,089	347,178,499
Total employees:			
Average number	21,321	20,295	19,197
Compensation	$150,577,190	$150,715,010	$145,108,799

[1] Excludes data for 5 companies in 1960; 5 companies in 1961; and 5 companies in 1962; as the annual reports filed by these companies relate to pipeline departments of large oil companies and these items are not segregated for the pipeline departments.
[2] Includes "Amortization reserve" as follows: 1960, $47,911,634; 1961, $55,965,856; and 1962, $56,690,620.

TABLE K.—*Revenues and traffic of carriers by water, 1961 and 1962* [1]

Item	1961	1962
Freight revenue	$262,020,866	$258,097,682
Number of tons of revenue freight carried	105,353,952	108,751,232
Passenger revenue	$8,800,076	$9,419,697
Number of revenue passengers carried	2,678,155	2,922,054

[1] Compiled from quarterly reports of 105 carriers of classes A and B.

TABLE L.—*Selected financial and operating data of electric railways, 1960, 1961, and 1962*

Item	1960	1961	1962
Miles of road operated	469	402	394
Investment in road and equipment	$87,719,770	$74,248,293	$73,514,310
Capital stock	23,298,409	22,495,601	22,456,100
Unmatured funded debt	862,500	1,068,750	873,021
Accrued depreciation—Road and equipment	26,157,404	21,535,683	22,236,120
Railway operating revenues:			
Freight revenue	10,354,240	10,123,335	9,888,752
Passenger revenue	8,486,525	8,134,329	7,952,672
All other revenues	3,993,532	4,039,804	3,915,012
Total railway operating revenues	22,834,297	22,297,468	21,756,436
Total railway operating expenses	21,848,931	21,421,740	20,917,797
Taxes assignable to railway operations:			
Other than U.S. Government taxes	674,124	637,796	601,659
U.S. Government taxes	1,152,726	1,167,359	1,132,647
Operating income	*811,314*	*933,827*	*879,377*
Net income	*545,387*	*747,418*	*692,224*
Dividends declared	78,554	42,278	63,004
Employees:			
Average number	2,301	2,258	2,040
Compensation	$12,880,674	$12,926,146	$12,110,420

Deficit shown in italics.

APPENDIX I

Number of carriers subject to Uniform Systems of Accounts and required to file annual and periodic reports as of June 30, 1963

Railroads, class I_____ 102
Railroads, class II_____ 295
Railroad switching and terminal companies, class I_____ 42
Railroad switching and terminal companies, class II_____ 153
Railroad lessor companies_____ 143
Motor carriers, class I passengers_____ [1] 222
Motor carriers, class I property_____ 1, 148
Motor carriers, class II property_____ 2, 495
Oil pipelines_____ 91
Water carriers_____ 93
Maritime carriers_____ 21
Electric railways_____ 16
Freight forwarders_____ 60
Protective service companies_____ 7
Express companies_____ 2
Sleeping car companies_____ 1
Stockyard companies_____ 39
Holding companies (rail)_____ 4

   Total_____ 4, 934

Number of carriers and organizations filing annual reports but not subject to prescribed Uniform Systems of Accounts as of June 30, 1963

Car lines (companies which furnish cars for use on lines of railroads)__ 166
Class II and III motor carriers of passengers_____ 874
Class III motor carriers of property_____ 12, 078
Water carriers (less than $100,000 gross revenue)_____ 104
Freight forwarders (less than $100,000 gross revenue)_____ 21
Holding companies (motor)_____ 23
Street electric lines_____ 5
Rate bureaus and organizations_____ 82

   Total_____ 13, 353
   Grand total_____ 18, 287

_____

[1] Includes combination property and passenger carriers.

236

INDEX

242   INDEX

Page